COLLAPSE

A WORLD IN CRISIS

AND THE URGENCY OF

AMERICAN LEADERSHIP

DOUGLAS E. SCHOEN

Encounter
BOOKS

New York • London

First American edition published in 2019 by Encounter Books, an activity of Encounter for Culture and Education, Inc., a nonprofit, tax exempt corporation.
Encounter Books website address: www.encounterbooks.com

Manufactured in the United States and printed on acid-free paper. The paper used in this publication meets the minimum requirements of ANSI/NISO Z39.48–1992 (R 1997) (Permanence of Paper).

FIRST AMERICAN EDITION

LIBRARY OF CONGRESS CATALOGING-IN-PUBLICATION DATA
Names: Schoen, Douglas E., 1953– author.
Title: Collapse : a world in crisis and the urgency of American leadership / by Douglas E. Schoen.
Description: New York : Encounter Books, 2019. |
Includes bibliographical references and index.
Identifiers: LCCN 2018043851 (print) | LCCN 2018047231 (ebook) |
ISBN 9781641770354 (ebook) | ISBN 9781641770347 (hardcover : alk. paper)
Subjects: LCSH: World politics—21st century. |
United States—Foreign relations—21st century.
Classification: LCC D863 (ebook) | LCC D863 .S384 2019 (print) |
DDC 909.83/12—dc23
LC record available at https://lccn.loc.gov/2018043851

Interior page design and composition: BooksByBruce.com

CONTENTS

WHEN THE WORLD KNEW

"The larger point is that this is something we are seeing all over, the top detaching itself from the bottom.... Something big is happening here with this division between the leaders and the led. It is very much a feature of our age."

—PEGGY NOONAN[1]

It was Pennsylvania that put him over the top, and it was past two in the morning on the East Coast on November 9, 2016, when Donald Trump won the presidency, much to the shock—and dismay—of the media, the political class, millions of Americans, and countless millions around the world.

"This was a primal scream on the part of a lot of voters who are disenchanted with the status quo," David Axelrod, Barack Obama's former top adviser, told CNN.[2] Many others just wanted to scream—not all of them liberal Democrats, by any means. "America has now jumped off a constitutional cliff," wrote Andrew Sullivan. "This is now Trump's America. He controls everything from here on forward. He has won this campaign in such a decisive fashion that he owes no one anything."[3]

However one viewed it, Trump's win represented the crescendo of half a decade or more of anti-establishment politics around the world, a raucous era of audacious terror attacks, global financial panics and economic recessions, technological disruptions, and political and institutional upheavals that have made the early twenty-first century as unpredictable and unstable as any recent era in at least a century. For years before 2016, electorates in other countries had been flirting with, or choosing, anti-establishment parties and leaders—but no one truly believed that someone quite as disruptive as Donald Trump could really become president of the world's superpower and de facto leader of the free world.

We're still getting used to it. But the problems and trends that led to Trump's shock emergence have been festering for years, in the United States and around the world.

In 2013, in my book *The End of Authority*, I warned that the loss of legitimacy and broken trust in institutions—from the United States to Europe, from the Far East to Africa and Latin America—posed grave threats to the future of free societies, the stability of the international system, and global security. "The most significant global crisis since the 1930s," I wrote, "could lead in any number of damaging directions if governments don't work to regain the trust of their citizens."[4]

Back then, I was writing in the wake of an international financial crisis that was testing governments around the world fiscally, economically, and politically; eroding confidence and trust in institutions, in the United States and internationally; and leading to the rise of anti-systemic parties and politicians worldwide. But I was writing *before* the outbreak of the Syrian civil war and refugee crisis, the emergence and eventual decline (at least militarily) of ISIS, the Brexit vote, and other forces of division impacting European unity—and, needless to say, before voters in the United States sent the most anti-systemic candidate in American history to the White House.

The global situation is far darker now—and so unstable and volatile that a war breaking out at almost any time cannot be ruled out. Rather than a decline of authority and an erosion of trust, we risk full-scale collapse of both, especially as reflected in popular contempt for established institutional authority.

In short, it is clear to me that we are now well beyond the crisis point that inspired *The End of Authority*, when I warned that "nothing less than global stability and a functioning international order are at stake." Indeed, global *instability* has become the norm rather than the exception. In recent years, we have seen a mounting barrage of terror attacks, failed states and governments, anti-systemic political candidates, rising tides of nationalism and nativism, and economic sclerosis.

We didn't reach this point of global populism, populist political movements, and accelerating institutional illegitimacy through any one path. Rather, a series of interlocking developments brought us to where we are:

- Failed leadership, especially in the West, has delegitimized political and social institutions, alienated millions from the political process, and fostered impassioned, broadly supported populist movements, which range in orientation from hard left to hard right, anti-systemic to neo-Nazi.
- The failures of democratic governance have emboldened authoritarian leaders worldwide, especially Russia's Vladimir Putin but also China's Xi Jinping—and, worse, as democracy loses its luster, even among some in the West, the allure of authoritarianism grows as an alternative political model and a foundation of order and security in a world seemingly spinning out of control.
- Cybersecurity and the threat of hackers—as reflected in Russian hacking of the Democratic National Committee (DNC) emails and other efforts to undermine the 2016 election in the United States—pose threats that, by every indication, Western governments are not prepared to meet; cyber warfare is another component of the authoritarian challenge.
- Security challenges from rogue states, like Iran and North Korea, continue to mount, especially as they enjoy critical backing from antidemocratic powers like Russia and China.
- Terrorism and radical Islam remain a fundamental challenge to the security of Western societies, as well as a scourge of millions of peace-loving Muslims around the world, whether in the Middle East, Africa, or elsewhere; ISIS's reign of terror, even if now essentially defeated, reminded complacent Western observers of the appeal of millenarian Islam to millions of disaffected Muslim young men, and of its deadly consequences.
- Beyond Islamist terror, the rise and proliferation of narco-fueled terror among international criminal gangs in the developing world, especially in Latin America, adds a

new dimension of disruption, violence, and anti-Western sentiment.

- Massive inequality of wealth and disparity in education and opportunity are eroding social cohesion and seeding the ground for continued revolts and disorder worldwide.
- The global collapse of oil prices may well cause unpredictable consequences in already-volatile countries like Russia, Venezuela, and Saudi Arabia, but this issue is just one component of a broader struggle in the years ahead for dominance of world energy markets—a struggle in which the United States' emergence as a leading player is both an enormously promising and a potentially destabilizing development.
- Nations in the developing world, especially in Latin America and Africa, continue to struggle mightily to develop functioning, lawful, effective governments, as they face a host of problems including extreme poverty, terror and criminal-gang activity, and institutional and infrastructural failure; if one malady unites all these challenges, it is the problem of corruption, which exists in these societies to a degree that Westerners would find difficult to fathom.
- The nation that remains the world's best hope for leadership to turn this around—the United States—labored for years with no strategy, no discernible conviction, and no viable leadership; it has fallen to Donald Trump, a president detested by at least half of the American electorate, to reverse these trends, if he can.

Let's take a brief look at some of these key areas.

REJECTION OF ELITES WORLDWIDE

If there is a central organizing principle driving all of this, it is the pervasive, global rejection of elites. It takes different forms in different countries—whether in the rise of left- or right-wing political leaders and movements, rebellions in the streets, referenda like Brexit, or the emergence of Trump in the United States—but the underlying premise that institutions don't work, that governance has failed, and that people are, essentially, on their own, can be seen everywhere one looks.

Consider the way that Western governments handled the Syrian refugee crisis. The key figure in the story is German chancellor Angela Merkel. Without any democratic consultation with her constituents, she approved the entry of about one million refugees into Germany. When incidents of violence and sexual molestation occurred—as they did most infamously at Cologne over New Year's 2015—Merkel lectured her countrymen that they needed to learn to master "the shadow side of all the positive effects of globalization."[5] Merkel and her peers likely don't come into contact with many Syrian refugees. It is ordinary people who live with the consequences of self-righteous elite decision-making, in Germany and elsewhere. In the United States, which has allowed only a fraction of the German quota of refugees, a recent report showed that Syrian refugees now living in Virginia have been settled in the poorest communities—far from the bedroom suburbs of Washington and Arlington.

"The larger point," Peggy Noonan writes, "is that this is something we are seeing all over, the top detaching itself from the bottom."[6] She believes that "something big is happening here with this division between the leaders and the led. It is very much a feature of our age."[7] Glenn Reynolds finds a contemporary analogy: *The Hunger Games*. "The Capital City, and its hangers-on, flourish, while the provinces starve."[8]

This top/bottom breakdown has other definitive characteristics. Rampant elite corruption has shattered popular confidence. The Panama Papers, for example, revealed a system of unbridled self-dealing among the world's elites, including 12 current or former heads of state. Most dramatically, the documents suggest a secret offshore money network, involving banks and shadow companies, tied to Russian president Vladimir Putin. Also implicated in self-dealing are a member of the Fédération Internationale de Football Association (FIFA), Icelandic prime minister David Gunnlaugsson, and Argentinian president Mauricio Macri. The International Consortium of Investigative Journalists, which published the Panama Papers, found that the families of at least eight former or current members of the Chinese Politburo Standing Committee had offshore companies. Wealthy Chinese have developed sophisticated networks and systems to evade currency controls and get cash out of the country.

Globalists and elites champion transnational efforts and institutions, but one wonders what game they're watching. International institutions have fared no better than nation-states in recent years. The British opt-out from the European Union was the most dramatic recent statement of no confidence, but imagine how Haitians must feel about the U.N., which admitted in 2016—finally—that its incompetent relief efforts after the 2010 earthquake in Port au Prince *helped cause* the subsequent cholera epidemic, which killed more than 10,000 people. It is bad enough that the U.N. is so ineffective at bringing peace to world trouble spots; the Haiti debacle shows that it cannot even be trusted with straightforward humanitarian relief.

Adding to popular despair is the sense that even dramatic change—or what seems like dramatic change—doesn't appear to make a difference. A revolt against government corruption in Thailand helped a junta, the National Council for Peace and Order, take power in a 2014 coup. The council quickly censored the nation's broadcasting system and suspended its constitution—but it now faces its own corruption scandals. Thais had welcomed the intervention of the military, but now that so little has changed, disillusionment is setting in.

Failed leadership seems to be the common denominator everywhere.

It's no wonder then, that we're seeing such anti-systemic, anti-elite motivation in country after country. It arises from elites' wholesale failures of leadership and governance, their inability to address the challenges of our age and serve the people they represent.

THE ONGOING JIHAD

The Western democracies, including the United States, face a challenge from radical Islam that is likely to continue for at least another generation. In the West, leaders' public messages have tended to alternate between effusive statements about diversity, multiculturalism, and how Islam means "peace," and defiant statements of resolve and pledges to crack down on Islamists whenever one of their cities is attacked. Millions of citizens in Western capitals have grown weary of the whole routine, especially when they sense that their governments don't seem in any hurry to change the policies that enable the problem to fester and grow.

And when Westerners look abroad, they can see the horrors that such unchecked savagery of sharia-driven Islam can wreak. The future of ISIS, if it has a future, remains to be seen; but we have learned painfully since 2001 about how terrorist forces rebound and reconstitute themselves, so it is unlikely that we have seen the last of the extreme violence and cruelty that was ISIS's hallmark, even if it appears under a different name. And the disturbing lessons of the group's history cannot be forgotten. At its peak, from about 2013 through 2015, it turned the Middle East, never a peaceful region, into a hell of violence and savagery. By the time President Obama left office in 2017, the region was in far worse shape than how he had found it, thanks in part to his disinterest in exerting American leadership there. Only near the end of his second term did Obama finally recognize the challenge that ISIS posed and take the requisite steps to ramp up American efforts to fight the group—an effort that President Trump augmented and accelerated, to inspiring results in 2017, when ISIS had to abandon its major territorial claims in Iraq. But the group's adherents will likely remain a going concern in the Middle East, especially in Iraq and Syria, and moreover, its international fighters, thousands from European countries, are now coming home, eager to strike at the societies that welcome them and which they detest.

For years, ISIS operatives or supporters have been attacking targets in Europe. In 2016 alone, jihadists struck in Paris, Nice, Brussels, and Munich, among others. A French official declared that terrorism had to be accepted as a part of life; he may as well have waved a white flag. Obama's minimization of the threat essentially sent the same defeatist message—but his indifference was not shared by ordinary Americans or citizens elsewhere, who braced for the next strike from ISIS and looked to their governments to protect them. Until Trump's national security team changed the rules of engagement and turned up the pressure, the United States appeared to have no strategy for victory, even in the short term.

Even now, with the subduing of ISIS, the West (and especially the United States) still needs a comprehensive and long-term program, not just to "degrade" ISIS and other jihadi groups, to use Obama's phrase, but to destroy them.

THE LOSS OF LEGITIMACY

In the years to come, we may look at 2016 as the watershed year, the year in which voters in the two primary English-speaking countries—Great Britain and the United States—made shocking breaks with traditional politics, setting their nations on courses that cannot yet be predicted or fully understood. Donald Trump's ascension to the presidency is one of the most astounding political developments in American history, a political earthquake with global implications. Trump's rise tells the story of Americans' total rejection of the political class; Bernie Sanders's near-miss in getting the Democratic nomination in 2016 is part of the same narrative. Together, Sanders and Trump inspired tens of millions of voters who felt completely estranged from the system. Trump—a political neophyte, fiery populist, and reckless articulator of aspirations and resentments—is beginning to leave his mark as president, on which I'll have more to say. However one views his record, it is impossible to deny that he has changed American politics forever.

At the same time, it is also impossible to deny that the worsening polarization of American politics, and indeed of American society, is eroding—and potentially even negating—the United States' advantages as a democratic society, its appeal to outsiders, and its legitimacy as a beacon of freedom around the world.

In Great Britain, too, the move to leave the European Union shatters precedent and history. Its roots may well lie in the failure to manage the challenges posed by radical Islam, especially as they relate to migration, a failure that may yet bring down the entire European project. Brexit came as a direct result of the Syrian refugee crisis, which has sent thousands of migrants—many of whom adhere to sharia law and feel no allegiance to Western political ideas—into Europe at the open invitation of political leaders like Germany's Merkel. Merkel's unswerving devotion to the European open-borders ideal has eroded her support nationally, and we've seen a wave of populism, national-ism, and Euroskepticism—think of it as Trumpism, European-style—in many countries, including France with Marine Le Pen and Hungary with Prime Minister Viktor Orbán. Even when these movements don't win—and most haven't, yet—they reflect the far-ranging and deep-seated nature of public discontent.

Why have the Western democracies proved so unequal to the current moment? Across the board, their governments and institutions have lost legitimacy with the public. Leaders are paralyzed, and popular consent and social cohesion are breaking down. For instance, in the United States, it isn't just the political system that Americans are rejecting. Gallup finds that Americans' trust in 14 key domestic institutions, from Congress to banks, is down to an average 32 percent. The only two institutions outperforming their historic averages are the military and small business. American confidence in international institutions is waning, too.

This contempt for elites extends worldwide. The 2018 Edelman Trust barometer surveyed 28 countries and found that among ordinary citizens, trust levels in government, business, media, and nongovernmental organizations (NGOs) remained low. Trust in these institutions has risen among just one segment of the population—elites themselves.

This huge disparity in how the world is viewed by insiders and outsiders—or, in Peggy Noonan's formulation, the protected and the unprotected—spells nothing but trouble. As the gap widens, the trouble expands and worsens. That has been the story of the last decade, which has seen not only escalating violence and political instability but also a worldwide financial crisis worse than anything since the 1930s, in which fortunes, life savings, and carefully planned futures were wiped out. The financial crisis, in tandem with expanding inequality and economic stagnation, especially for the middle class, has done untold damage to the prestige of free market economies.

AUTHORITARIANISM ON THE RISE

Against this backdrop of the West's political and economic failure, it should come as no surprise that authoritarian and antidemocratic governments are consolidating their power and seeing a surge in momentum.

Russia's Vladimir Putin has massed at least 77,000 troops, and by some estimates many more, on the Russian/Ukrainian border, in what American officials fear may be an invasion in the making. He continues to send menacing signals in Eastern Europe, and his aggressive international campaign of cyber warfare continues. In no country have his machinations proved more contentious than in the United States, which remains embroiled in an ongoing investigation into Russian meddling in the 2016 presidential campaign, along with long-running allegations that the Trump campaign team colluded with Moscow in an effort to secure victory in the election. Compelling evidence for such charges has failed to materialize, but Trump has not made his own case easier with his repeated statements that seem to praise or even encourage Putin, with whom, some critics suggest, he feels an authoritarian kinship. Too often, Trump's words, if not his deeds, have seemed to empower or at least excuse authoritarian leaders, and seemingly without a countervailing passion for the cause of democratic leaders around the world. Trump's gentleness toward Putin reached its low point in Helsinki, in July 2018, when, in a roundly condemned performance, he seemed to accept the Russian president's denials of election meddling, a direct contradiction of the conclusion of his own intelligence agencies.

Whatever Trump might think of Putin, under the Russian president's leadership, Russia remains anti-Western, antidemocratic, and unpredictable. Passive American leadership has ceded vast diplomatic power to Putin in Ukraine and Syria; in both places, his boldness and vision have made Russia a power player in determining the future, while the United States isn't even at the table. The seeming successes of Putin's authoritarian model have attracted legions of admirers, including in the West. Researchers in Western countries have noted a growing public tolerance for, and even admiration of, authoritarian brands of leadership.

Meanwhile, Russia's partner, China, increasingly sees itself as the real pacesetter of a new antidemocratic and statist model of governance and world leadership—in direct counterpoint to the United States. In a marathon, three-hour-plus speech to the Communist Party Congress in Beijing in October 2017, Xi Jinping, marking five years in office, declared the dawn of a "new era" in Chinese history. This new era, he said, would see "China moving closer to center stage" in world affairs and mark a victory for "Socialism with Chinese Characteristics"—a model, he took pains to point out, that was free of the taint of Western influences. "It offers a new option for other countries and nations who want to speed up their development while preserving their independence," he said.[9]

"Independence" is an ironic term for Xi to tout, of course, when his regime wantonly violates human rights, manipulates currency, and disregards international court decisions. China is ignoring a U.N. tribunal ruling regarding its aggression against the Philippines in the South China Sea. In the East China Sea, meanwhile, China is facing a tense standoff with Japan, reigniting an ancient rivalry. And, like Russia, China does not seek to oppose the West just in deed but also in ideology: the China Dream, as President Xi Jinping calls it, includes an explicit goal to surpass the United States as the world's preeminent military power by 2049. And Xi's One Belt, One Road Initiative in Eurasia—a $1 trillion economic and trade initiative with the goal of giving Beijing economic leadership in the region—reflects a kind of Chinese Marshall Plan for the globe. Indeed, the initiative is seven times the size of the American Marshall Plan that was put into effect in Europe after World War II. It offers an explicit counter-model to America's, and the West's, retreating approach.

Given their size and power, Russia and China represent the world's two definitive models of authoritarian leadership in the world today. But other nations join them in a swelling antidemocratic tide: according to Freedom House, the number of countries that can be considered "free" continues to decline around the world.

THE ROGUE MENACE

Russia and China aren't only rivals to Western values and the Western way of life. They also actively support and facilitate the world's rogue regimes, through which so much of the world's terrorist mayhem and other destabilizing activity occurs. Putin's uncompromising backing of Syria's Bashar al-Assad not only has ensured the survival of one of the world's most brutal dictators and sponsors of state terror; it has also struck a blow for authoritarians worldwide. And Iran and North Korea—both enjoying support from Moscow and Beijing—continually test Western resolve and influence, whether through their sponsorship of terrorist organizations across the globe or their pursuit of nuclear capabilities. President Trump, to his credit, has taken major steps to push back on both of these rogue nations—detailed in chapter 5—but his predecessor left him with a big cleanup task.

Eight years of President Obama's "strategic patience" with North Korea did nothing to minimize the dangers that Pyongyang poses to its

Asian neighbors or to disentangle the regime from Beijing's embrace. Before Obama, George W. Bush and Bill Clinton also tried waiting and hoping, to no avail. But North Korea kept building nuclear warheads and stepping up its development of ballistic missiles. In July 2016, North Korea ran ballistic missile tests described as a dress rehearsal for a nuclear attack on South Korea, as well as on U.S. ports and airfields. North Korean dictator Kim Jong Un "expressed great satisfaction over the successful drill," according to the Korean Central News Agency. Then, on September 3, 2017, North Korea detonated a powerful device underground that it claimed was a hydrogen bomb, which could be placed, Kim claimed, on an ICBM (an intercontinental ballistic missile), and that the missile could reach the United States. The blast equaled the magnitude of a 6.3 earthquake, according to the U.S. Geological Survey, and was described as a "city buster" by an MIT nuclear expert. And to add to the sense of menace, President Trump and Kim taunted one another on Twitter, adding to the sense of an unstable situation being overseen by unstable actors.

The Obama administration's ruinous nuclear deal with Iran has all but guaranteed that Tehran will become a nuclear power—offering the mullahs a crucial bargaining chip and blackmail tool in their quest to become the ruling power of the Middle East. A 2016 Heritage Foundation assessment declared, "By far the most significant security challenge to the United States, its allies, and its interests in the greater Middle East" comes not from ISIS or al-Qaeda, but from the Islamic Republic of Iran.[10] This judgment is sound, not only based on the certainty that Tehran will soon be a nuclear power, but also because of its broad range of destabilizing activities across the region—including establishing Shia revolutionary groups in Iraq and Lebanon, shipping arms to Palestinian militants in Gaza, and making common cause with Shia and Taliban militants in Afghanistan.

THIRD WORLD: DESTABILIZATION, DYSFUNCTION, AND THE RISE OF KLEPTOCRACY

A complete vacuum of political leadership and institutional legitimacy plagues the developing world, with deadly and destabilizing effects.

Latin America is in chaos, as Brazil, Venezuela, and Bolivia struggle to combat corruption and economic decline, which have driven people to steal food from their neighbors and even eat their pets. If Venezuela looks for help, it will likely look not to Washington but to Beijing, to whom the United States is losing influence (though the Chinese are growing impatient with the Venezuelans over unpaid debt). The drug trade has fueled increased terrorism in the region, and some reports suggest that police have killed people in exchange for promotions and rewards in Peru. The 10 cities with the highest murder rates in the world, and 18 of the top 20, are in Latin America.[11]

Brazil celebrated its 2016 hosting of the Summer Olympics, while the world watched tensely, worried about potential terror attacks in Rio. That danger was averted, but the Olympic spectacle helped overshadow a national crisis: Brazil's Congress voted to impeach the president, Dilma Rousseff, after charges that she used creative government accounting to cover up the deficit problem during her reelection campaign. How deep does corruption run in Brazil? More than half of the 65 members of the impeachment commission face serious charges themselves. Hundreds of members of the lower house of Congress are also under investigation.

Many nations in Africa continue to suffer from failed governance, pandemics, and murderous ethnic strife. Without sustainable political institutions, the continent will remain impoverished and subject to the dozens of wars that currently rage there. Its developmental weaknesses have made Africa a natural target for Chinese economic expansion, which not only serves Beijing's self-interest but also makes Africa more susceptible to Chinese political and economic influence.

The word "kleptocracy" was coined in Africa, in reference to Congo, known as Zaire when it was run by Joseph Mobutu, who looted the national treasury of tens of millions of dollars. Unfortunately, the Mobutu model still has many adherents on the continent today. In Uganda, government officials accused of graft are routinely "just shifted to other government positions," as Africa specialist Maria Burnett puts it. Seven out of ten Liberians have had to pay bribes to get health care and education. Afrobarometer, which studies African governance, estimates that 75 million people in sub-Saharan Africa have paid bribes in the last year. Citizens of the continent's biggest economies are the most skeptical. "Corruption is the single biggest threat to Africa's growth," says Ali Mufuruki of the International Monetary Fund (IMF).[12]

OTHER ISSUES

While political leadership has failed across the board, the engine that so often compensated for other problems—economic growth—has only recently begun to show signs of recovery. The global financial crisis of 2007–2008 hit every major national economy hard; but for more struggling economies, its effects were truly devastating. Now, for the first time in years, indicators are looking more generally positive. "Every major economy on earth is expanding at once, a synchronous wave of growth that is creating jobs, lifting fortunes and tempering fears of popular discontent," wrote Peter S. Goodman in the *New York Times* in January 2018.[13] Indeed, as the Trump administration settles into its second year, the United States appears poised for a major economic boom; European economies are rallying, too. "In general terms," as Goodman sees it, "improvement owes less to some newfound wellspring of wealth than the simple fact that many of the destructive forces that felled growth have finally exhausted their potency."[14]

Of course, we're talking about broad, macro indicators here. Whether a new round of economic growth will alter the dynamic that drove so much of the popular discontent of recent years—a top-to-bottom economy, in which most of the income gains accrued to the affluent and well-educated—remains to be seen.

And even in the context of more encouraging growth forecasts, it's important to keep in mind how expectations have changed post-crisis. The IMF projects that the global economy will grow at 3.9 percent in 2018, continuing an upward trend from 3.7 percent in 2017 and 3.2 in 2016. But global growth more commonly exceeded 4 percent in the years before the financial downturn. If the growth forecasts fail to pan out, the impact will be felt far and wide, especially with rising income inequality.

Poor economic growth always brings costs and risks, particularly in an adverse climate. Slower growth will likely yield lowered productivity and investment, less demand, fewer jobs, and stagnant incomes. Any significant economic slowdown will widen the gaps between the wealthy and the poor. Further hardship for those of modest means—especially when the well-off continue to prosper—could spark even more dramatic rejection of conventional politics, deepening the crisis of institutional legitimacy.

Any stalling of economic growth will also cripple governments' ability to get their balance sheets in order and deal with mounting deficits and debt. Depending on the severity of the slowdown, we could experience another crisis of financial confidence, with ramifications for everything from currency to interest rates. In short, with the intense political volatility worldwide, looming economic stagnation couldn't come at a worse time.

Even if the global economy is headed for a sustained surge, we're likely to continue to hear about economic inequality. Bernie Sanders made inequality the centerpiece of his presidential campaign—and look how far it took him, in the world's bastion of free-market capitalism. In the United States, the gap between the wealthiest 10 percent of the country and the rest of the population is staggering, and the gulf continues to widen. The growing gap between the rich and the poor affects millions, fuels anti-systemic movements, and threatens the future of developed and third world nations alike.

Failed leadership, political and social instability, and financial and economic deficits: we are poorly positioned to address the great challenges of our age.

Principal among them is the future of the young, particularly unemployed young men, and especially in the Middle East and the developing world, where governments seem to view them as a threat, not a resource. By failing to cultivate young people, Arab rulers are stoking the flames of another revolt that is bound to come. In democratic societies, the crisis of the young takes the form of starting from a disadvantage economically, losing confidence in the ethic of upward mobility, and adopting radical or marginal politics, in a rejection of the democratic system they have inherited.

Looming over all of this for the West is a crisis of faith: not just of belief in the Western way of life and in our political ideals—which, all too often, we either fail to actualize or openly denigrate—but actual spiritual belief as well. Around the world, religion remains a defining force in people's lives, but in most parts of the globe outside of the West, oppression goes hand in hand with faith: either because the state represses open religious activity, as in China; the state favors one church at the expense of others, as in Russia; or militant, sharia-based Islam endorses and enables brutal treatment of children, women, and dissenters, as an everyday staple of life—entirely apart from the problem of terrorism. Only in the West does religious faith flourish without opposition from the state, but religious faith is declining in the West, even in the United States. That the decline of religious faith would transpire roughly in tandem with a loss of faith in Western ideals, history, and culture, I believe, is no accident.

WHAT THIS BOOK IS ABOUT

As this book appears, the international environment remains volatile—between nuclear tensions, Islamist ferment, harrowing poverty and instability in the third world, and the growing power of populist and nationalist parties in the West, including major European countries and the United States—which, in the person of Donald Trump, has elected a populist president. I will make the case that there are reasons for what we're seeing—grounded in the failure of institutions, which I've been writing about for years now—but that the cost and stakes continue to grow higher and more serious. As disturbing as it is to contemplate the mounting momentum of authoritarianism around the world, or the dissolving governmental authority in places like Latin America or Africa, or to reflect soberly on the sub-replacement birthrates of the European continent, even as its countries continue to welcome hundreds of thousands of new residents from Islamic countries—is it any more reassuring to look close to home, where the political and social divisions that began to explode during the Obama era now have some people talking, during the Trump presidency, of some kind of new American civil war? Where are we headed? I wrote this book to shed some light on these issues.

In the first section of this book, "Broken Structures," I'll examine some of the causes and results of our current predicament, focusing mostly on the West—where, as my chapter titles indicate, the failure of institutions, a revolt against elites, and a breakdown of the alliance system all threaten not only public confidence but also governmental functioning. In the second section, "Escalating Threats," I'll look beyond the West to see what we're confronting: authoritarian powers (especially Russia and China) that are on the move not only in a material (and territorial) sense but, even more disturbingly, in an intellectual sense—winning loyalists to their antidemocratic, anti-Western, and anti-American ideological systems; the ongoing and chilling challenges presented by the world's rogue regimes and its deadly and determined Islamist terror groups; a third world in crisis, with escalating problems—economic, political, infrastructural—across swaths of Latin American and Africa; and the sobering prospect of a global energy war sometime in the future, Russia working overtime to preserve its energy economy even as the United States, a new world energy leader, threatens not just its market prerogatives but also an entire delicate balance of power. Finally, in the third section, "A Way Forward," I'll examine how religion, at the heart of so much tension around the world today, sees its potential realized most fully in the West—and only in the West, even as Western citizens seem increasingly indifferent to Christianity, the defining faith. This tension has particular relevance in the United States because, as it turns out, religion has always been central to Americans' ideas about themselves. That leads to my final chapter, which I call "assertive democratic idealism" and in which I argue that the only true prospect for stabilizing the global climate will come from a renewed commitment to leadership from the United States, a commitment informed by an idealistic, moral, yet practical outlook toward the rest of the world.

A president whom I served, Bill Clinton, said in his first inaugural address, "There is nothing wrong with America that cannot be cured by what is right with America." This is not just true at home but abroad: in an aspirational sense, the vast majority of the world's people continues to identify with the values and goals identified with America—liberty, freedom, and the right to pursue one's own destiny—even as we Americans lose confidence in ourselves and as our increasingly sclerotic politics work to delegitimize our system internationally. I believe that Clinton's words still apply, even amid the tumultuous and often demoralizing political climate that now prevails in the United States. Moreover, I am convinced that believing it is central to the goal of a more stable, democratic, and peaceful world. We're a long way from that scenario at the moment, though, and there is much work to do.

PART I

BROKEN STRUCTURES

CHAPTER ONE

THE COLLAPSE OF INSTITUTIONAL LEGITIMACY

"Europe is going through a deep crisis, it is like a sleepwalker heading towards a cliff."

—GREEK PRIME MINISTER ALEXIS TSIPRAS, SEPTEMBER 2016[1]

"We are now observing the inequality of trust around the world. This brings a number of potential consequences including the rise of populist politicians, the blocking of innovation and the onset of protectionism and nativism."

—RICHARD EDELMAN, PRESIDENT AND CEO OF EDELMAN RESEARCH[2]

Never in modern Western history has there been a moment when entrenched institutions are weaker, less trusted, and more subject to volatile public movements than now. What I call the collapse of institutional legitimacy is wholesale and broad-based, and it has run on remarkably parallel tracks in the United States and in Europe. (These will be our focus for this chapter; later chapters will explore the state of things in other parts of the world.)

"Pick an adjective to describe the current political mood—angry, anxious, populist—and one thing about the descriptor is certain: It will fit the atmosphere on both sides of the Atlantic equally well," wrote Gerald Seib in the *Wall Street Journal* in January 2016, just as the United States presidential election season was about to begin in earnest. "Political trends in Europe and the U.S. often move in synchronization, and rarely has that been more true than right now. In both places, the political establishment is shaking, fringe actors are moving to center stage, parties are changing face and voters appear to be tearing themselves loose from their traditional moorings."[3]

Driving the popular mood, then and now, is contempt for elites. The public has grown increasingly disgusted with elite institutions, especially government but also business and the media. This collapse of institutional trust is a phenomenon of the mass public—the kinds of people who voted for Brexit or for Trump—but not of the elites themselves, who, surveys show, continue to hold government and other leading institutions in high esteem. And why wouldn't they? They run these institutions. The gap between the general public and its leaders—call them governing elites, the political class, or what you will—is considerable, and it generally reflects an even deeper gap: that between haves and have-nots. In more than two-thirds of the countries surveyed in the 2018 Edelman Trust barometer, the general population did not trust mainstream institutions to do what is right.[4]

"If you've got money, you vote in," a pro-Brexit voter told the *Guardian*. "If you haven't got money, you vote out."[5] And this attitude extends far beyond Great Britain. "We are now observing the inequality of trust around the world," said Richard Edelman, president and CEO of Edelman Research, in 2016. "This brings a number of potential consequences including the rise of populist politicians, the blocking of innovation and the onset of protectionism and nativism."[6]

The United States and Western Europe have always had income inequality; in free societies, massive gaps in income between society's wealthiest individuals and its poorest are inevitable and, to a certain extent, desirable: they reflect mobility and the opportunity for advancement. But the wealth disparities are wider now, in many places, than they have been in many years; and in those earlier periods, leading institutions were broadly able to maintain the confidence and trust of citizens—even poor citizens. Now such confidence and trust have been shattered, and not just among the poor but across a broad swath of the middle class as well.

Where did this collapse in institutional legitimacy originate? It is ultimately the result of two decades of elite decision-making—in economics, finance, politics, and war and peace—that have failed, and failed repeatedly, to deliver positive results for the vast majority. In the mid-1990s, for example, the United States, Mexico, and Canada entered into the North American Free Trade Agreement. Critics and economists still say that NAFTA has brought substantial benefits, especially to the

United States, but today the average American middle-class worker doesn't feel that way. A quarter-century after its adoption, NAFTA has become one of the most detested trade agreements in history. Contempt for NAFTA colored public views of the Trans-Pacific Partnership (TPP), which President Obama championed in vain—Congress refused to authorize it and President Trump formally killed it during his first week in office.

It wasn't just anti-free-trade sentiment that sunk TPP: it was also public anger at elite arrogance. The deal was negotiated behind closed doors; officials would not publicly disclose its terms. President Obama expected to sign a complicated deal, get Congress to pass it, and get Americans to live by it—all without ever telling them what was in it. Some remembered then House Speaker Nancy Pelosi's infamous line, before the passage of Obamacare: "We have to pass the bill so that we can learn what's in it." Not this time, the public said. Not again.

Public dissatisfaction extends far beyond trade deals. The 2008 financial crisis was precipitated by elites: policies devised in Washington and London and supported on Wall Street and in European financial capitals led to the worst financial panic since the 1930s. Government came to the rescue—of elites, not ordinary people. Huge financial-sector bailouts rescued elite leaders like the CEOs of financial services companies; only the general public paid any real price, and it is still paying. In 2015, six years into an economic recovery, 64 percent of Americans told pollsters that they felt like the Great Recession was *still* going on.[7] The financial crisis has eroded confidence in institutions across the globe. It damaged confidence in economists for not predicting the crash, banks and financial firms for helping cause it, and politicians for bailing out the banks while Main Street suffered. Above all, the crisis eroded the credibility of experts—and of expertise itself.

In Europe, ordinary citizens see elites protecting themselves at every turn. The Greek debt crisis could have been put to rest years ago, with short-term pain but much less far-reaching suffering, had the government permitted defaults on private bank debt. Instead, the banks, with their government enablers, engineered a bailout paid for by the public. Greek taxpayers have borne the primary burden. Though there have been encouraging signs in recent years, and the country was cleared by its eurozone partners to exit its bailout terms in 2018, default remains a possibility; even without default, EU creditors hold most Greek debt, and they will demand austerity reforms.

And even as the global economy has recovered substantially from the worst of the financial crisis, for millions in the United States and Europe, the recovery seems thin or nonexistent. While the U.S. economy is now thriving, economic growth in Europe has been tepid, jobs are scarce, and the income gap continues to grow across Western societies. Making people still angrier is that elites in government, business, and media still don't seem to understand the public mood. Thus, events like Brexit, and especially the Trump candidacy and Trump victory, left them bewildered—and worse, contemptuous of the "masses" for responding in this way.

In a sense, the schism between elites and the general public operates in a kind of feedback loop: elites make decisions that cause hardship; the public pushes back; elites don't listen and continue pursuing policies that the public detests; the public responds by making populist or radical political choices; elites, disgusted by the public's lack of gratitude for their wise leadership, mock and denigrate ordinary people, calling them "deplorables" among other things; and the divide grows. Or, as the *Los Angeles Times*'s Vincent Bevins wrote on Facebook, "The elites in rich countries have overplayed their hand, taking all the gains for themselves and just covering their ears when anyone else talks, and now they are watching in horror as voters revolt."[8]

Accompanying financial and economic woes are national security fears, especially fears of Islamist terrorism. These fears are exacerbated by a powerful sense among citizens in multiple countries that they are losing their national culture and identity to outsiders, even being colonized. The main fear here concerns Muslims, and these fears have grown over a generation of extremely liberal European immigration policies but also, more recently, during the Syrian refugee crisis. Two of the attackers behind the 2015 Paris attacks posed as Syrian refugees to gain entry into Europe. After the recent string of terror attacks and other incidents involving migrants, the tensions continue to deepen. In the United States, the Obama administration's plan to resettle 10,000 Syrian refugees sparked intense opposition from the public and from Republican officials—and Trump used the issue, among others, to rally support to his "America first" campaign.

The refugee crisis is another instance not just of bad policy judgment on the part of elites but also of their lack of responsiveness to public concerns. "Our ruling elites are globalists," wrote Guy Randolph, an American, in a letter to the *Wall Street Journal*. "They have abandoned the idea that they belong to a country. They are detached from the man on the street."[9] Millions of Europeans voice similar sentiments about their national governments and the EU.

Electorates in the United States and the United Kingdom also remember the Iraq war, how their governments took them into a conflict that proved bloody, staggeringly costly, and globally destabilizing—and they remember how it was the sons and daughters of families of modest means who were called upon to fight it, not the sons and daughters of elite parents. Then they saw continued damaging judgments from the Obama administration, whose foreign policy failures show that disaster can come equally from recklessness or passivity: its withdrawal from Iraq left a vacuum filled by the rise of ISIS, and its refusal to assert itself in Syria led to more bloodshed in that country's savage civil war and allowed Russia's Vladimir Putin to attain power-broker status in the Middle East; meanwhile, its foolhardy adventuring in Libya helped create another radical Islamist stronghold in North Africa.

Again and again, we see failures of governance, with ordinary people paying the price.

Nor does the media, supposedly the interpreters of the public mood, have a handle on the situation. So deeply embedded, by now, in their own hardened assumptions about the world and about ordinary people, they can do little more than parrot elite talking points. Thus they were blindsided by Brexit and by Trump, as well as by developments on the European continent, where anti-EU sentiment is rising and anti-systemic, populist parties are gaining momentum. As John Harris wrote of Brexit, in the *Guardian*, "Most of the media...failed to see this coming.... The alienation of the people charged with documenting the national mood from the people who actually define it is one of the ruptures that has led to this moment."[10] More and more, citizens see the media not as information sources or interpreters of news events but as part and parcel of the same elite apparatus that they despise. Yes, it was undignified and undiplomatic when Trump's former chief strategist, Steve Bannon, told the media to "shut up" and described them as "the opposition party"—but millions of Americans cheered.

This rejection of media, however justified, is also a destabilizing force, as it raises the question of whether any common narratives can be accepted anymore. People don't believe what they're told for good reason: they have been poorly served, at best, and outright lied to, at worst. For years, from governing administration to governing administration, by media and by politicians, in country after country, elite, established institutions have been losing all credibility. Their authority has collapsed—as I warned was happening five years ago, in my book *The End of Authority*.

This chapter will examine the collapse of institutions in the United States and Europe and why we can't understand our present moment without an understanding of this wholesale erosion of authority in the West.

FAILURES OF GOVERNANCE IN THE WEST

If there is an original cause for these woes, it is the failure of governance across the board—to solve problems, to honor commitments, and to perform with anything resembling competence. At the core of the issue in the United States for many years has been economic stress, stagnation, and dislocation—a broad sense of malaise about economic growth, wage levels, and growing inequality. In 2016, fed-up American voters bucked the prognostications—and mockery—of nearly the entire mainstream media and put Donald Trump in the White House. Trump would not be president if a broad base of the American people hadn't become convinced that the institutions of their government were broken and that there was no other alternative. Trump's first year in office saw a more rapidly growing economy and more robust job growth—in part due to his administration's business-friendly regulatory, tax, and trade policies—but the underlying tensions that run underneath the U.S. economy, and those of most advanced nations, remain largely in place.

In the United States

"For too long, a small group in our nation's capital has reaped the rewards of government while the people have borne the cost," Trump said on January 20, 2017, in his inaugural address. "Washington flourished—but the people did not share in its wealth. Politicians prospered—but the jobs left, and the factories closed. The establishment protected itself but not the citizens of our country." He went on: "Their victories have not been your victories; their triumphs have not been your triumphs; and while they celebrated in our nation's capital, there was little to celebrate for struggling families all across our land."[11]

A poll shortly thereafter showed that 53 percent of Americans rated the speech "excellent" or "good" and just 20 percent called it "poor" or "terrible."[12] No doubt they were responding, in part, to the economic message. Barack Obama was the first modern president not to have a single year of even 3 percent economic growth. By traditional indicators, Obama could claim success: the unemployment rate reached a peak of 10 percent during his first year in office; when he left, unemployment had plummeted to 4.9 percent. But many observers no longer find such traditional figures meaningful, pointing out that millions had simply stopped looking for work and were thus not accounted for in the totals. The labor-force participation rate is the real story here, and in the Obama years, it reached 62.7 percent, the lowest since 1977.[13]

Slow growth and low labor-force participation have produced stagnant wages and salaries, especially among those in the middle class and below. According to inflation-adjusted Census data, the typical middle-class American family has seen no boost in its earnings over 20 years ago; men working full-time are making slightly less, on average, since then.[14] Households at the bottom of the economic ladder are making less, in real dollars, than they were in 1989—more than a quarter of a century ago. Those at the top continue to race ahead: the top 5 percent of households make 37.5 percent more than they were earning in 1989.[15]

Income inequality continues to widen in the United States. The top 20 percent of income earners in the United States earn a little more than half (51.3 percent) of all national income (they also pay 84 percent of the taxes).[16] The top 1 percent earns about 17 percent of the income (and pays about 46 percent of the taxes).[17]

Discontent about the present and gloom about the future—atypical traits for Americans—have characterized the public mood, with more people telling pollsters that they see a less promising future ahead for themselves and especially for their children, whom many believe won't have the same opportunities they themselves have.[18] In late September

2016, a little more than a month before the presidential election, 58 percent of respondents in a Gallup survey said that economic conditions in
the United States were "getting worse."[19]

Though economics remains at the center of national discord, the
United States has troubles across the board. The American elementary
and secondary education system is a flat-out failure. The United States
spends an average of $10,768 per pupil on primary and secondary educa-
tion annually, more than any other OECD (Organisation for Economic
Co-operation and Development) country except Switzerland.[20] In fact,
the United States has *doubled spending on education* over the past 40
years—but test scores in reading, math, and science have remained stub-
bornly flat.[21] School dropout rates, especially in poor areas, are staggeringly high; we're creating generations of unemployable people. American
students' performance rates poorly internationally, especially on the
Programme for International Student Assessment (PISA), a respected
triennial international survey that tests the skills of 15-year-olds in
mathematics, science, and reading in over 70 countries, including the
United States. In the most recent PISA assessment, published in 2015,
the United States ranked nineteenth in science, twentieth in reading, and
thirty-first in mathematics out of 35 OECD countries.[22] On standardized
tests, reading and math scores for American 17-year-olds have *shown no
improvement whatsoever* over the last 40 years.[23]

The American health care system was upended by Obamacare, the
most sweeping, undemocratic federal attempt to control a large portion
of the economy in the nation's history. Obamacare has failed; the only
question is what will replace it. Under President Trump, the replacement
process has begun: the administration's Tax Cuts and Jobs Act of 2017
repealed Obamacare's individual mandate starting in 2019 and ended the
cost-sharing reduction payments to insurers, which the administration
considers a bailout for the insurers and "another example of how the
previous administration abused taxpayer dollars and skirted the law to
prop up a broken system."[24] The health care dilemma is even more acute
in the context of an aging population, longer lifespans, and mounting
public health crises, from untreated mental health populations to a massive and hugely destructive plague of opioid addiction.

U.S. border and immigration policy played a central role in the 2016
campaign, thanks to Trump's pledge to build a wall that would keep

migrants from Mexico out of the United States. Trump capitalized on Americans' frustration with hearing politicians promise to control the border and stem the flow of illegal entrants into the United States—but failing to deliver. The problem seemed to crystallize in summer 2014, when thousands of minors streamed across the United States' southern border with Mexico, fleeing gang violence in South and Central America. Their arrival created a humanitarian crisis and underscored for millions of Americans—especially those living near the border—the utter failure of governing elites to protect national sovereignty.

Concern about the border only deepened at the news that the Obama administration wanted to resettle at least 10,000 Syrian refugees. Governors in about two dozen states quickly announced that they would close off their states to refugees. Popular opposition was strong; 60 percent of Americans opposed taking in so many refuges in a November 2015 Gallup poll.[25] The opposition only hardened when it became evident that most of the refugees were slated to be moved into poor communities, not well-to-do ones—a dramatic illustration of the divide between elites, who make these rules, and ordinary citizens, who have to live with them.

In opposing asylum for the refugees, many cited terror concerns, and with good reason. Then FBI director James Comey admitted to Congress that the refugees couldn't be thoroughly vetted. "If we don't know much about somebody, there won't be anything in our data," Comey said. "I can't sit here and offer anybody an absolute assurance that there's no risk associated with this."[26]

And the risks of terrorism, as far as Americans were concerned, were already multiplying, refugees or no refugees. The waning Obama years saw an outbreak of domestic terror attacks: the 2013 Boston marathon bombing, the July 2015 Chattanooga shootings at a military recruiting center, the December 2015 San Bernardino massacre, and the June 2016 Orlando nightclub shooting. All were committed by Islamist terrorists. Despite Obama's assurance that the country was safe, Americans sensed a rising tide of domestic terror during his presidency, and they weren't put at ease by the president's calm demeanor or by the troubling fact that he seemed more interested in warning against virtually nonexistent attacks on Muslims than he was in protecting the country.

The Obama years took a toll on Americans' sense of well-being in many areas, and national security was no exception. Two months before the 2016 presidential election, just 27 percent of survey respondents said the nation was safer than before 9/11. More than half—55 percent—said they did not think the country was safe, and 50 percent were not confident that the government could protect citizens from future attacks.[27]

Economic distress, educational failure, social problems, health care woes, national sovereignty challenges, and terrorism fears: it was a deeply troubled American electorate that went to the polls in November 2016.

Failure in Europe

For all its problems, America still has a better hand to play than anyone else. That is most apparent when looking across the Atlantic at our traditional allies: Great Britain and the democracies of Western Europe.

The big story here in 2016 was Brexit, of course, but Brexit comes in a much larger context of the impending failure of the European Union amid economic, political, social, and cultural divides that continue to widen. Europe's problems run the gamut of financial instability and poverty (Greece, Italy), unemployment (Greece, Spain, some former Eastern Bloc countries), immigration (most EU member states), threats from a resurgent Russia on Europe's eastern periphery (the Baltic states), and fears about terrorism (everywhere). As in the United States, however, many of these concerns might be less intense if economic growth were more robust.

"Europe is going through a deep crisis, it is like a sleepwalker heading towards a cliff. If we do not make employment a priority, Europe could disintegrate," Greek prime minister Alexis Tsipras told *Le Monde* in September 2016, warning that the future could soon see "other referendums rejecting the European Union."[28] In particular, Tsipras was referring to the scourge of unemployment, which, though it doesn't get the headlines of the refugee crisis or terrorism, might be the issue that tops all others.

The improving global economy offers some hope for the future, but unemployment remains considerably higher in almost all EU countries than in the United States; the average EU unemployment rate was 8.3 percent in June 2018.[29] Some countries are doing well: in June 2018, the

U.K., the Netherlands, Norway, Malta, the Czech Republic, Poland, Germany, and Hungary had lower joblessness rates than the United States, but three EU countries topped 10 percent unemployment. In Greece, unemployment stood at 20.2 percent; in Spain, it was 15.2 percent. Unemployment is particularly glaring among the young. Across the EU, the youth unemployment rate averages 16.7 percent; in Greece, Spain, Croatia, and Italy, the rates range from 27 percent to more than 43 percent. These figures are among the worst anywhere in the world.[30]

Unsurprisingly, a bleak jobs picture has affected the public outlook on the future. More than three-quarters of Greeks told a poll for *Real News* that they feared that they wouldn't be able to maintain their living standards in a year; 70 percent of young Greeks said that they would look for work elsewhere.[31] The young have often formed a key constituency for the right-wing and left-wing populists who are gaining such momentum in Europe.

Another tectonic plate that is starting to shift in Europe is the social safety net. Its crippling costs put its future solvency in doubt, especially with shrinking native-born populations to pay for it. Many EU governments have by necessity moved toward austerity measures, but these steps have by and large only deepened social and political divisions.

With stagnant employment and a troubled social safety net, standards of living have suffered, especially in countries facing potential fiscal crises, like Greece and Hungary. After years of EU-mandated austerity, Greek citizens have seen their purchasing power decline by one-third and their income by one-quarter. In 2014, when asked if they had trouble making ends meet, 95 percent of Greek survey respondents said yes. The "extreme" poverty rate in Greece exploded from just 2.2 percent in 2009 to 13.6 percent in 2016.[32]

One Hungarian member of Parliament described the country's middle class as living in a "vegetative state."[33] The Hungarian Central Statistical Office (KSH) estimates that more than one-third of the nation's population lives below the poverty line—a chilling figure, especially in that nation, where qualifying as "poor" by official standards takes extraordinary deprivation. The KSH considers a family of four as below the poverty line only if it lives on an income of about $900 per year.[34] In Hungary and in Romania, half the population lives in overcrowded apartments, according to estimates.[35]

In Italy, the economy has barely grown since the formation of the euro nearly 20 years ago, and the economy is more than 10 percent smaller than it was before the 2008 financial crisis.[36] Nationally, unemployment exceeds 10 percent; in southern Italy, it is nearly double that rate;[37] and among young people, it exceeds one-third.[38] In a nation with the third-largest economy in the eurozone, this is crippling stagnation. Some believe that an Italian banking crisis is imminent. Italy formed a panel in September to examine the causes of the collapse of several large financial institutions.[39]

France's unemployment rate, slightly under 10 percent, is comparatively modest but still very high when compared with the much lower jobless rates in the United Kingdom and Germany. And France, too, suffers from very high youth unemployment—21.8 percent in October 2017.[40]

With this kind of economic duress, it's not surprising that immigration, whether legal or illegal, has become such a furious issue across Europe, dividing governments from their citizens in many cases. In Germany, Chancellor Angela Merkel has thrown open the doors to more than one million migrants fleeing war, poverty, and instability in North Africa and the Middle East. "Merkel made a mistake letting everyone in," said Moritz Daul, 48, a Berlin resident. "She will pay the price and so will Germany, our children."[41] Merkel has stood firm, but strong feelings about the migrant policy have a lot to do with the rise of the nationalist Alternative für Deutschland (Alternative for Germany or AfD) party. The AfD's views resemble those of citizens in many other European countries, where native-born populations fear that their leaders do not understand or care about the cultural and economic impact these migrants will have on their communities, while the leaders themselves are shielded from the consequences. In Germany's September 2017 elections, AfD won enough seats to enter Parliament for the first time, becoming the third-largest party in the legislature—and apparently forcing Merkel to make a concession: she has agreed to cap refugee admissions into Germany at 200,000 per year.[42] In July 2018, in another major concession, Merkel agreed to set up "transit centers" on the Germany-Austria border that will make it easier to turn immigrants away.

The case of Sweden, long recognized as one of the most welcoming nations in Europe to outsiders, is instructive. Sweden granted residency to nearly ten times as many newcomers in 2015 as it did in 1980, but this open-door policy has finally generated a backlash. Anti-immigrant sentiment is on the rise, and numerous violent incidents have been reported against newcomers. The climate wasn't improved by the terror attack in April 2017, when a jihadi drove a truck into a shopping area and department store in Stockholm, killing five and injuring at least a dozen more. Many Swedes fear the arrival of Middle Eastern and North African migrants.[43]

So do citizens in other Scandinavian countries. "I've become a racist," says Johnny Christensen, a retired bank employee in Denmark who once considered himself pro-immigrant. But after years of watching Muslim newcomers flood into Denmark, he has changed his mind. Denmark's culture minister, Bertel Haarder, puts it bluntly: because of fundamental cultural differences on matters including free speech and the role of women, Muslims do not assimilate as easily to Denmark as other newcomers do.

"It's not racism to be aware of the difference," Haarder says. "It's stupid not to be aware."[44] A Danish historian, Bo Lidegaard, puts it best: "We are a multiethnic society today…but we are not and should never become a multicultural society."[45]

But that indeed is the danger: without a common cultural norm, which for centuries most European nations could fall back on without even thinking, newcomers from more alien cultures, like the Middle East and North Africa, will destabilize European societies. To some extent, this is already happening. Recent years have seen an upsurge in terror attacks on the Continent—from Paris and Nice to Brussels and Berlin. And Barcelona, too, where, in August 2017, a terrorist drove a van into pedestrians on La Rambla, a popular tourist thoroughfare in the capital city, killing 13 people and injuring at least 130 others.

Few French citizens will forget 2015, which began with the *Charlie Hebdo* massacre, when the Kouachi brothers, French citizens born to Algerian immigrants, murdered the staff of the satirical magazine, which had often ridiculed Islam (and other religions) and had printed Muhammad cartoons. In November 2015 came the worst terrorist massacre in French history, when ISIS-coordinated attacks killed at least 130 people, most at the Bataclan nightclub and others at cafes around Paris. Then in July 2016, on Bastille Day, a French citizen of Tunisian descent drove a 19-ton truck into a crowd of revelers, killing 86. For France, 2017 was quieter on the terror front, with police killing a machete-wielding attacker yelling "Allahu Akbar" at a mall near the Louvre before the jihadi could kill anyone, and a terror attack on the Champs-Elysées in April, where an attacker fired at a police van, killed an officer, and injured two others by firing at pedestrians on the sidewalk before being killed by police.

France has the largest Muslim population in Western Europe, with Muslims making up about 7.5 percent of the population.[46] Anti-Muslim attitudes in France are on the rise in the wake of these attacks. More than half of French citizens told Pew in 2016 that they don't believe that Muslims want to assimilate into French society.[47] In June 2017, 96 percent of French citizens told Gallup that attacks against France, whether carried out by residents or nonresidents, were a serious problem.[48]

Germany has also borne the brunt of a rising tide of attacks. Notoriously, on New Year's Eve 2015 in Cologne, dozens of women were groped or sexually assaulted by men described as North African or Middle Eastern. Merkel's government had no meaningful response. Multiple small-scale terror attacks have broken out, including some committed by Syrian refugees—like the machete-wielding man who murdered a pregnant woman in Reutlingen or the Afghan refugee who attacked passengers on a German train while shouting "Allahu Akbar." An 18-year-old Islamist went on a shooting spree at a Munich mall, killing seven. And in December 2016, a Tunisian migrant drove a truck into a Christmas market, killing 12 and wounding dozens.

But Great Britain had the grimmest 2017 of the Western European democracies. In March, a British Muslim terrorist killed 4 people and injured more than 50 when he drove his car into pedestrians on Westminster Bridge. ISIS claimed responsibility. In May, one of the worst attacks in British history took place at Manchester Arena, where, just as an Ariana Grande concert was ending, a terrorist detonated a homemade bomb, killing 22 people, including children, and injuring hundreds. In June, three jihadis rammed their van into pedestrians on London Bridge, killing seven and injuring dozens, and in September, a "bucket" bomb detonated in the London Tube, injuring 22.

To millions of Europeans, the carnage of recent years is intimately tied to the refugee crisis and the lax attitude of European elites toward national borders and immigration. Eight out of 10 respondents in a 2016 Pew Research poll of residents of European countries believe that the inflow of refugees will increase the likelihood of terrorist attacks in their countries.[49] That same year, 70 percent of respondents in a poll from the Hungarian Századvég Foundation saw increased Muslim immigration as a serious threat to security in Europe; 86 percent said that a terrorist attack was likely in their country.[50]

Elite policies—on the economy, on finance, on immigration and refugees—have been divisive enough. Worse, however, are elite attitudes toward public objections to these policies. As exemplified by Chancellor Merkel, the general message seems to be: we know best; do what we say; stop being so narrow-minded. Peggy Noonan summed it up well:

> Ms. Merkel had put the entire burden of a huge cultural change not on herself and those like her but on regular people who live closer to the edge, who do not have the resources to meet the burden, who have no particular protection or money or connections. Ms. Merkel, her cabinet and government, the media and cultural apparatus that lauded her decision were not in the least affected by it and likely never would be. When the working and middle class pushed back in shocked indignation, the people on top called them "xenophobic," "narrow-minded," "racist." The detached, who made the decisions and bore none of the costs, got to be called "humanist," "compassionate," and "hero of human rights."[51]

The bill is coming due, however, both materially and otherwise. The most far-reaching effect of these failures of governance—and the arrogant attitudes of the leaders who have perpetrated them—is not economic woe, cultural tensions, or even the body count from terror attacks. It is the collapse of public faith in the institutions of government and civil society.

THE COLLAPSE OF TRUST

What is the result of two decades (at least) of failed governance and elite myopia? A thoroughgoing, wholesale erosion, and in many cases outright collapse, of popular support for institutions across a full spectrum of government, education, media, religion, health care—you name it. Consider the numbers.

The Edelman Trust Barometer has been publishing the results of its annual survey of public trust in institutions for a decade and a half. In 2017, it found the most dramatic drop in trust in major institutions— government, business, media, and NGOs—in the survey's history. "Trust in media (43 percent) fell precipitously and is at all-time lows in 17 countries, while trust levels in government (41 percent) dropped in 14 markets and is the least trusted institution in half of the 28 countries surveyed," the organization's press release stated. "The credibility of leaders also is in peril: CEO credibility dropped 12 points globally to an all-time low of 37 percent, plummeting in every country studied, while government leaders (29 percent) remain least credible." Moreover, "the Trust Barometer found that 53 percent of respondents believe the current overall system has failed them—it is unfair and offers little hope for the future—while only 15 percent believe it is working."[52]

These figures represent overall survey results—but when sorted by subgroups, the results are even more troubling. It turns out that elites have not suffered the same loss of confidence. What Edelman calls the "informed public"—those with college educations, who are highly engaged with media, and who earn incomes in the top 25 percent—have *never had more faith in established institutions*. Among the general public, however, the picture is very different. Edelman surveys citizens in more than two dozen countries worldwide; in over 60 percent of these nations, the mass population—the non-elites, that is—registered trust levels below 50 percent. The average trust gap between the elites and the general public was 12 points.[53] In the United States, the trust gap was 19 points; the United Kingdom, France, India, Australia, and Mexico weren't far behind.[54]

Income inequality is crucial to this divide. The trust gap between low-income and high-income respondents is even greater than that between non-elites and elites. In the United States, the trust gap by income is *31 points*. In more than two-thirds of the countries Edelman surveyed, more than half of respondents didn't think that they would be better off in five years.[55] That is a crushing blow to future prospects.

Globally, averaged over all the countries it surveyed, Edelman found government the least trusted of all institutions—with just 42 percent expressing trust.[56] Trust levels in business fared best among the four main institutions, though its overall figure (53 percent) is hardly overwhelming. As for the media, less than half of all respondents (47 percent) expressed confidence.

In the United States

According to Edelman, the United States has the biggest trust divide of any country between its elite "informed public" and its "mass population." While trust levels are at a 16-year high among the informed public, they have barely budged for the remaining 85 percent (mass population). Again, the gap should be seen through the lens of economics: less than half of the mass population think that they will be better off in five years. By contrast, 63 percent of the informed public in the United States think that they will be better off by then.

Indeed, outside of elite circles, American skepticism has become widespread—and it played a crucial role in Trump's election. Two-thirds of Americans said that the country had "pretty seriously gotten off on the wrong track" in a CBS News poll as the 2016 presidential election approached; seven in ten told Gallup that they were dissatisfied with how things were going.[57] In this context, it makes sense that Trump's "Make America Great Again" slogan resonated with so many Americans.

On other surveys, Americans' confidence in the nation's major institutions continues to lag behind historical averages. Of the 14 institutions Gallup asked about, a majority of the public expressed confidence in only two—the military (72 percent) and the police (57 percent). Only 36 percent have trust in the public schools, 32 percent have confidence in banks, 27 percent in the criminal justice system, 24 percent in TV news, 27 percent in newspapers, 21 percent in big business, 41 percent in churches and organized religion. Just 12 percent have confidence in Congress.[58] That number comes perilously close to Senator John McCain's oft-repeated crack that, if Congress's approval rating got much lower, its supporters would consist solely of family and paid staffers.

According to a December 2017 Pew survey, "Only 18% of Americans today say they can trust the government in Washington to do what is right 'just about always' (3%) or 'most of the time' (15%)."[59]

Americans see government leaders and politicians generally as much less honest than average people. Just 29 percent said that the word "honest" could describe elected officials, while 69 percent said average Americans could be described that way.[60] Nearly three-quarters say politicians are out for themselves, not the national interest.[61] Fifty-nine percent assert that the government needs "major reform"—an increase of 22 points since 1997. And 55 percent believe ordinary Americans would do better than the government at solving the nation's problems.[62]

Meanwhile, Americans' trust in the mainstream media "to report the news fully, accurately and fairly" dropped to its lowest level in Gallup polling history in 2017, when just 27 percent said that they had "a great deal" or "quite a lot" of confidence in newspapers; just 24 percent had high confidence in TV news and just 16 percent in Internet news.[63] Distrust in media ran across age groups, and people's views on this matter are a good hint of their views on the bigger picture. In the homestretch of the 2016 presidential campaign, 88 percent of Trump supporters told Rasmussen Reports that news organizations skew the facts; most Hillary Clinton backers (59 percent) trusted the media.[64] Therein hangs a tale.

In the U.K.

On the morning of June 23, 2016, British voters went to the polls to vote on the Leave or Remain referendum that would determine whether the United Kingdom stayed in the European Union. Polls forecasting the outcome of the so-called Brexit vote were close, but British betting markets gave a heavy edge to the Remain forces, and polls among British voters themselves showed that most thought that the Remain side would win. All the backing and support of Western heads of state, including President Obama, was aligned with the Remain forces and behind British prime minister David Cameron, who had called the vote to put to rest the agitation from the British Right for a popular referendum on EU membership.

By late in the day, however, the betting markets, the smart forecasters, and Western governing elites all had egg on their faces: by 52 to 48 percent, the British people had voted to leave the European Union, throwing the EU's future into question. It was a stunning political result in a year whose most stunning outcome was yet to come, across the Atlantic.

"Never has there been a greater coalition of the establishment than that assembled by Prime Minister David Cameron for his referendum campaign to keep the U.K. in the European Union," wrote Fraser Nelson in the *Wall Street Journal*. "There was almost every Westminster party leader, most of their troops and almost every trade union and employers' federation. There were retired spy chiefs, historians, football clubs, national treasures like Stephen Hawking and divinities like Keira Knightley. And some global glamour too: President Barack Obama flew to London to do his bit, and Goldman Sachs opened its checkbook. And none of it worked." The Brexit vote, Nelson wrote, was "probably the biggest slap in the face ever delivered to the British establishment in the history of universal suffrage."[65]

Why did Britons vote to leave the EU, despite the best efforts of every establishment organ and leader to convince them to stay? In short, because millions had lost confidence and faith in their leading institutions, especially their government and political leaders. The British experience has notable similarities with the American one. In short, the Brexit vote came down essentially to a have v. have-not split. There is "a huge gap between the haves and have-nots of Britain in the trust they place in their government," said Edelman in 2016.[66] More than half (54 percent) of "high-net-worth" individuals—those earning more than £100,000 a year and with liquid assets of more than £650,000—expressed confidence in government, while just 26 percent of those with incomes of less than £15,000 said the same.[67] It's not surprising, then, that those with higher incomes were much more likely to vote Remain; those with lower incomes were much more likely to vote Leave. Seventy percent of university graduates voted Remain, while 68 percent of those without high school diplomas voted Leave. An urban/rural split and the split between millennials and older voters, with which Americans are familiar, played a role, too: Remain votes drew heavily from London residents and voters under 30, while Leave relied on the support of voters over 60 and residents of Northern England.[68]

This class breakdown essentially propelled Britain out of the European Union. But it wouldn't have happened if it didn't correlate closely with a trust breakdown: as in the United States, the Edelman

Trust Barometer found in the U.K. what it called "a yawning gap" in trust between the elite "informed public" and the "mass population."

In 2016, for the fifth year in a row, Edelman found government the least trusted institution in Britain, and this lack of trust played a decisive role in Brexit.[69] In a YouGov poll, 81 percent of Leave voters said they didn't trust the views of British politicians; 85 percent said they didn't trust foreign political leaders.[70] President Obama's visit to the U.K. shortly before the Brexit voted, in which he warned Britons that leaving the EU would put them at "the back of the queue," clearly didn't help and may well have backfired.[71]

And it isn't just government. Trust in business has grown to record highs, reaching 60 percent—that is, among elites. Among the mass population, trust in business has barely budged since the crash, and in fact, among all U.K. institutions, the trust gap is biggest in business.

Likewise, trust levels between Britain's elites and the mass population diverges when it comes to media. In 2016, 52 percent of Edelman's "informed public" expressed trust in media, while only 36 percent of the mass population felt the same way.[72] The mainstream British media overwhelmingly supported a vote to Remain. Britons didn't listen. And even after the vote, British elites were flummoxed by the result. Former prime minister Tony Blair, for example—a symbol of New Labour and the globalist consensus—was said to be baffled. "Tony doesn't get it," said a Blair colleague. "He increasingly resembles a ghost. He keeps saying that after Brexit what is needed is simply to have better policies and ideas to appeal to voters when he doesn't seem to realise that something much bigger has happened."[73]

Indeed, most broadly, the Brexit vote indicated a wholesale loss of trust not just in elite institutions but also in the idea of expertise itself—another similarity with the American election, in which the United States elected the first president in its history without political or military experience. A majority of Leave voters told pollsters that they trusted the common sense of ordinary people more than the views of experts. They showed it on voting day, when they rejected the dire warnings about what would happen if Britain voted to leave the EU.[74]

The Brexit battle lines were more or less replicated five months later in the American presidential election. Once again, it was economic and intellectual elites versus the working class; urban dwellers versus rural residents; those with college and advanced degrees versus those without; those whose incomes continued to rise versus those whose incomes had stagnated or declined.

In the European Union

In Europe, where life in general has been much more difficult than in Great Britain—outside of Germany, say—public skepticism of elite institutions also runs broad and deep. The most elite institution of all, the EU itself, enjoyed the trust of just 33 percent of European citizens, according to the spring 2016 Standard Eurobarometer survey.[75] Fifty-five percent of Europeans, meanwhile, said explicitly that they do not trust the EU.[76] One key reason is the EU's antidemocratic nature: only 38 percent of Europeans surveyed agreed that their voice "counts in the EU."[77] The EU's unresponsive model of governance has lost support at a time when citizens across Europe are concerned about immigration, the terrorist threat, economic stagnation, and cultural upheaval; in more severe cases, such as Greece and Italy, they worry about poverty and the stability of the financial and political system. Economic concerns remain well-founded, even as 2018 looks like a better year on the Continent, relatively speaking. Making its latest economic forecast for EU member states in the fall of 2017, the European Commission projected GDP growth of 2.2 percent—an exceedingly modest rate that nevertheless would be its best in a decade.[78]

WHEN PEOPLE DON'T BELIEVE IN SOMETHING, THEY WILL BELIEVE IN ANYTHING

Where do people go, then, when their governments, economies, and leaders have proved inept, corrupt, or unresponsive, failing to deliver positive results; when these failures are long-term and systemic, with no sign that a routine change of leadership will make any difference; and when the ultimate effect, as we have seen across multiple countries, is a collapse of public faith in leaders, experts, and institutions?

They look elsewhere. They reach out to strange, renegade, anti-systemic, and sometimes dangerous prophets who promise not to "shake up" the system but to break it—and to build something new and different in its place. To paraphrase an old saying, when people stop believing in something—in this case, the institutions of free societies—they will believe in anything. And increasingly, with the populist, nationalist, and radical movements that have been growing in power and momentum in the United States, in Britain, and across Europe, that is precisely what we're seeing.

"It has reached a point where there is so little trust that many voters will instinctively back whatever their leaders tell them to reject," Daniel Larison writes in *The American Conservative.* He was writing specifically in regard to the British and Brexit, but his observations could apply to all of Europe: "The political classes...have neglected their constituents and dismissed their concerns (especially on immigration), presided over multiple debacles for which almost no one was held accountable, and then expect the public to believe them when they say that they know what is in the best interests of the country.... Political leaders have squandered the public's trust often enough that few will listen to anything they say, or will immediately assume that what they're saying is false."[79]

That's not just where Donald Trump comes from, and that's not just the explanation for Brexit. "The implications of the global trust crisis are deep and wide-ranging," says Richard Edelman. "The consequence is virulent populism and nationalism as the mass population has taken control away from the elites."[80] Indeed, while the world was shocked by the election of Trump, the years ahead may have even greater surprises in store, especially on the European continent, where nationalist and populist parties are growing dramatically in appeal and threatening to upend the political status quo.

It has become a worldwide movement against elites, and where it ends is anyone's guess.

CHAPTER TWO

A WORLDWIDE MOVEMENT
AGAINST ELITES

"[In Europe] you're seeing, as in the U.S., that the political center has collapsed. Collapsed and discredited. That's why you're seeing the increase on the far right and the far left."

—HEATHER CONLEY, CENTER FOR STRATEGIC AND INTERNATIONAL STUDIES[1]

"The mainstream media has often spoken of Pannocchia [Trump] in the same way they speak of our movement. Do you remember? They said that we were sexist, homophobic, demagogues, populists. They do not realize that millions of people no longer read their newspapers or watch their TVs. Trump capitalized on all this."

—BEPPE GRILLO, LEADER OF ITALY'S POPULIST FIVE STAR MOVEMENT[2]

"I will not ask for instructions from Mrs Merkel! Not from Mr Juncker! Nor from Mr Draghi! I will not submit."

—MARINE LE PEN[3]

In the United States and overseas, November 8, 2016, was one of the most shocking days of a young century. Donald Trump won the presidency: no self-respecting media pundit, no conventional political operative, and few even within Trump's own campaign would have predicted it, but somehow, the real estate developer and reality television star had pulled off an American first: unlike the 43 men who had preceded him into the White House, he would take the reins as the nation's chief executive with no previous political or military experience. In the world's most powerful nation, Trump's victory was the culmination of a worldwide movement against elites, established institutions, and long-held political arrangements. It was final confirmation that a new day has dawned in politics—and in history—around the world.

The people on the receiving end of this upheaval—established politicos like Hillary Clinton, Trump's vanquished opponent; media organs from the *New York Times* to the BBC; and powerful corporate and cultural figures—would spend months trying to absorb the reality that Trump had won, let alone understanding what it all meant.

But for others, there was no mystery about the significance of Trump's victory. Marine Le Pen, head of France's right-wing nationalist party, the National Front, understood it quite well. "Americans have voted," she said. "They have rejected the status quo. They showed, through a decision which surprised those who believe situations are unchangeable, that the world moves, that the world changes and that movement is part of the life of nations. What happened last night was not the end of the world—it was the end of a world."[4]

And Florian Philippot, a high-ranking National Front official, tweeted, "Their world is collapsing. Ours is being built."[5]

By "ours," Philippot was speaking specifically to France and the National Front, the party that, on the night Trump was elected, was less than six months away from its own try at taking power in the French elections. But his words expressed the sentiments of millions not just in France or in the United States but across Europe—a continent riven with nationalist, populist, and sometimes extremist movements aimed at toppling the status quo. The Brexit vote in June 2016 gave these movements hope, and proof that they could win; Trump's victory in November 2016 convinced them that the impossible was achievable—and maybe even inevitable.

Trump is the most dramatic and, given the power of the United States, the most consequential result of these movements. But he was comparatively late in arriving, declaring his presidential candidacy only in June 2015. By then, populist and nationalist movements had been percolating for years in most European countries, and some, like the National Front and others, had been around for decades. All share one thing in common: they have seen major surges in support in recent years, threatening to move past a fringe existence into major-party status and perhaps even take the reins of power. In country after European country, the collapse of faith in institutions has led more and more citizens into the arms of alternative, nationalist, or populist parties. As with a good number of Trump voters, many of the Europeans supporting these various parties aren't always sure about what they want done or what they support. What they do know is that they want change. What they do know is that they no longer have faith in the governing consensus that has prevailed in Europe since the end of the Cold War. Many are willing—as American and British voters proved willing—to reject safe, established choices in favor of high-risk alternatives. As Trump himself asked voters during his campaign, "What have you got to lose?"

"European populism is here to stay," wrote Matthew Goodwin, author of *Brexit: Why Britain Voted to Leave the E.U.*, in October 2017.[6] He appears to be correct. Consider the gains such parties have made in European politics in recent years:

- Austria has elected 31-year-old Sebastian Kurz of the right-wing populist Freedom Party (motto: "Austria first") as chancellor; he took power in December 2017.
- UKIP, the United Kingdom Independence Party, played a central role in championing Brexit; though the party itself more or less collapsed afterward, it has more recently rebounded in polls as dissatisfaction with Prime Minister Theresa May's "Brexit Lite" grows.
- Though it has fallen back since, the Danish People's Party increased its share of the vote from 12 percent in 2001 to 21 percent in 2015, and it remains a powerful player in the nation's politics.
- Finland's nationalist Finns Party is the fifth most-supported political party in Finland.[7]
- Though the National Front is dead in France—the party voted to rebrand itself Rassemblement National (National Rally)— its ideas live on powerfully in the country; 63 percent of French said in a February 2018 survey that the nation had "too many immigrants."[8]
- In 2017 federal elections, Germany's AfD party won 13 percent of the vote, an eight-point increase from the previous election, and has become the nation's third-largest political party.[9]
- Golden Dawn won 7 percent of the Greek vote in 2015 and retains this share, and fifth place overall among the nation's parties, in current polls.[10]

- Hungary's Fidesz, the governing party of Prime Minister Viktor Orbán, remains the leading national party; Jobbik, a neofascist party, claims 13 percent support.[11]
- In a May 2018 poll, the nationalist Sweden Democrats registered 20 percent support.[12]
- Geert Wilders, a fearless and defiant critic of Islam and Islamic terrorism, has seen his Party for Freedom surge in the Netherlands; in the March 2017 elections, his party won 13 percent of the vote, increasing its parliamentary seats from 15 to 20.[13] Yet the Party for Freedom has a new rival on the Euroskeptic Right: the Forum for Democracy, which is polling at about 8 percent support.[14]
- Poland's Law and Justice Party increased its vote from 10 percent in 2001 to 36 percent in May 2018; it now controls the government.[15]

As the list above indicates, the power of these movements is largely coming from the political Right, where concerns over immigration, terrorism, economic stagnation, and national sovereignty have fueled the rise of nationalist movements. Indeed, in two countries—Poland and Hungary—right-wing parties have won governing power. Right-wing parties are also surging in Scandinavian countries, from Denmark to Holland to Sweden. These countries, generally associated with liberal social attitudes and placid temperaments, have become hotbeds of right-wing nationalism and hostility to immigration, especially from the Islamic world.

"Three things make me consider voting for the Sweden Democrats," says Oscar Lind, a 43-year-old Swedish economist, "even if I find the party's historical links to white supremacy repugnant and don't agree with their anti-E.U. and anti-NATO membership stances: mass immigration and open borders, identity politics, and 'establishment' propaganda for the previous two."[16] One member of the Swedish Parliament from the Sweden Democrats party has a one-word response to arguments that immigration is a positive for the country: "Bullshit."[17] The Sweden Democrats want to block any new immigration and even remove some of the migrants who have already arrived in the country.

In Germany, the AfD, or Alternative für Deutschland, a party that defines itself against Angela Merkel's refugee policy and that barely existed before 2013, has become a serious electoral player. "People here read that everything is done for the refugees, and they ask themselves: What is being done for us? Where does that leave the poorer and weaker from our community?" asks Andrea Wiedmer, an independent local councillor in the village of Kaltwasser. "Whether this is true or not doesn't matter. This is what the people feel."[18]

And in France, of course, Le Pen's National Front has become a central force in national politics, so formidable that the Republican and Socialist parties banded together to beat National Front candidates in regional elections.

And yet, the populist surge is not just a right-wing phenomenon. Particularly in Southern Europe, left-wing populism has surged. Italy's Five Star Movement, Spain's Podemos, and especially Greece's Syriza, the country's governing party, have rallied against the EU's austerity dictates—delivered from Brussels but identified closely with Frankfurt. They rail against financial elites while insisting that the social welfare state not be shredded. Even in the U.K., the Labour Party, while not in power, has swung hard to the left under leader Jeremy Corbyn, refuting the centrist path of earlier Labour leaders Tony Blair and Gordon Brown.

Though each national party has its own unique characteristics, they share broad common traits, and in fact some convergence exists between the Right and Left. Certainly, opposition to immigration unites most of these parties, though not for the same reasons. The left-wing parties tend to oppose immigration for reasons of economic competition and devotion to jobs for domestic citizens; or they oppose the political system more generally for its corruption and failure to provide economic opportunity. The right-wing parties stress the dangers of the "Islamization" of their countries, fears of terrorism, and loss of a common culture. (Some right-wing parties also make the economic argument.) Interestingly, however, Right and Left often converge on the welfare state: the right-wing parties rarely sound the traditional American free-market themes but rather stress that if anyone should get the benefit of public money, it is native-born citizens. That's why Geert Wilders wants money that would be spent on housing migrants to go instead to cancer treatment for native Dutch citizens. Le Pen's party is devoted to shoring up the French welfare state—for native French, that is, even promising to lower the retirement age. In short, Right and Left want more for their native citizens.

"What we're seeing is the breakdown of traditional party systems and the rise of protest parties all over Europe," says Dmitry Abzalov of the Moscow-based think tank the Center for Strategic Communications. "Left-wing candidates are taking the positions of the right wing—on immigration, for instance."[19]

Another important common theme is the idea of frankness. Again, this is often heard on the Right—especially where political correctness about Islam has silenced many critics but made heroes out of figures like Wilders and Le Pen, who are willing to voice the private thoughts and fears of millions. "We say what people think," says a Sweden Democrat, Julia Kronlid. Wilders is legendary for his frankness and even had to stand trial for it—winning the devoted allegiance of his supporters. "He tells it like it is. Speaks truth to power, you know?" said a Wilders supporter in Amsterdam.[20]

This chapter will take a close look at the populist and nationalist movements that have washed over both the United States and Europe—highlighting common themes, identifying common goals, and looking for the connections between these hugely disparate national movements. But one truth should remain simple and fundamental: neither elites nor everyday people should be confused about why such parties and movements have sprung up or why they have garnered so much appeal. Whatever one thinks of these movements, these parties, these leaders—and some are deeply troubling indeed—they would never have found the oxygen to breathe or the political space to operate had not the failures of elite governance been so total and the collapse of institutional legitimacy so all-encompassing.

HOW POPULISM TOOK AMERICA

The 2016 presidential election in the United States is destined to be remembered as unprecedented in American history. It featured, on the Republican side, perhaps the largest field ever—17 candidates, most with impressive traditional political credentials—but it was dominated from the beginning by a nonpolitician and celebrity whose populist message would vanquish 16 opponents on his way to the nomination. On the Democratic side, a woman won a major party's nomination for the presidency for the first time in American history—but not before enduring a sustained battle with a lifelong Socialist who inspired millions of voters, especially the young, with a populist message directed against financial elites and the wealthy. In the 2016 general election, the Hillary Clinton v. Donald Trump contest shattered records for presidential debate and election night viewership—while also smashing barriers of decorum, eroding civility, and making millions of Americans wonder what had happened to their political system.

When the dust cleared, it was Trump's populism that prevailed over Clinton's establishment-oriented message of modest reform. Trump won because enough Americans concluded that Clinton's incrementalism simply wouldn't do—not in the face of economic stagnation, social decay, cultural tumult, and fears of terrorism. Her positions simply didn't suffice, and her attempt to rally people via identity politics of feminism fell flat, even with millions of women, who voted Trump. (In fact, Trump won a majority of white women.)

Or maybe it is more accurate to say that the identity politics of feminism were overcome by other kinds of identity politics—in 2016, the identity politics of the white working class, which became Trump's main voting bloc. Trump's populist message—especially his contempt for the media and his willingness to ridicule ruling elites and policy failures of both political parties—appealed enormously to these voters. Trump's style was slash and burn; it had no middle gear. He called the media liars, he branded politicians corrupt puppets of big donors and special interests, slammed them for being "all talk and no action," and then lambasted the results of their action—from free trade agreements to Middle East wars to a porous border. "We have people that are selling this country down the drain," he said. "The American dream is dead."[21] He promised, again and again, to bring jobs back to the United States. He would make America great again, he pledged.

Trump's rise would not have been possible without the loss of trust in government and institutions chronicled in the previous chapter. This is *the* development that undergirds everything else about his candidacy, and its reality was starkest among the working class, particularly those voters without college degrees, whom polls showed distrusted the government, media, and other elite institutions profoundly. (White, college-educated voters supported Clinton over Trump, 52 percent to 40 percent; white voters without college degrees went for Trump, 57 percent to 36 percent.[22]) Moreover, these people disproportionately told pollsters that they did *not* expect to be better off five or ten years from now. This stark outlook made for a receptive audience for Trump.

At the core of the discontent was the issue of jobs. "A lot of people can't get jobs, because there are no jobs," Trump said when he announced his run for president. "Because China has our jobs and Mexico has our jobs."[23] With his typical bluster, Trump vowed to be "the best jobs president God ever created."[24] These pledges resonated with millions of struggling working-class voters in the nation's heartland, as did Trump's opposition to NAFTA, which he blamed for many of these job losses, calling it "the worst trade deal in history"[25] and suggesting it was negotiated by elites and for elites—and against the working class. That viewpoint jibed with how many had felt for years, yet they hadn't heard a presidential candidate from either party come out and say it. On the contrary, NAFTA and other free trade deals enjoyed full bipartisan support, thus confirming the sense for many Americans that governing elites, whatever their differences on other policy matters, were essentially in alignment on big global matters. Among Trump supporters, 67 percent said that free trade agreements had been bad for the country.[26]

Another issue that Trump supporters felt was bad for the country was the failure to secure the border with Mexico. Here, millions were thrilled by Trump's unvarnished, gleefully politically incorrect willingness to talk about border security, about illegal immigration, and about the right of the United States to determine who does and doesn't get to come into the country. It was all symbolized with his boastful pledge to build a wall sealing off the United States' border with Mexico—and to make Mexico pay for it. The border issue resonated on multiple levels: economic, as many saw illegal immigrants taking low-wage jobs from Americans; political, as a mass influx of non-English-speaking, illegal residents was altering the fabric of the country and affecting its policy priorities; and on crime and national security, as the porous border had allowed illegal immigrants to come in and commit crimes, including murder, in American "sanctuary cities" and also presented an opportunity for Islamist terrorists to get into the United States. And like some European populists, Trump made his border pitch from an unconventional position for a Republican: he cited the need to control the border and illegal immigration as a way to shore up reserves for Social Security and Medicare, which, he suggested, were being drained by too many immigrants, illegal and otherwise. For all these reasons, Trump's pledge to "build a wall," much to the dismay of media pundits, found broad support.

Concerns about security—from the border and elsewhere—also made Trump's call for a temporary ban on Muslims entering the United States appealing to voters. Once again, the mainstream media, which assumed that the call would end Trump's campaign, was caught by surprise. "Despite an international uproar and condemnation by President Obama and nearly all of those running for the presidency," Rasmussen research reported, "Donald Trump's proposed ban on Muslims coming to the United States has the support of a sizable majority of Republicans—and a plurality of all voters."[27] Indeed, 67 percent of Republicans voters supported the idea, while among all voters, 46 percent supported it compared to 40 percent who opposed it. And Trump continued to hit a deep vein among the public by going, verbally, where no candidates would dare go. Hitting Clinton for her pledge to increase the number of Syrian refugees coming into the United States far above what President Obama had allowed, Trump said, "We don't know who these people are. We don't know where they're from. They have no documentation.... We can't let this happen. But you have a lot of them resettling in Rhode Island. Just enjoy your—lock your doors, folks."[28]

The fears of illegal immigration and Muslim infiltration went to a broader concern among many middle Americans: fear that they were losing the country they had known. In the 2015 American Values Survey, 53 percent of respondents (of all races) said that American culture and way of life had "mostly changed for the worse since the 1950s."[29] These feelings were even more pronounced among white Americans, who, as David Frum wrote, "often don't think in ideological terms at all. But they do strongly feel that life in this country used to be better for people like them—and they want that older country back."[30]

They looked to Trump—a billionaire but a political outsider in every way that counted—for deliverance. Trump self-financed his primary run, slamming his opponents and Hillary Clinton as prisoners of political donors and money. "They are controlled fully by the lobbyists, by the donors, and by the special interests fully.... It has to stop," he said. "It is destroying our country!"[31] He often described the political system, from the deal-making in Washington to the vote-counting at the polling places, as "rigged." The media was aghast and excoriated him for this rhetoric, but Trump never modulated, and his defiance won the loyalty of his supporters, who tended to see media opposition to Trump as confirmation that he was on the right path.

Indeed, whatever one thinks of Trump, an objective observer couldn't help but be struck by the all-out media onslaught against him. "The number of mainstream media reporters who are out there expressing their explicit opinions, that tend to be decisively pro-Hillary and anti-Trump, to me is scary," said Politico cofounder Jim VandeHei. "Donald Trump gives you a lot of things to fear and a lot of things to dislike. But you cannot, cannot, cannot as a reporter be taking sides in a public forum whether it's on Twitter or whether it's on email or whether it's on TV."[32] Yet the media kept at it, all the way through to Election Day (and beyond). They seemed wholly unaware of how their overt opposition played into the very critique that Trump was making.

Given the widespread popular disgust with politicians, it's not really surprising that Trump, a globally famous businessman, would have such appeal. Americans have always admired strong business figures, and business as an institution has rebounded more strongly than most others since the financial crash. The idea that Trump could "drain the swamp" in Washington and "get things done" held broad appeal. America's political leaders were incompetent, Trump said repeatedly. "Politicians are all talk, no action. Nothing ever gets done."[33]

And finally, Trump's appeal played into Americans' disgust with experts. Here was a candidate who spoke with ruthless simplicity about the major issues of the day, who frequently made misstatements of facts but who sounded themes that resonated with voters. The frequent charge that Trump's was a campaign without ideas was always fraudulent. Trump's campaign was rife with ideas: close the border; renegotiate trade deals; bring manufacturing jobs back home; repeal Obamacare; destroy ISIS. These ideas may have been crude—and they often lacked policy detail—but they were certainly *ideas*. Moreover, they were ideas that many mainstream politicians did not want to address. And voters knew it.

"I'm not down with any more politicians—we need some common sense in this," said Darrin Hahn, a 45-year-old Trump supporter in Louisiana. "We bring them into office to do certain things, and they're not doing it—so why the hell am I going to make 'em president?"[34]

Even as Election Night approached, most pundits still couldn't quite grasp how Trump was getting traction. It's remarkable how badly they missed it, especially given the two movements during the Obama years that clearly foreshadowed Trump's rise: the Tea Party on the right and Occupy Wall Street on the left. The Tea Party was an internal rebellion within the Republican Party against the policies of George W. Bush that, Tea Party adherents argued, had betrayed fundamental conservative principles and left the country mired in war, up to its neck in debt, and with hollowed-out working-class communities where good jobs had fled. The Tea Party sounded many of the themes that would become Trump's: stop the wasteful spending, stop playing by two sets of rules—one for elites and one for everyone else—and start governing the country in the public interest. Occupy Wall Street was more narrowly focused, and it proved shorter-lived, but its focus—on Wall Street bailouts and income inequality, and, memorably, on the division of the country between the 1 percent and the 99 percent—would provide the template for Bernie Sanders's campaign, which won the hearts of millions of young Democrats, whom Hillary Clinton would struggle to keep in her camp.

It all culminated with the shocking evening of November 8, 2016, when the world's most powerful nation elected a full-fledged populist to the presidency. Around the world, other populists and nationalist were taking notes, and taking heart, for their own struggles.

"THE LITTLE TRUMPS": THE RISE OF EUROPEAN POPULISM

"In nearly every European country they are on the move now, the little Trumps," wrote a commentator in the German paper *Süddeutsche Zeitung*.[35] But most of Europe's little Trumps have been on the scene for a while. They have spent years, sometimes decades, on the margins of political life, and some remain there; but most have gained political strength and public appeal over the last decade in response to the problems of the euro, the financial crisis, high unemployment and income inequality, Euroskepticism and rising nationalism, and the Syrian migrant crisis.

Germany

Angela Merkel was as shook up as anyone by the British Brexit vote in June 2016, but the German chancellor's real wake-up call came three months later, on September 4, 2016, when her party, the Christian Democratic Union (CDU), came in third place in local elections in her home state, Mecklenburg-Vorpommern. It wasn't hugely shocking to see that the CDU's main rival, the Social Democratic Party, came out on top. What *was* shocking was that the CDU came in third—beat out for second place by the nationalist AfD party, which took nearly 21 percent of the vote to the CDU's 19 percent. It was the AfD's second big moment of 2016; in March 2016, the AfD took 24 percent of the vote in Saxony-Anhalt and performed credibly in other local elections, riding popular momentum because of its stance on immigration and Islam, Merkel's handling of the refugee crisis, and attitudes toward the European Union. "We see the political climate changing toward the AfD and against the established parties, especially the Christian Democrats," said Frauke Petry, the AfD's youthful and attractive 41-year-old leader. "21 percent in the northeast of Germany is an absolutely brilliant result."[36]

In the 2017 federal elections, the AfD became the first right-wing party to win seats in the German federal Parliament since the end of World War II.

An anti-Europe, nationalist party in Europe's most powerful and prosperous country, the AfD is a recent phenomenon. It was founded only in 2013, but since then, with discontent rising, it has been building momentum as the leading voice for Germans who oppose Merkel's immigration policies and who also see no help coming from the Social Democrats. The AfD originally was spurred by anger at EU bailout policies, especially regarding Greece, but more recently its focus has been on nationalism, on preserving German culture and opposing the influx of Muslims. The AfD's party platform calls for a ban on the building of mosques, declaring that "Islam does not belong in Germany."[37] Petry suggested that border guards should be willing to use their guns on migrants trying to cross the German border illegally.

Perhaps such appeals would have been rejected more decisively by Germans five or ten years ago, but fear of the threat of Islamic populations has grown. Merkel's welcoming of perhaps one million Syrian refugees between 2015 and 2016 may stand as a grand historical example of compassion from the leader of a powerful nation, but it has also helped scramble German politics, unsettle public attitudes, and spark growing anger and resistance to newcomers. Several high-profile incidents have also contributed—especially the brutal terror attacks in 2016 and the infamous sexual assaults on New Year's Eve 2015 in Cologne and other cities, attributed to men "of North African or Middle Eastern appearance." Germans felt that the Merkel government did nothing to protect them and little to prevent future outbreaks. Within this tense climate, violence against Muslim newcomers is on the rise. German police reported more than 1,000 attacks on refugee homes in 2015[38] and more than 900 in 2016.[39] German Federal Police Office (BKA) chief Holger Münch blamed the AfD's rhetoric for helping to make antagonism toward foreigners more "socially acceptable" in Germany.[40]

That's not how Petry and her supporters see it. "Basically we are a very necessary corrective in German and European politics," she says.[41] Support for the party surged after Cologne, leading to its gains in the various 2016 races. Recent estimates put AfD's public support at about 13 percent—an enormous gain from where the party started but still a far cry from what would be needed to wield real power. Still, what Petry and the AfD have achieved in a brief time is sobering for those who believe deeply in Merkel's pro-European, pro-integrationist, centrist model of governance. Germany remains a stalwart for the idea of a united Europe, but should Merkel falter and the AfD continue to gain, almost anything is possible on the Continent.

France

With the exception of Bulgaria, no EU country has a higher proportion of Muslims as a percentage of the population than France. And no country in the EU has faced more shattering terrorist attacks perpetrated by homegrown Islamists—the *Charlie Hebdo* slaughter in January 2015, the

Paris massacres of November 2015, and the Nice carnage of July 2016. The difficult equation of French life plus an increasing Islamic population has put millions of French citizens on edge, especially since younger French-born Muslims are not integrating into French life in the way that their parents did. They have become increasingly isolated in the *banlieues*, some of which resemble independent Islamic provinces more than they do anything like traditional France. France is a country perched on a sword's point: famously tolerant, a nation of immigrants and outsiders, it is coming face-to-face with not only the costs of a stagnant economy and a declining birthrate, but with the sobering possibility that there are, indeed, limits to multicultural tolerance—at least when that tolerance puts the population at risk from those who do *not* share an allegiance to liberal, secular values.

It is this fault line that explains the support for the National Front, France's right-wing nationalist party, which has been around since the 1970s but has never had such a broad audience nationally as it does now—even if its June 2017 parliamentary election showing was weaker than expected. The party's leader, Marine Le Pen, is the daughter of the party founder, Jean-Marie Le Pen, whose flirtations with outright fascism and even Nazism ensured that the National Front would always remain a fringe party. Le Pen has publicly rejected her father's dark legacy and brought the National Front into a more mainstream position, though it remains a hard-edged, right-wing force. Whether it has crested for now in terms of support, as some analysts believe, remains to be seen.

It was not just Le Pen's nationalist message that resonated with voters. It was also her frankness and her willingness to take on political sacred cows. Though she bears little resemblance to Donald Trump—she is far more composed and thoughtful, and a much more polished, even conventional, politician—she, like the American president, has won loyal backing from listeners thrilled to hear her speak frankly.

"Our leaders chose globalization, which they wanted to be a happy thing. It turned out to be a horrible thing," Le Pen told a huge crowd in Lyon, in southeastern France, in February 2017. "They made an ideology out of it: economic globalization, which refuses any regulation.... It sets the conditions for another form of globalization: Islamist fundamentalism." Linking globalization to "Islamization" is a shrewd Le Pen tactic—it allows her to tap into voters' economic discontent, and their anger at financial elites, with their fears of terrorism and concerns about losing a common French culture. Both forces, Le Pen went on to say, "are working to make our nation disappear, by which I mean the France in which we live and that we love. These ideologies want to subjugate our country, one in the name of financial globalization, the other in the name of fundamentalist Islam."[42]

At the center of Le Pen's candidacy was a pledge to leave the euro currency and lead a "Frexit" out of the European Union for France. "The euro has not been used as a currency, but as a weapon," she said, "a knife stuck in the ribs of a country to force it to go where the people don't want to go. Do you think we accept living under this threat, this tutelage? It's absolutely out of the question."[43]

Like populist candidates in other countries, Le Pen wins converts—and loyalists—with her boldness. "She is the only candidate who dares to say what the others do not, who dares to speak frankly about the danger of Islamization in France," said Sylvie Bianchi, a retired factory worker. "We used to vote for Socialists but now we don't see anyone else who represents us."[44]

Whether Le Pen can grow her support in the years ahead, however, depends on somewhat contradictory factors. To maintain the loyalty that she enjoys from her most devoted voters, she must stay staunch on her positions. But to broaden her appeal, she will need to trim the harsher edges—and she has already begun to do so, backpedaling from her frequent earlier pledges to leave the euro and lead a Frexit. Frexit does not enjoy majority support among the French, though dissatisfaction with the EU is widespread.

The future of the National Front is now crucial to France's future as well. Once again, a nationalist and populist party has placed itself at the center of a nation's political fate—a feat not possible without the continued failure of leadership from more mainstream political leaders and a widespread popular rejection of the same.

United Kingdom

It is somewhat ironic that the U.K. would be the catalyst for the various calls for "exit" on the European continent—not only because the U.K. is not physically part of the Continent but also because, with the exception of Germany, its political culture has been, until fairly recently, the least roiled by nationalist and populist movements. The U.K. Independence Party (UKIP), which became closely affiliated with the Brexit movement, never had tremendous power or appeal politically. In 2006, David Cameron infamously derided the party as a collection of "fruitcakes, loonies and closet racists."[45] Nigel Farage, the party's longtime leader, who stepped down after the Brexit victory, made many missteps during the run-up to the referendum, and some observers felt that the victory of the Leave forces came as much despite Farage and UKIP as because of them. Yet the Brexit referendum would almost certainly never have happened without UKIP, and Farage had his day of glory on June 23, 2016, when he called Brexit "the first victory against an international political elite who have led us into an endless series of foreign wars and seen politics effectively purchased by the big banks and the multinationals."[46]

Still, with the success of Brexit, UKIP can now be said to have achieved its single-issue goal—an impression supported by subsequent events, in which the party has basically unraveled. UKIP won just 2 percent of the general election vote in 2017. Even if UKIP goes the way of other British fringe parties, British nationalism and Euroskepticism will endure. There is no question that the anti-EU feelings among the British electorate, along with the contempt felt for both major parties, is widespread and in some ways reminiscent of the sentiments in the United States. And with new frustration about the process and status of Britain's Brexit, UKIP has more recently seen something of an upsurge. Prime Minister May has tried to strong-arm her cabinet into a "softer" Brexit, but that effort led to a crisis in her government in 2018. To buy time, the U.K. and the EU have agreed to a 21-month Brexit "transition."

Regardless of what UKIP's future might be, its landmark success in 2016 has emboldened Euroskeptic parties across the Continent, some of which are perched on the very precipice of taking power.

The Netherlands

Look for a single figure who represents the power and appeal of European nationalism, populism, and Euroskepticism, and Holland's Geert Wilders is hard to beat. Here is a man who has stood trial for things that he has *said* about Muslims; who has spoken of Islam in the frankest and, to many, most objectionable terms; who has been the target of hostility ranging from political condemnation to assassination plots. Like Donald Trump, he is larger than life, wears his hair in a distinctive and vaguely ridiculous bouffant, and revels in saying things that invite the condemnation of elites in media and government—while winning hosannas from legions of ordinary citizens, who admire him for his guts. Geert Wilders is the face of European populism.

Wilders heads Holland's Party for Freedom (PVV), the main platform of which is the "de-Islamization of the Netherlands." The PVV openly preaches the superiority of the West's traditionally Judeo-Christian culture; it wants to shut down mosques, ban the Qur'an—Wilders has likened it to *Mein Kampf*—and close the doors to asylum-seekers. Wilders and others in the party rail against the EU's open-borders policy, as encapsulated in the Schengen Area. Cheering on the Brexit result, Wilders calls for a "Nexit" of the Netherlands from the European Union.[47]

Such is the mood in the Netherlands, as with so many other European countries, that the populist fire of Wilders and the PVV has influenced the "respectable," mainstream political parties—even those currently in power. How else to explain why Holland prime minister Mark Rutte felt inspired to take out a full-page ad calling out people in the Netherlands who "refuse to adapt, and criticise our values"? He was talking about Islamists, even if he didn't name them directly, and he made clear what their choice was: "behave normally or go away."[48]

Such words would never have been uttered among mainstream Dutch politicians without the influence of Wilders.

Like other nationalists, Wilders has long conflated the Islamist threat with the broader question of the European Union, drawing a straight line between what he and his followers see as Brussels' antidemocratic, globalist dictates and the infusion of Muslims into European societies once associated with the term "Christendom." Wilders asks his listeners if they want to preserve a Dutch identity. They answer overwhelmingly yes. Then not only do they need to embrace the PVV, he suggests; they need to reject the established elite political order, which is largely responsible for all that ails them—politically, economically, and socially. The Dutch Parliament? A "phony parliament," Wilder says. The Dutch judiciary? A "phony judiciary."[49]

And he is willing to say intemperate, even vile things to get his point across. Like Trump, he shoots from the hip, offending many; only later does he qualify remarks that often come across as incendiary. Launching his presidential campaign in February 2017, Wilders said, "If a Dutch person driving in a car drives five miles too fast, he will be fined within a minute whereas the Moroccan scum in Holland—once again, not all are scum, but there is a lot of Moroccan scum in Holland who makes the streets unsafe, mostly young people and they are not taken seriously."[50]

Wilders and the PVV are the very apotheosis of European nationalism and populism. Though he is not likely ever to gain electoral control of the Netherlands, Wilders has been a force in national politics for more than a decade, and with the issue of Islamic integration in Europe very much unresolved, as well as other questions about the longevity and viability of the European Union, he and his party figure to be crucial players for years to come.

Austria and Hungary

In December 2017, 31-year-old Sebastian Kurz was sworn in as Austria's youngest chancellor in history. His ascension completes the triumph of nationalist politics in Austria; his governing coalition includes not only his own center-right Austrian Peoples Party (ÖVP) but also the country's most right-wing party, the populist Freedom Party (FPÖ), a political organization founded by former Nazis in the 1950s. Young and boyish and politically savvy, Kurz has managed to take the rougher edges off of policies that virulently oppose additional migration to Austria from the strife-torn countries of the Middle East. To critics, he has merely packaged the Freedom Party's ideology into a friendlier wrapping.

Only a year earlier, these critics thought they had dodged a bullet.

"Austria saves the world!" exulted a veteran Austrian diplomat on December 4, 2016, when the country turned back the presidential challenge of the FPÖ's Norbert Hofer. In the Austrian system, the president represents the official head of state but not the head of government; the real authority lies with the chancellor. Still, for a Far Right candidate such as Hofer—he has been variously described as a right-wing nationalist or a quasi-fascist—to be within arm's length of the presidency represented a potential watershed in the nation's history. Hofer wound up losing by a solid six-point margin, bringing relief to many.

His campaign motto, "Austria First," which echoes Trump's "America First," emphasized what he called "identity"—which was understood to mean native Austrian identity, not immigrants or outsiders. Making clear his anti-immigration outlook, Hofer expressed a desire to see Austria join the Visegrad Group, a four-nation group—comprising the Czech Republic, Hungary, Poland, and Slovakia—of EU members and former Eastern Bloc nations that have taken hard lines against immigration and especially against Merkel's refugee policies. In another era, a man like Hofer would likely have lagged at single digits in polls, a marginal outlier espousing discredited blood-and-soil themes.

But the Syrian refugee crisis reenergized the FPÖ, and even though Hofer lost, his issues had framed the election—and, as Kurz's triumph a year later demonstrates, those issues still carry the day with Austrian voters.

Austria is a country of just 8.6 million people, yet in 2015 it saw nearly 90,000 applications for asylum—the second-most, per capita, in Europe, and the most in the country since the Hungarian Crisis of 1956 and 1957.[51] Before the first round of the presidential election in April 2016, just 12 percent of Austrians told pollsters that the country was on the right track, while 52 percent said that it was on the wrong track.[52] Like many other nationalist parties, the FPÖ, which will have a role in Kurz's government, does best in rural regions and lags in urban districts. But among its minority share of urban voters, one hears familiar themes. "I've voted for the F.P.Ö. for many reasons related to foreigners, but in most cases, the foreigners are not guilty," said Werner Farkas, a 36-year-old construction supervisor from Vienna. "Our government is responsible for the hate against foreigners, because many Austrians feel like second-class citizens in their own country."[53] This refrain—that governing elites have betrayed their own citizens—is familiar across Europe, and in some countries, its adherents are expressing it in darker terms.

Austria's onetime partner in empire, Hungary, has traveled further still along the road of protest politics. To his supporters, Viktor Orbán, leader of Hungary's governing party Fidesz, is a charismatic leader fighting for the needs of average Hungarians and upholding the traditional values of Hungary's Christian past against a (potential) onslaught of largely Muslim migrants. His critics see him as an authoritarian demagogue who, as prime minister of an EU country, confers a dangerous mantle of legitimacy on populism, nativism, and xenophobia.

Orbán put a marker down on July 26, 2015, when, speaking at the Bálványos Free Summer University and Youth Camp, he called for "illiberal democracy" in Hungary. The "Hungarian nation is not a simple sum of individuals," he said, "but a community that needs to be organized, strengthened and developed, and in this sense, the new state that we are building is an illiberal state, a non-liberal state.... When I mention the European Union, I am not doing this because I think it is impossible to build an illiberal nation state within the EU. I think this is possible. Our EU membership does not rule out this option."[54] The speech horrified elites and proponents of moderate politics while thrilling populists and nationalists. In Hungary, Orbán's popularity surged.

So far, he has proved to be a man of his word. In 2015, when the refugee crisis reached its peak, he shut down transit routes in an effort keep migrants out. Eventually, he erected a razor-wire fence. "Who commissioned European leaders," he asked, to "not only let in but ship into Europe by the hundreds of thousands groups that are culturally different from European culture?" He had the people's ear. "I believe Hungary needs to protect its own borders," said Mate Sebok, a 21-year-old Hungarian student. "A few months ago the eastern railway station was still teeming with migrants and now the country is nice and empty, luckily, so I think the border fence was a good measure."[55]

In April 2018 elections, Fidesz secured more than 49 percent of the vote, with some 2.6 million voting for the party and its Christian Democratic allies. That was roughly the same as the seven largest opposition parties combined. Fidesz also secured a two-thirds majority in Parliament. Orbán has also been fighting a rearguard action against Jobbik, a radical, right-wing populist nationalist party that appeals more overtly to the darker tribalist impulses—and harbors serious ambitions of becoming the nation's second-leading party. In the 2018 elections, Jobbik appeared to achieve that goal, winning 26 seats, good for second place, followed by a left-wing coalition that won 20 seats. Jobbik began in 2002 as a right-wing youth movement on the margins of the nation's political life. It won just 2 percent of the vote in the 2006 national election. But by the 2010 parliamentary elections, Jobbik had surged to 12 percent of the national vote, becoming the country's third-largest party in Parliament on the strength of its nationalist appeal, encapsulated in its party slogan, "Hungary belongs to the Hungarians." Its basic outlook can be summarized in two core precepts: first, opposition to globalization, including market capitalism; and second, opposition to multiculturalism.

In Jobbik's early days, the sole focus of its anti-multiculturalist agenda was on the nation's Roma, or Gypsy, people. "The situation in certain parts of the country is akin to civil war," said Jobbik's young leader, Gabor Vona, who ran for prime minister in 2010. "Now only drastic interventions are capable of helping.... We must produce an environment in which gypsy people can return to a world of work, laws and education. And for those unwilling to do so, two alternatives remain: they can either choose to take advantage of the right of free movement granted by the European Union, and leave the country, because we will simply no longer put up with lifestyles dedicated to freeloading or criminality; or, there is always prison."[56]

Jobbik also indulges in anti-Semitism. Some party members have made incendiary anti-Semitic remarks that have drawn denunciations from mainstream Hungarian politicians. One Jobbik member gave a speech in Parliament repeating the old "blood libel" against Jews; some Holocaust memorials were desecrated. The situation has gotten so tense that "some Jewish families are considering emigrating."[57] Marton Gyongyosi, a senior leader of Jobbik, called for a tally of Jews in the country in 2012: "[It is] time to tally up people of Jewish ancestry who live here, especially in the Hungarian Parliament and the Hungarian government, who, indeed, pose a national security risk to Hungary."[58]

And even when the party itself isn't railing against outsiders, it is cheering on those who do. In August 2016, György Budaházy received a 13-year sentence in Budapest for leading a group of right-wing thugs, the Arrows of Hungarians, in bombings of gay clubs and Molotov cocktail attacks on the homes of liberal and socialist politicians. When the convicted Budaházy walked out of the courtroom, he was cheered by a group of Jobbik supporters.[59]

Finally, there is the matter of Islam. Up until very recently, Jobbik had spoken positively of Islam. Vona even called Islam "the last hope for humankind, in the darkness of liberalism and globalization," praising

Muslims for their efforts to resist multiculturalism and preserve a uni-
fied heritage. But that was before the rise of ISIS and the harrowing
attacks in France, Germany, and Belgium. Hungary's Muslim population
remains very small, but the Syrian refugee crisis has brought Muslims
pouring in, and Jobbik has taken a firm stand against taking in any
refugees. The party has not as yet come out with explicitly anti-Islamic
pronouncements, but Hungarian imams sense that the party is not their
friend, and that seems like a sound instinct.

There is also a longing for old (Habsburg) values, such as those of
"faith, strength and will." Jobbik seeks to restore these, by force if necessary. Since 2007, it has fielded a uniformed paramilitary organization,
the Hungarian Guard, which has been involved in frequent episodes of
street violence.[60]

What is most concerning to Hungary's more mainstream parties—
whether Fidesz or the socialists—is Jobbik's appeal to the young. Fidesz
remains the most popular party in all age groups except those under 30,
for whom Jobbik is the leading choice.[61] The views of someone like Mark
Cserepes, 24, a management student, are typical. He told the *New York
Times*, "As a young adult, I would like to vote for something fresh with
no or few connections to the previous regime. Only the far-right party
is speaking about real problems, e.g., the two largest parties promise to
solve Gypsy-related issues (their low education, their low income), but
they never do anything. As a master's student, I can say most of my
friends, most of the people I know, think in the same way. They want to
support something new, because neither Fidesz nor the Socialist Party
works, and we would like to see the country improve."[62]

Fresh off its encouraging performance in 2018, Jobbik will clearly
see opportunity to make further gains: dissatisfaction runs deep among
the public. And Jobbik has clearly been pushing Orbán farther right—so
far right that the EU itself has threatened expulsion due to Hungary's
hard-line refugee policies.[63] In one form or another, the nationalist right
is ascendant in Hungary.

Italy and Greece

In Italy, the power of populism was made clear on December 4, 2016,
when a constitutional referendum, put forth by Prime Minister Matteo

Renzi, went to a national vote. The referendum would limit the power of the upper chamber of Parliament, make it easier to pass legislation, and change the way legislators were elected. Promising to resign if the referendum wasn't passed, Renzi put his political career in the voters' hands.

He lost. More than 59 percent of Italians voted "no," believing that the referendum was more about centralizing political power than constructive reform.[64] But the popular verdict was about more than legislative procedures. In the words of the BBC, the referendum was also "a chance to reject establishment politics," and, as such, it was "a resounding victory for the No camp, a medley of populist parties headed by the Five Star Movement, which capitalised on Renzi's declining popularity, years of economic stagnation, and the problems caused by tens of thousands of migrants arriving in Italy from Africa."[65]

Sound familiar? It should. And once again, at the heart of a rejectionist movement was a populist party—this time the Five Star Movement (M5S), an anti-immigration, anti-establishment, and, yes, Euroskeptic party led by a former comedian, Beppe Grillo. While Renzi's Democrats remained in power for the moment—he was succeeded by Paolo Gentiloni—M5S was poised for victory, and in the March 2018 election, victory came.

The election results were a mess, by American standards: No political party or coalition achieved a majority, though Five Star emerged with the most votes. Matteo Salvini's right-wing Lega Nord took a plurality of seats in the Chamber of Deputies and in the Senate, while Renzi's Democrats came in third. The result was a hung parliament, but a coalition government was formed between Five Star and Lega Nord. Messy or not, by any standard, Five Star's position of co-leadership in the Italian government represents a stunning ascent.

Like other European populist parties, Five Star Movement also borrows from the Left: it is a pro-Green party, and its economics are more left than right. The party takes its name from what it describes as its five core issues—public water, sustainable (eco-friendly) transport, sustainable development, Internet access, and environmentalism—all of which sound more left than right.[66]

Greece, too, has populism with elements of left and right, but as might be expected with a country that has struggled so dramatically with fiscal disaster, the extremes tend to run harder to both poles. More than five years after the Greek debt crisis began, the economy is still in shambles, unemployment runs toward 25 percent, asylum-seekers and migrants are arriving daily by boat to Greece's shores—and Greeks don't trust that their government can handle it. Like Hungary, Greece is a country with such deep problems that one of its protest parties has in fact already taken control of the government—but this time from the Left, not from the Right. Syriza, the governing party in Athens, began as a protest movement. Prime Minister Alexis Tsipras remains at the head of the party, which has harnessed popular outrage at the "Eurocrats" in Brussels—and Frankfurt—pushing austerity measures on a crippled economy. Syriza has also railed at Greece's "oligarchs."

The problem for Tsipras is that he and his party are becoming unpopular themselves, in part because they have had more time to get results than other populist parties—after all, Greece's crisis was more severe, and thus its revolt against the centrist consensus took place earlier. But up until recently, Greek citizens weren't seeing much of a payoff; the promised economic recovery has not arrived. Tsipras's approval rating plummeted to 19 percent in a September 2016 survey, with 85 percent of Greeks viewing him unfavorably.[67] That was just one year after Syriza and Tsipras won reelection. Voters still want no part of the establishment parties that they blame for the country's financial meltdown, but Syriza is running out of time to prove itself.

And waiting in the wings is a party with radical solutions of its own—from the Right. Golden Dawn has been around much longer than many of the European nationalist parties. It was founded in 1980, but it only began breaking through in 2012, when it won 18 seats in the Greek Parliament, entering the body for the first time in its history. Of course, it is no accident that Golden Dawn took this long to gain traction; before the Greek financial crises, the party held little appeal and existed on the margins.

Now it's a different matter, and with the party gaining ground, its odious views are getting more scrutiny. It has openly campaigned against the "Islamization" of Greece. It denounces representative democracy and calls for direct democracy—in essence, a plebiscite on all public questions. Perhaps one reason it believes in such measures is its confidence that it can intimidate enough people to vote its way: party members have often engaged in street violence. "Parts of Athens feel like a war zone," wrote William Wheeler in the *New York Times*. "Racist gangs cruise the streets at night in search of victims."[68]

The Council of Europe's human rights commissioner denounced the party in 2013 as "neo-Nazi and violent."[69] The party rejects these charges, though it has used Nazi symbolism and even praised some Nazi figures. The party's symbol resembles a swastika, and party members deliver a Nazi-like salute when its leader, Nikos Michaloliakos, gives speeches. But with the kinds of hardships Greeks are facing today, a movement pledged to help Greeks and only Greeks was bound to win public support.

Greece is the basket case of Europe not just fiscally, but economically and socially as well. The fear of immigrants and the desire to protect the Greek welfare state have made Golden Dawn more appealing to ordinary citizens. "They're doing what the politicians should be doing," says Nikos Katapodis, a funeral home owner in Athens. "There's a hole, and they fill it."[70]

However, 2018 might shine a light at the end of Greece's long tunnel—and not a moment too soon. Greece's economy is, tentatively, on a path to recovery at last. S&P increased the nation's credit rating from B- to B; Greece's third bailout program is ending; and the economy is projected to grow by 2 percent—modest, to be sure, but something to build on.[71] There may yet be time for Greece to avoid a descent into a political wilderness.

CONCLUSION

"Populists have always brought calamity to Europe," declared an op-ed in *Die Welt*, a daily German newspaper.[72] One could substitute "nationalists" in that sentence and be just as accurate. Yet for the broadly encompassing reasons already described—fundamentally, the failure of institutions to address the challenges of our age—populists and nationalists are on the march. The result is further fragmentation. "There is not enough Europe in this Union," said European Commission president Jean-Claude Juncker, and "not enough union in this Union."[73]

The fragmentation doesn't end at national borders, however. We're also seeing a fundamental fracturing of the international alliance system, an issue also rooted in institutional failure but with potentially global, not just national, consequences.

CHAPTER THREE

THE BREAKDOWN OF ALLIANCES

"Superpowers don't get to retire. Look around you will see a world on fire. Syria torn by war and conflict. Iraq on the brink of collapse. Libya a failed state in North Africa. Russia attacking Ukraine and destabilising Eastern Europe. China flexing its muscles, the rogue state North Korea threatening nuclear attacks. All that requires a world policeman to restore international law and order."

—ANDERS FOGH RASMUSSEN[1]

"One hundred years after the entry of American forces into World War I, the transatlantic bond between the United States and Europe is as strong as ever and maybe, in many ways, even stronger," President Trump told a Warsaw audience in July 2017. He was standing in Krasinski Square, considered a symbol of Polish resistance to totalitarianism, before a large and friendly crowd that frequently chanted his name. Nearly six months into his presidency, Trump was making his second visit to Europe, and on his way to Hamburg for the G20 summit, he had stopped in the Polish capital to give what has been, so far, the most-discussed speech of his presidency. After months of refusing to commit himself to an unconditional endorsement of NATO or of the Western alliance, Trump finally spoke words millions had longed to hear.

"Americans know that a strong alliance of free, sovereign and independent nations is the best defense for our freedoms and for our interests.... The United States has demonstrated not merely with words but with its actions that we stand firmly behind Article 5, the mutual defense commitment. We have to remember that our defense is not just a commitment of money, it is a commitment of will."[2]

And Trump did not stop there. He defended not only NATO and the broader Western alliance but also Western civilization itself, in a remarkable tribute:

We write symphonies. We pursue innovation. We celebrate our
ancient heroes, embrace our timeless traditions and customs, and
always seek to explore and discover brand-new frontiers.

We reward brilliance. We strive for excellence, and cherish inspiring works of art that honor God. We treasure the rule of law and
protect the right to free speech and free expression.

We empower women as pillars of our society and of our success. We put faith and family, not government and bureaucracy,
at the center of our lives. And we debate everything. We challenge
everything. We seek to know everything so that we can better know
ourselves.

And above all, we value the dignity of every human life, protect
the rights of every person, and share the hope of every soul to live in
freedom. That is who we are. Those are the priceless ties that bind us
together as nations, as allies, and as a civilization.

Our citizens did not win freedom together, did not survive
horrors together, did not face down evil together, only to lose our
freedom to a lack of pride and confidence in our values. We did not
and we will not. We will never back down.[3]

The oratory was made even more stirring by Trump's framing of
what he called the "fundamental question of our time: whether the West
has the will to survive."

Trump's appearance in Warsaw heartened conservatives in the
United States long worried about his commitments to American allies,
and it bolstered many in Europe who, with an assertive Russia to the
east, have reason to worry more viscerally about this question. But as
powerful as his rhetoric was in Warsaw, the speech remains an outlier
in the Trump canon.

And even in his Warsaw speech, Trump sounded a theme that angers
Merkel and other European leaders: that NATO member countries aren't
paying their fair share to support the alliance and that America is bearing
too much of the financial costs.

That suggestion was prominent during a far more typical Trump
episode: his trip to Europe in July 2018, a seven-day excursion to
visit with NATO allies and have a summit meeting, in Helsinki, with
Russian president Vladimir Putin. Even by the eventful standards of

Consider that NATO guidelines call for each member of the alliance to spend 2 percent of its GDP on defense spending, to build up its military in case a conflict should arise. However, only five NATO members currently meet the alliance's 2 percent target for defense spending: Poland, Britain, Estonia, Greece, and the United States.[7] The United States spends far more money on defense than any of the 28 other nations that belong to NATO, or any other nation on the planet, for that matter.[8] NATO's goal is for each member nation to reach the 2 percent target by 2025. So the cost structure is a legitimate issue for Trump to highlight, even if he goes about it like the proverbial bull in a china shop—particularly when it concerns wealthy and powerful members of the alliance, like Germany, whom Trump suggests is dawdling in its responsibilities.

"I think these countries have to step it up, not over a 10-year period, but they have to step it up immediately," Trump said, pointing to Germany as a "rich country" that "could increase [defense spending] immediately tomorrow and have no problem."[9]

Likewise, Trump's lambasting of NATO members for being ineffectual on terrorism has a basis in reality, as the spate of horrific Islamic terror attacks in Europe in recent years testifies—especially when taken in the context of the now nonexistent borders between countries and Merkel's open-door refugee policies. What Trump sees, and millions of Americans see as well, are European partners who seem to lack the will to make essential but politically incorrect decisions about national security. Enough voters in the United States, with its own porous borders with Mexico, thought this problem was so serious that it was worth putting Trump, with his pledge to "build a wall," into the White House.

The problem: Trump has not yet shown the political savvy to make his views known without alienating allies. This was perhaps best symbolized a few days after the inauguration, when Trump, according to inside reports, got into something of a shouting match on the telephone with Australian prime minister Malcolm Turnbull over a refugee-resettlement agreement brokered by the Obama administration. Trump was probably right that the deal was bad; but again, his means of dealing with it seemed more likely to exacerbate the problem and drive a wedge between the United States and one of its closest allies. One can imagine how presidents ranging from John Kennedy to Ronald Reagan and

Bill Clinton to George W. Bush might have handled such a call: with warm words and pledges of cooperation, and perhaps some resolution of unresolved business that could create goodwill, before getting to the hard stuff. Instead, Trump went for the jugular.

Both before that phone call and after, Trump's behavior has caused unease and even fear among alliance partners. Merkel was said to be "preparing for the worst" even before Trump's inauguration, and she has probably felt little cause to think differently since. The best encapsulation of the mood in Europe came from Anne Applebaum, who, writing in the *Washington Post*, described the angst among Swedes, which can readily be seen as a stand-in for feelings across Europe: "Sweden's economic and political model depends on Pax Americana, the set of American-written and American-backed rules that have governed transatlantic commerce and politics for 70 years—and they fear Trump will bring Pax Americana crashing down. Nor are they alone: Variations of this conversation are taking place in every European capital and many Asian capitals too."[10]

Writing in the *Wall Street Journal*, Simon Nixon described four key anxieties that Europeans have about Trump: first, that he will try to weaken the dollar, which would stall Europe's economic recovery; second, that his America First stance could result in policies of explicit protectionism; third, that Trump's interest in financial deregulation will loosen capital rules, potentially creating the same conditions that led to the financial crisis; and fourth, that Trump's anti-EU and anti-euro rhetoric will bolster Euroskeptics and nationalists and foster deeper social and political divisions. These remain reasonable concerns.

It seems a fair bet that Trump's relations with major European leaders will remain tenuous. And yet, it bears repeating: as destabilizing a force as Trump might prove to be, his presence in some ways is a distraction from the broader problems that the Western alliance system faces—no matter who the American president is.

IS THE WESTERN ALLIANCE DYING?

The numbers don't lie. In 2006, NATO allies set a target to spend 2 percent of their gross domestic product on defense. Today, the United States covers 72 percent of NATO's budget, while only five other countries spend the recommended 2 percent of GDP on defense.[11] That's a prescription for American dominance, American frustration, and, in the Trump era, American threats to alliance members that they better start pulling their weight financially. NATO's secretary general even called Europe's miniscule defense budgets "unsustainable" when compared with the Russian ramp-up in defense spending. But so far, progress is slow on getting NATO countries to step up, perhaps because none of these countries have it written into law that they must contribute 2 percent or more.[12] Without an enforcement mechanism for contributing more, it's easy to fall back on U.S. largesse.

The consequences of this non-commitment to common defense can be seen in Syria, where the West stood by and essentially watched a brutal carnage take place, year after year, since 2012. When critics excoriate the weakness of NATO and the European Union, Syria is the lead exhibit, because it is in that war-torn country that the paralysis of NATO under American leadership—at least during the Obama administration—has been most powerfully demonstrated. To be fair, leaders in France and Britain pushed for a military response after Bashar al-Assad's regime used chemical weapons against Syrians in August 2013. And, briefly, it looked like Washington was with them, until President Obama infamously pulled back from his red line. Soon enough, the British Parliament had voted down military force, too, and any Western response was dead. Europe chose not to intervene in a situation in which, it could be argued, it had greater interests at stake than the United States did.

If Europe's passivity is a problem, American disengagement has been another, more consequential one. "Experience shows that when the United States retreats or retrenches, it will leave behind a security vacuum, and that vacuum will be filled by the bad guys. And that's what we are seeing," said former NATO secretary general Anders Fogh Rasmussen. "While America and Europe slept, President Putin attacked Ukraine and he launched a reckless military operation in Syria."[13] Rasmussen didn't bother to add that Putin has achieved his objectives in Syria—no small thing, and an achievement hard to imagine had the Western alliance been operational and determined.

So far, the prevailing concern among American allies in Europe regarding Trump is the fate of Article 5, the NATO clause that guarantees collective security for members of the alliance; it pledges that an attack on one country will be taken as an attack on all, and that member nations will come to the aid of their partners. While few observers doubt that the United States would step in to defend, say, Britain or France after an attack, the gray area, especially with Trump, is what might happen with more recent NATO allies—especially those nations located in Vladimir Putin's traditional zone of influence.

In a sobering article in *Foreign Affairs*, "How World War III Could Begin in Latvia," Paul D. Miller sketches out a disturbingly plausible scenario. Miller, who predicted the Russian invasion of Ukraine, makes another prediction: "the Baltics are next." He doesn't mean a traditional invasion: the Baltic nations, unlike Ukraine (and, before Ukraine, Georgia), are NATO members, so Putin would need to move more subtly. What Miller sees Putin doing instead is instigating an "ambiguous militarized crisis using deniable proxies," which sounds like another iteration of Putin's hybrid-war tactics. Indeed, Miller sketches it out:

> Perhaps Russian-speaking Latvians or Estonians (a quarter of Latvians and Estonians are ethnically Russian) will begin rioting, protesting for their rights, claiming to be persecuted, asking for "international protection." A suspiciously well armed and well trained "Popular Front for the Liberation of the Russian Baltics" will appear. A few high-profile assassinations and bombings bring the Baltics to the edge of civil war. A low-grade insurgency may emerge.
>
> Russia will block all United Nations Security Council resolutions, but will offer its unilateral services as a peacekeeper. The North Atlantic Council will meet. Poland will lead the effort to invoke Article V, declare the Baltics under Russian attack, and rally collective defense against Russian aggression. The Germans and French will fiercely resist. Everyone will look to the United States to see which way the alliance leader tilts.
>
> If the Alliance does not invoke Article V, NATO's mutual security guarantee becomes functionally meaningless. No alliance member will put any faith in the treaty to guarantee its own defense against Russia in the future. The geopolitical clock will rewind to 1939. Some Eastern European states may choose to bandwagon with Russia. Others, starting with Poland, will begin arming to the teeth.

Putin's dream of a fractured West and an open field in Europe will be realized.

But if the Alliance does invoke Article V, it will be tantamount to a declaration of war by the West against Russia. And that's when Trump will have to decide if the defense of Latvia is worth risking World War III.[14]

Trump himself entertained such hypotheticals, this time involving NATO member Montenegro, in a July 2018 interview with Tucker Carlson on Fox News. Carlson asked why his son should go to Montenegro to defend it in the event of an attack.

"I understand what you're saying," Trump responded. "I've asked the same question. Montenegro is a tiny country with very strong people. They have very aggressive people. They may get aggressive and congratulations, you're in World War III, now I understand that. But that's the way it was set up."[15]

Like many of the comments Trump makes about NATO, especially its mutual-defense agreement, this one caused consternation far and wide.

Article 5 has been invoked only once in NATO history—by the United States, after 9/11—but like many principles and clauses, its effectiveness lies in *not* being invoked. That is, the prospect of collective defense, a foundation of the alliance, is widely viewed as an effective deterrent against aggression. A potential Russian challenge, in Europe, to the NATO principle of mutual defense is not an unfamiliar fear, of course—such scenarios dominated strategic thinking during the Cold War, after all. What's different this time is that the American president's commitment to the mutual-defense principle is unclear.

In Warsaw, as we have seen, Trump spoke the words that many have called on him to deliver since he was inaugurated. It was an encouraging, even inspiring moment. Yet Trump has shown himself to be changeable; he can deliver prepared speeches one day and then tweet something in apparent contravention of the speech later that day or the next. Or he tweets positions that seem at odds with what his own administration officials are pursuing. So Trump's 2017 words in Warsaw, while beneficial, shouldn't be seen as the last word on this matter—especially in light of his subsequent tumultuous European trip in 2018.

Making matters even more perplexing, Trump's inner circle seems as devoted to Article 5 as any other administration. During his confirmation hearings, Trump's first secretary of state, former Exxon Mobil CEO Rex Tillerson, broke with Trump's previous assertion that he would defend NATO allies only "if they fulfill their obligations" to the United States.[16] Tillerson called Article 5 "inviolate." Republican senator Rob Portman asked Tillerson, "Just to be clear, because I know there was a discussion about NATO earlier, particularly about Article 5, which talks about 'an armed attack against one or more members shall be considered an attack against them all.' Can you just clarify that you believe Article 5 creates a binding obligation to assist any member of the alliance who is a victim of aggression regardless of their size or geographic location?"

"Yes, sir, I do," Tillerson replied.[17]

When Portman asked if Tillerson would ever "threaten to break the U.S. commitment to Article 5 as a means of pressuring allies to spend more on defense," Tillerson said that he would "not recommend that." These, too, are encouraging words—but more is needed from the administration, in both deeds and words, to put allies' concerns to rest.

In the meantime, though, some in Europe have begun at least to plan for the possibility that United States security support might not be what it has been in the past. Some longtime observers of the EU believe that its member nations have been "infantilized" by decades of dependence on the United States' protections, and that it is past time for these nations to take a hard look at their budgets and begin figuring out how they can invest more in their own defenses. President Merkel wants to see more military integration between her country and France; if the two both get their budgets above the 2 percent NATO minimum, they would be spending, together, about two-thirds of Russia's defense budget. That's getting somewhere.

One lingering problem that European defense specialists have pointed to for years is the bewildering array of defensive systems, some outdated and redundant, that the various nations possess. In Europe, 17 different families of battle tanks are manufactured; in the United States, there is just one. In Europe, there are 20 different types of fighter aircraft, compared with just 6 in the United States, and 29 kinds of destroyers and frigates, compared with just 4 in the United States. That is no way to run efficient or effective procurement. But with the new challenges on the horizon from Russia—and, it must be said, the pressure that Trump is exerting—the EU's leading countries might finally be ready to take a more active role in their own defense.

It remains to be seen, then, how NATO and the European alliance will fare under Trump. On the one hand, the president talks tough; and his willingness to challenge elites both domestically and internationally, which sets him apart from Obama and other presidents, could achieve some real benefits. On the other, sometimes his tough talk is directed against America's allies. In either case, even if Trump becomes an eleventh-hour convert to the importance of the Western alliance, fault lines are prevalent, from nationalist movements and institutional failures to financial and economic challenges—all having the effect of eroding public confidence and support.

American alliances outside of Europe have also grown more uncertain.

For 60-plus years, the U.S. relationship with South Korea was about as strong as alliances can be, and for good reason—the United States wanted to support its democratic ally on the Korean peninsula, while for Seoul, Washington's protection was a safeguard against the tyrannical (and nuclear-armed) North Koreans, along with their benefactor, Communist China. More recently, though, tensions have appeared in the alliance—at just the moment, amid rising fears of Pyongyang's nuclear threat, that the partnership is most needed. When Kim Jong Un was firing off ballistic missile tests in summer 2017, and eventually tested what North Korea claimed was a hydrogen bomb on September 3, 2017, Trump needlessly and provocatively criticized South Korea for not doing enough to defend itself. "Talking is not the answer!" he tweeted, in reference to South Korean president Moon Jae-in's interest in holding talks with the North. "South Korea is finding, as I have told them, that their talk of appeasement with North Korea will not work, they only understand one thing!" the president blasted.[18] He even threatened to withdraw from a bilateral trade agreement. South Korea hasn't been deterred by Trump's bluster; in January 2018, North Korea announced that it had accepted Moon's offer to meet for talks. Trump didn't miss a beat, taking credit for forcing the talks by being "firm, strong and willing to commit our total 'might' against the North."[19]

U.S.–South Korea watchers were further dismayed when Trump suspended some military exercises with South Korea after his Singapore summit with Kim in June 2018. Fortunately, Congress passed a bill that "prohibits the use of funds to reduce the U.S. troop size from the current 28,500 to below 22,000 without certification from the secretary of Defense that the reduction is in the national security interest of the United States and its allies in Northeast Asia," according to *The Hill*. Trump's instincts, again, seem indifferent or even opposed to traditional U.S. alliances, but officials in his own administration and in Congress often have other ideas.

The Washington-Seoul relationship is vital to whatever happens on the Korean peninsula; one can only hope that Trump does not needlessly damage it at such a perilous time. Japan, the world's third-largest economy and another longtime U.S. ally, remains a crucial check on China's presence in the South China Sea and a powerful advertisement for a democratic, market-based society. And yet, Trump caused concern in Japan, as well as in South Korea, with numerous statements during the campaign, including his complaint that neither country was paying enough for the security protections it enjoyed from the United States. More troublingly, he even suggested that both should get nuclear weapons—which sounded like a precursor to telling them that they were on their own, defense-wise. Trump also complained about the terms of the defense commitments that the United States has made.

"You know we have a treaty with Japan where if Japan is attacked, we have to use the full force and might of the United States," Trump said, but should the United States be attacked, "Japan doesn't have to do anything. They can sit home and watch Sony television."[20] There is simply no excuse for such appallingly ignorant statements; Japan was demilitarized as a condition of surrender after World War II. The conditions of the agreement that the two nations drew up were set by the United States.

Defense Secretary James Mattis was dispatched to Japan and South Korea to smooth things over with officials there. Mattis made clear to Japanese prime minister Shinzo Abe that Washington remained committed to the U.S.-Japan Security Treaty, including as it pertains to the Senkaku Islands in the East China Sea—a source of deepening tensions in recent years between Japan and China; Beijing also claims the islands, which it calls the Diaoyu Islands. Mattis's assurances mean that the United States will stand by its treaty commitments to come to Japan's aid if the islands are attacked.

Abe was also thrown off by Trump's surprise announcement of his summit meeting with Kim. The Japanese president had strongly supported Trump's campaign to curtail North Korea's nuclear program, but the Trump-Kim summit itself, filled with the vaguest promises and warm rhetoric, couldn't have reassured him. Indeed, skepticism and anxiety run high in Tokyo regarding the prospects for North Korean denuclearization.

The most dislocating Asian experience in recent years for the United States has been the rise of President Rodrigo Duterte, who has been, in his brief time in office, a loose cannon of anti-American rhetoric, levied in part to respond to U.S. criticism of his human rights abuses in the Philippines' drug war—he has voiced support for killing drug dealers and other criminals without due process. Duterte's crackdown resulted in 3,000 deaths in three months, and he boasted that he could kill three million, even comparing himself with Hitler.

"Hitler massacred three million Jews," he said. "There's three million drug addicts. There are. I'd be happy to slaughter them."[21]

The Obama administration's criticism of the Philippines sent Duterte into a rage. A month before the 2016 presidential election in the United States, Duterte said, "Instead of helping us, the first to criticize is this state department, so you can go to hell, Mr. Obama, you can go to hell." (At another point, he called Obama the "son of a whore.") Then he turned his attention to the also-critical European Union: "Better choose purgatory, hell is filled up." For what remained of Obama's time in office, it seemed like the Philippines was not drifting but racing out of the American orbit and into the arms of China—an astounding development. Duterte made overtures to China and even Russia.

In a visit to Beijing, Duterte gave a speech at the Great Hall of the People and announced, "I've realigned myself. Maybe I will also go to Russia to talk to Putin and tell him that there are three of us against the world: China, Philippines, and Russia.... I announce my separation from the United States. America has lost now."[22] Duterte said that he wanted to terminate long-standing defense agreements with the United States, under which American soldiers have access to Filipino military bases. He said that he wanted American troops out, and he canceled joint military exercises.

But just as it seemed that the Philippines was ready to consummate these new relationships with China and Russia, Trump won the White House, and his administration has reached out to Duterte. Relations have improved substantially, in no small part because Duterte himself seems to believe that he will have a more sympathetic ally in Trump than he had in Obama. (I'm not one to circulate Trump-as-fascist formulations, but one must acknowledge that as a statesman, he clearly seems more comfortable dealing with authoritarian leaders than with democratic ones.)

By August 2017, Duterte was sounding a different note. "I am your humble friend in Southeast Asia," he told Secretary of State Rex Tillerson when the two met in Manila. Tillerson was visiting Duterte to discuss regional issues including counterterrorism measures against radical Islamists, who have a serious presence in the southern Philippines. Duterte was one of the first world leaders to call Trump to congratulate him on his election; Trump has praised Duterte's efforts against drugs, soft-pedaling the human rights questions. The main change that the Trump administration appears to have made is decoupling continued military and counterterror assistance for the Philippines from the question of Duterte's human rights record.

"We see no conflict at all in our helping them with that situation and our views of the human rights concerns we have with respect to how they carry out their counter narcotics activities," said Tillerson. That approach may or may not prove sustainable; past precedents of American support for pro-Washington dictators are not happy ones. But at least for the moment, the Trump administration has succeeded in slowing down the deterioration of the vital American-Filipino alliance.

CAUSE FOR CONCERN—AND CAUSE FOR HOPE

Ever since the collapse of Berlin in 1945 and the surrender of the Japanese, later that year, on the USS *Indianapolis*, the United States has been the guarantor of global security for democratic nations around the world, but especially those in Western Europe and in Asia. There is no question that this liberal world order, as some have called it, is facing enormous challenges right now, and perhaps even breaking apart, under the strain of a host of developments: the failures of institutions, which have eroded popular support for government, free enterprise, and even democracy itself; the rise of populist and nationalist movements; the continued destabilizing effect of Islamist terror in Europe and in the United States, along with the unsolved problem of how to integrate (if such integration is truly possible) newcomers from parts of the world that do not share a commitment to a secular, democratic, open society; and the rise of aggressive, antidemocratic powers, like Russia and China, who are moving boldly in their regions of influence while also troubling Western allies and ratcheting up fault lines in the alliance.

I have written in the past that Russia and China pose the greatest challenge, overall, to the Western alliance, and I still believe that. This is not to dismiss or diminish the Islamist threat—nor, for that matter, the nuclear-tinged dangers of rogue nations like Iran or North Korea— but in my view, nation-states remain the fundamental power centers in global politics, and Moscow and Beijing have enormous resources at their command. They have used them ruthlessly, artfully, and successfully, and their successes only point up the current state of disarray among the Western democracies, especially the United States, in how to respond. Since Russia and China see it as their mission, in different ways, to present alternatives to the Anglo-American model of open societies and democratic governance, their successes have had not just material consequences but ideological ones—as I write about in chapter 4, on the rising tide of authoritarianism.

Unless the Western alliance reasserts itself, the world could very soon begin to resemble the kind of nationalist, tribal rivalries of an earlier time. That world was marked by hugely destructive great power competitions that culminated in catastrophes such as the world has never seen. "It has been the great accomplishment of the U.S.-led world order in the 70 years since the end of the Second World War," Robert Kagan writes, "that this kind of competition has been held in check and great power conflicts have been avoided."[23]

But the U.S.-led world order looks to be tottering, in no small part because the United States itself has seemed so uncertain and changeable. Over the last decade and a half, we have had three presidents: the first, a confident and hugely ambitious interventionist who launched an invasion that redrew the Middle East map, but not to Western advantage, and in the process discredited American intervention for millions of his own countrymen and political allies; the second, a devoted internationalist who preferred multilateral to bilateral agreements, adjudication of disputes via international bodies rather than through unilateral or bilateral decision-making, and who, believing deeply that American intervention had caused just as much trouble as it had alleviated, argued that America must "lead from behind"; and the third, a political neophyte who has so far given more lip service to nationalism and isolationism than his actual policies reflect, but whose rhetoric has, nonetheless, refigured the political landscape in America and abroad.

U.S. allies aren't entirely sure what to make of America's role anymore, and they worry that America's own problems and divisions will cripple it as a leader. Close American allies have told pollsters that they worry that America is in decline. Their level of confidence in their own capabilities is hardly more robust, and for good reason: their internal problems, ranging from economic stagnation to financial crisis to declining native-born populations to enormous difficulties in integrating newcomers, make America's challenges appear entirely manageable. Their long dependence on American leadership (and arms) has not suited them for alliance leadership, and it seems clear to me, anyway, that the future of the Western alliance remains in American hands.

How should we look at it? An important thing to remember is the strengths that we retain and the serious weaknesses of our adversaries. I have written three books warning about the dangers posed by Putin's Russia, but in none of them do I suggest that he is not beatable or that he lacks vulnerabilities; the same applies to China. Listen to the wisdom of Michael J. Green of the Center for Strategic and International Studies (CSIS):

> Russia is a declining power that is using the fissures in the Western alliance and its own asymmetrical cyber and paramilitary capabilities to sow limited chaos in Western political systems and to block former Soviet states from consolidating their security and economic relationships with NATO. China, like rising powers throughout history, is free-riding on American leadership globally while engaging

in limited revisionism regionally. Beijing will do what it can to assert its control over the East and South China Seas, but unlike Russia has a great stake in the current international economic order and limited appetite for direct confrontation with the United States.[24]

He's right, and he's right as well that Iran's rise, and especially its looming nuclear status, seems to be having the effect of rearranging relationships between longtime Middle East adversaries, like Saudi Arabia and Israel. And North Korea remains a grave danger but a containable one: it can cause havoc, and it might yet cost many lives, in a nuclear exchange, before the regime is finally replaced, but North Korea is not going to remake the world map.

Moreover, the West's economic power remains preeminent, as Goldman Sachs's decision in 2015 to shut down its BRICS investment fund made dramatically clear. Remember the BRICS—Brazil, Russia, India, China, South Africa? They were going to replace the West, and especially the United States, as the leaders in investment and innovation. It's not happening. The unrivaled leader in foreign direct investment and technological innovation remains the United States. And the Western democracies remain the places where most of the world's migrants want to live, for very good reasons.

What is the problem, then? One is that, as Green puts it, "there is no coherent geopolitical concept of 'the West' any longer in Washington, London, or Berlin." That brings us back to Trump's Warsaw speech, cheered on the Right but jeered on the Left, which saw it as nativist and even "racist"—this about a speech that merely praised Western civilization for its towering accomplishments and pledged devotion to that culture and civilization. Trump's speech was stirring mainly because our political leaders don't talk this way anymore; that contemporary liberals found the speech "hateful" and racist shows the truth of Green's words. If the West doesn't believe in itself as the "West," all the hard work of alliances and diplomacy and deterrence is going to be much, much harder to pull off.

In the end, though, it's going to come down to the United States. "Superpowers don't get to retire," said NATO's former chief, Rasmussen, in November 2016. "Look around: you will see a world on fire. Syria torn by war and conflict. Iraq on the brink of collapse. Libya a failed state in North Africa. Russia attacking Ukraine and destabilising Eastern Europe. China flexing its muscles, the rogue state North Korea threatening nuclear attacks. All that requires a world policeman to restore international law and order."[25]

It's up to America—and that means, in turn, that it's up to America's leaders. That's where the game will ultimately be decided. The United States and the Western alliance will look to the man in the Oval Office to set the tone and direction for the years ahead. Having visionary, brave leaders in Europe will be essential, too. No doubt, in recent years, millions of European and American citizens have been disappointed in the leaders they've gotten, and populist and nationalist movements are one by-product of that. But the clock is ticking on the Western alliance to reformulate itself appropriately to the challenges of a new and potentially deadly age.

For now, at least, it comes down to Donald Trump. Is he up to it? Does he want to be? The answers to those questions will tell us much.

PART II

ESCALATING
THREATS

CHAPTER FOUR

AUTHORITARIANISM RISING, DEMOCRACY DECLINING

"You get the feeling that President Xi cares about the little guy. He gives you hope that the government can solve your problems."

—YANG TIANRONG, RETIRED SOLDIER, HEBEI PROVINCE, CHINA[1]

"Eighty-two percent of Russians support the myth or the revival of the Great Russia status, as Putin makes people feel proud of Russia's greatness since the fall of the USSR."

—LEV GUDKOV, DIRECTOR, LEVADA POLLING CENTER[2]

I n 2017, for the twelfth year in a row, Freedom House's annual survey showed a decline in global freedom and liberty. Seventy-one countries showed a decline in freedom for the year, while just 35 registered gains. Over slightly more than a decade, more than 100 countries have taken backward steps, with the worst areas for decline being the rule of law and general freedom of expression. Overall, Freedom House classed a mere 39 percent of the global population as "free," with 24 percent "partly free" and 37 percent not free—the latter list including China, Russia, Iran, Afghanistan, and much of the Middle East except for Israel.[3]

But the most troubling sign is the decline in liberty in democratic countries. "The world's most powerful democracies are mired in seemingly intractable problems at home, including social and economic disparities, partisan fragmentation, terrorist attacks, and an influx of refugees that has strained alliances and increased fears of the 'other.'" For the Freedom House authors, most concerning of all was the retreat that the United States seemed to be making, under the Trump administration, from its traditional role as defender and promoter of democracy around the world. "A long list of troubling developments around the world contributed to the global decline in 2017, but perhaps most striking was the accelerating withdrawal of the United States from its historical commitment to promoting and supporting democracy," the report read. "The potent challenge from authoritarian regimes made the United States' abdication of its traditional role all the more important."[4]

In its report the previous year, Freedom House had written that Turkey, where President Recep Tayyip Erdoğan oversaw a mass consolidation of power and purge of governmental institutions following a failed coup, illustrated the advent of an "unvarnished form of authoritarianism" in a country that had seen legitimate democracy before; that Venezuela and Nicaragua appeared to be on an "extended downward trajectory"; and that the rise of anti-establishment parties in Europe was "shifting the debate in ways that undermine the fundamental values of democracy." These assessments still hold.

As chronicled in earlier chapters, populist and nationalist parties are on the rise across Europe, some of them exhibiting indifference or even hostility to traditional democratic principles. And in the United States, under Donald Trump, the office of the presidency has lost some of its traditional luster as a defender of democracy around the globe. While I find many of the warnings about Trump's impending tyranny, let alone fascism, to be absurdly overstated, I too have been dismayed at his lackadaisical attitude toward America's alliances, his seeming ignorance of core democratic principles—often calling for "loyalty" from cabinet members who, like the attorney general, are sworn not to him but to the Constitution—and his reckless and chaotic management style, which suggests contempt for the patient deliberation and deal-making that democracy requires.

But the United States' retreat from its role as a democratic beacon didn't begin under Trump, and the United States is not alone in its shaken confidence in the virtues of the Western political tradition. Over the last five years, no place on earth has illustrated the West's lack of conviction better than Syria, where a ruthless and barbaric civil war has raged, abetted and exacerbated by Vladimir Putin's Russia—but also enabled by a demoralizing failure to act on the part of the United Nations and the Western democracies, especially the United States. The U.N. has been lambasted before by its many critics for a range of failings, but Syria stands glaringly as the international body's most abject failure of the twenty-first century. Its failure to prevent genocidal attacks and mass atrocities is simply breathtaking and presents a real challenge to the organization's future viability. "It is becoming clearer every day that the UN Security Council has failed the Syrian people," said Sherine Tadros, head of Amnesty International's U.N. office. "There have been almost half a million deaths, and each one is a stark rebuke of the Security Council, the supposed guardian of international peace and security, which has allowed a political deadlock to stand in the way of saving lives."[5]

One key reason that the international effort to save Syria has failed so abysmally is the lack of American leadership—and especially the loss of American faith in the idea of democracy promotion. This lost faith first manifested itself in the Obama administration, which, reacting to the Bush administration's failures in Iraq and Afghanistan, took a decidedly unsentimental approach to humanitarian intervention, preferring to "lead from behind." And then, under Obama's successor, Donald Trump, the United States has backed off for different reasons: hard-headed assessments of the national interest that, in the Trumpian vision, don't include such interventions, even in cases of enormous human suffering and where the only nation in the world that can truly tip the balance is the United States. The administration did launch a missile attack on a Syrian airbase in April 2017, to punish the regime for a deadly chemical weapons attack on civilians, but this was a one-off and has not been followed up meaningfully. By and large, Trump has followed Obama's Syria policy of tough rhetoric but little substantive action; the administration's incoherent policy has allowed Iran and Russia's role to go unchallenged.

Failure to prevent Russian aggression is another touchstone of decline. Under President Obama, the United States refused to export lethal aid to Ukraine to assist with combat against Russian-backed insurgencies in eastern portions of the country. Several senators wrote a letter to then president-elect Trump in December 2016 urging him to change this policy, noting, "Russia has launched a military land-grab in Ukraine that is unprecedented in modern European history. We believe it is in our vital national security interest to uphold these norms and values, and prevent America's commitment to its allies and ideals from being called into question." But while the urging has continued, as of July 2017, the Trump administration had still not approved lethal aid to Ukraine.

Two presidents make a trend: put simply, the United States no longer prioritizes democracy promotion as a key component of its foreign policy. And under Trump, it remains more unlikely than likely that the United States will elevate human rights as a primary priority. (I'll have more to say about this in chapter 10, "Assertive Democratic Idealism.")

Even more troubling is Trump's newfound friendliness, at least rhetorically, for strongmen and authoritarian leaders ranging from Putin in Russia to Duterte in the Philippines to Abdel Fattah al-Sisi in Egypt. It is pointless to deny that Trump feels such affinities; he has made numerous public statements dating back to his presidential campaign indicating such sympathies, which are jarring to hear from the leader of the free world, even if they represent no substantive policy shift, as yet.

Is the democratic model in genuine decline? The *Journal of Democracy* sees three reasons to worry: the economic and political instability in advanced democracies; a new self-confidence of some authoritarian countries; and a general shift in the geopolitical balance between democracies and their rivals, as the Freedom House data show.[6] Indeed, the 2008 financial crisis caused advanced democracies to suffer, while emerging-market countries grew rapidly; recession and high unemployment rates spread across Europe and the United States. China has made enormous economic strides, providing Africa with trade and military/development aid not contingent on human rights accountability in the recipient country. And Russia, Iran, Saudi Arabia, and Venezuela have been learning from one another and cooperating to slow Western democracy's progress. Authoritarian states like these and others have been steadily increasing their military spending; in democratic nations, military expenditures are on the wane.[7]

Another flashpoint: populist authoritarianism clashes with the liberal values of modern Western societies, which tend to regard these values as "universal." They're not. Data from the World Values Survey reveal how, as Western countries become more liberal regarding sex roles, LGBT rights, tolerance of diversity, and secular values, non-Western or non-advanced nations have not been traveling the same path—to the contrary, in fact.[8] Virtually all advanced industrial societies have been moving in the same direction, but while economically advanced societies have been changing rather rapidly, countries that remained economically

stagnant showed little value change. As a result, there has been a growing divergence between prevailing values in low-income countries and
those in high-income countries. The strongest emphasis on traditional
values is found in Islamic societies of the Middle East. By contrast, the
strongest emphasis on secular values and self-expression is found in the
Protestant societies of Northern Europe.[9]

In short, over the last decade or more, antidemocratic and even
outright authoritarian models of governance have been on the ascen-
dancy. And while I could devote this chapter to any number of countries
that represent troubling trends, I maintain that the two countries at
the center of the authoritarian appeal remain Russia and China. Not
only do their economic and military might exert influence around the
world; they also are governed by savvy, determined leaders, Vladimir
Putin and Xi Jinping, both of whom have achieved prestige, even awe,
at home. A 2014 Harvard Kennedy School survey asked residents of ten
countries—the United States, Britain, France, Germany, Japan, India,
Russia, China, Brazil, and South Africa—to rate the country's president
or top political leader. Among the ten leaders—on a list that included
Angela Merkel, President Obama, Shinzo Abe, David Cameron, and
Francois Hollande—Xi and Putin won the highest approval ratings from
their citizens: Xi scored 9 out of 10 points, while Putin rated an 8.7 out of
10. Americans can scoff at these ratings if they wish, and scoff at Putin
and Xi, too: but unless we understand better why and how they have
made substantive advances over recent years, and why they enjoy such
broad support among their people, we will lack crucial insight into the
newfound momentum of antidemocratic, authoritarian governance.

THE RUSSIAN SHADOW

"Life is still hard, but at least we have a real man in power now," residents of a remote village in the far Eastern region of Sakhalin told a
journalist from the *Independent* in 2008. "[Vladimir] Putin isn't like
the oligarchs, who just want to steal cash. He is working hard to make
Russia great again."[10]

Over more than 15 years at the helm of Russian leadership, whether
as president or prime minister, Vladimir Putin has steadily restricted
civil liberties and free speech while imposing harsher domestic media

control and deepening the militarism of Russian society. He has jailed—
and, some say, arranged the murder of—dissidents and sent his security
forces to crack down on political demonstrations. In fact, Putin's war on
the free press has been described by close observers at home variously as
worse than what the old Soviet Union did—even "Stalinist."[11]

And yet, Putin's political support at home remains robust. Between
2013 and 2014, Putin's popularity among Russians rocketed from 54
percent to 83 percent—a likely result of his invasion of Crimea. Western
economic sanctions, imposed after his annexation of Crimea, at first
only strengthened his domestic support. The sanctions have hit hard:
Russia's sovereign wealth fund had $87 billion in assets in December
2013, a month before the Crimean incursion; as of June 1, 2016, it was
down to $38 billion, following sell-offs by the Russian government to
account for budget deficits. And yet, in September 2016, two months
before the U.S. presidential election, Putin's approval rating in Russia
stood near 81 percent.[12] Between 52 and 55 percent of Russians saw
Putin as someone they could trust, whereas only 4–5 percent saw him
as untrustworthy.[13]

More recently, Putin's popularity in Russia, while still enviable by
the standards of Western democracies, has ebbed somewhat, dipping,
for example, from over 80 percent in April 2018 to 67 percent just a few
months later, in July 2018. Analysts attributed the cooling off, though,
not to Putin's provocative foreign policy but rather to his failure to live
up to promises he made about worker pensions.[14]

There is no question that Putin's defiance of the sanctions (his
refusal to reconsider his moves in Crimea even though the costs are
severe) has empowered him with the Russian electorate, which sees
him as standing for Russian greatness and a recovery of national power.
Moreover, with Trump's election in 2016, the Kremlin had the prospect,
at least, of seeing some relief from these sanctions. Nothing as yet has
come of it, but Trump has clearly attempted to set a new tone with
Moscow. His questioning of the United States' NATO commitments
and his pooh-poohing of Putin's authoritarian rule and human rights
abuses has sent a signal to Moscow that the American president differs
from his predecessors in a rhetorical sense, at the very least.

I have written at length about Putin's Russia for nearly a decade now.
He has been at the center of three of my recent books: *The Russia-China*

Axis, Putin's Master Plan, and *Putin on the March.* For the sake of space, I will presume that readers are generally familiar with the Kremlin leader's recent embroilment in the 2016 United States presidential election, as well as his aggressive geopolitical moves of the last half decade and more: his annexation of Crimea, his destabilization of Ukraine—including his support for separatists in Eastern Ukraine—and his staunch backing of Syrian dictator Bashar al-Assad, who owes his survival in power and triumph in the Syrian civil war to Moscow's intervention and bold defense of his regime.

"Russia is an independent, active participant in international affairs," Putin said in a 2014 speech. "Like other countries, it has its own national interests that need to be taken into account and respected."[15] It's important to recognize that Putin is not merely pursuing Russia's national interests; he is also doing so as part of a concerted, counter-Western philosophy, one that rejects the core premises of open democratic societies, pluralism, and international norms. I have written extensively about this. Putin is not merely an adversary of the United States due to competing interests; he is an adversary because he views the United States' democratic model as a threat to what he holds dear—Russian hegemony over its "near abroad," traditional Russian culture, and authoritarian political system not subject to the sometimes destabilizing influence of democracy.

When one strips away some of the euphemisms, the plain fact is this: Putin is attempting to avenge Russia's defeat and embarrassment at end of the Cold War. "He basically wants to make Russia great again," said Strobe Talbott.[16] And though he does not necessarily seek open conflict with the United States, he does see the United States, at least before Trump came on the scene, as engaging in a long pattern of behavior, post–Cold War, of building up its alliances at the expense of traditional Russian interests. Thus, he has become contemptuous of NATO and the broader Western alliance, and he is willing to "look for opportunities to discredit and eventually undermine the alliance," said U.S. general Martin Dempsey.[17]

The alternate Russian model of governance is bluntly and unapologetically authoritarian. Putin has instituted severe crackdowns on domestic democratic institutions within Russia: arresting protestors, purging the "liberal elite," censoring magazines and the Internet.[18]

Recently, top editors of RBC media group, an outlet that had infuriated Putin with some of its published stories, were forced to leave their posts for political reasons.[19] Editors of 12 other Russian media outlets were ousted as a result of government pressure over the past five years.[20] In 2014, Dozhd, described as Russia's one truly independent TV station, was nearly forced to halt operations. The reason was a law banning advertising on private cable and satellite channels. According to a letter penned by a group of advertising leaders, "excluding the advertising model will place about 150 [out of 270 cable and satellite channels] on the brink of survival."[21] In collaboration with the Russian Orthodox Church, Putin's regime has also made life increasingly difficult, and dangerous, for adherents of other religions—as I'll have more to say about in chapter 9.

Putin has consolidated his own power within the Russian political system, essentially eroding any democratic checks on his authority. This goes back a ways—back even before the Putin–George W. Bush relationship began breaking down. In 2004, Putin passed a law allowing the president to appoint regional governors.[22] In 2012, circumventing laws designed to prevent lengthy executive terms, he returned to power after Dmitry Medvedev's one-term presidency. In 2012, Putin signed the "foreign agent law," requiring international NGOs to register as "foreign agents" and be subject to routine audits. The move was seen as an attempt to demonize a broad range of organizations that includes election-watchdog groups.[23]

American readers might assume that such brutish moves would ensure Putin's demise at the hands of Russian voters—at least, in a fair election—but they would be wrong. On the contrary, Putin's strongman tactics have boosted his popularity. Some argue that Putin's high approval ratings demonstrate general Russian support for an authoritative strongman leader, rather than affinity for Putin himself: "The approval rating we see is not for Putin, it is for the tsar, and if tomorrow they replace him with a different leader, who will soon have the same approval rating, the majority will vote for the tsar appointed to sit on the throne," says Olga Bychkova of the independent radio network Echo of Moscow.[24] Seconding that view, Lev Gudkov, director of Levada polling center, says, "Eighty-two percent of Russians support the myth or the revival of the Great Russia status, as Putin makes people feel proud of

Russia's greatness since the fall of the USSR."[25] They might be right, but in practice, the distinction is meaningless. Perhaps Russians might yearn for a czar, any czar; but the fact remains that Putin has fulfilled that wish. Moreover, Putin's rule has been so distinctive, so clearly the product of a unique political personality and intelligence, that dismissing his broad national appeal as czarist nostalgia seems ill-considered.

Perhaps even more disturbing than Putin's popularity at home is his not-inconsiderable appeal to Westerners, including in the United States. In December 2016, 37 percent of Republicans in the United States told pollsters that they had a favorable opinion of Putin, a climb of 56 net percentage points from July 2014. Nine in ten Republicans called Putin a "strong leader."[26] Remarkably, in May 2016, more people in the United States held a "very negative" view of Trump and Hillary Clinton than they did of Putin.[27]

Even after the election, a "surprising number of people" saw Putin "in a positive light as a man of action," Russian expert Keith Darden told the *Christian Science Monitor*.[28] And Trump strategic guru Steve Bannon urged the West to support Putin's promotion of traditional values and ideas promulgating the "underpinnings of nationalism."[29] Far Right and alt-right leaders in the United States (including white nationalists), along with their counterparts in Europe, have also championed Putin and his rule.

As for Russia's intervention in the 2016 American presidential election, it is infamous and probably unprecedented. Here again, we should focus not merely on the well-known specifics—the email hacking and the like—or the effect of these actions (including whether they affected the ultimate outcome), but on the broader design behind Russia's activity. That broader, most ambitious goal was *not* the election of Donald Trump—which is not to say that Moscow may not have been happy when he won. (Indeed, at his 2018 joint press conference with Trump in Helsinki, Putin admitted that he had wanted Trump to win the election.) The broader Russian goal: to undermine the Western democratic model by demonstrating the corruption of the U.S. electoral system and "creating the image that [other countries] couldn't depend on the U.S. to be a credible global leader anymore," as one U.S. intelligence source put it.[30]

As I have written elsewhere—most recently in my 2017 book, *Putin on the March*—in my view, this goal has been accomplished to almost

100 percent effectiveness. Take a look at the state of American politics and public attitudes about the trustworthiness of institutions to get an idea of how things stand. Certainly, I am not attributing American disillusionment and distrust entirely, or even mostly, to Putin's efforts; as I have written before, Americans' loss of faith in institutions has been a gradual but inexorable process since at least the 1970s. But the levels of trust have never been lower than they are today, and Russia's intervention in the 2016 election—however deep it ran, whatever its ultimate impact—could represent a tipping point in the erosion of American confidence in democratic institutions.

THE CHINA DREAM

Meanwhile, under the strong, savvy, and non-democratic leadership of Xi Jinping, China has moved further away from any notions of liberal democracy—not that such a goal was ever imminent in Beijing. But under Xi, the sound one hears is of doors closing. He heads two policy coordinating bodies, the Leading Small Group for Comprehensive Deepening of Reform and the State Security Commission, which give him unparalleled power to advance his agenda. Under Xi's leadership, China has imposed greater restrictions on academic freedom,[31] tightened media controls,[32] and campaigned against "Western values" and "Western ideas" such as "Western Constitutional Democracy," freedom of the press, and human rights.[33]

Xi is a Chinese leader whose growing stature has been compared by some observers with that of Mao Zedong himself. The devotion millions of Chinese citizens and political allies seem to feel for him increasingly resembles a personality cult. Post-Mao, such overt personal glorification is officially prohibited by the Communist Party, but to Western eyes anyway, the distinction between Xi devotion and old-fashioned Maoism is getting blurrier. Xi's speeches are broadcast from enormous TV screens in public plazas and his image is widely seen (sometimes alongside Mao's) in private homes, restaurants, and taxicabs. Newspapers print excerpts from his speeches; highway billboards and electronic displays flash Xi slogans and aphorisms. "While there may be no 'Little Red Book' of quotations for mass consumption like in the bygone Mao era," writes Chris Buckley in the *New York Times*, "Mr. Xi's thinking will now infuse every aspect of party ideology in schools, the media and government agencies. In the near future, Chinese people are likely to refer to Mr. Xi's doctrines as simply 'Xi Jinping Thought,' a flattering echo of 'Mao Zedong Thought.'"[34]

Xi demands absolute loyalty to himself and to the state. He has visited China's state-run news agency, newspaper, and TV station in the same day to demand total loyalty to the Communist Party from employees. China has shut down numerous media outlets. Communist Party officials in Beijing have assumed essentially unquestioned power to control content on current affairs and political news sites, with a special focus on critics of the regime.

"He is worried that he will lose the rule of the Chinese Communist Party," says historian Zhang Lifan. "He is also worried that he might be replaced by his peers.... For those reasons, he must hold on to his power tightly. He's like a man who doesn't know how to swim. He is going to grab hold of whatever he can."[35] Lifan's words are compelling—most dictators govern at least in part through fear—but the fact remains that Xi is making a pretty good go of it. He is remaking China in his image.

A major part of that project involves the projection of Chinese power overseas—especially in the sea lanes of the Far East. In 2012, Xi seized previously unoccupied territory to begin construction on artificial islands in the disputed Spratly Islands archipelago, as he seeks to extend China's economic and military reach. Satellite images showed weapons systems placed on Spratly, refuting earlier Chinese claims that construction on the islands was to be civilian in nature. A CSIS report noted "large antiaircraft guns and probable close-in weapons systems" on the islands.[36] China's state *Global Times* newspaper warned against attempts to prevent China from building on the islands, saying that interference would produce a "devastating confrontation."[37] And Xi defended the construction, saying that the islands in the South China Sea had been "China's territory since ancient times," as the *New York Times* reported. "The Chinese government must take responsibility to safeguard its territorial sovereignty and legitimate maritime interests."[38] Xi pledged not to accept any ruling from an international court or tribunal regarding jurisdiction in the South China Sea.[39]

While Beijing's moves in the South China Sea initially threatened only its Asian neighbors, in time Beijing's ambitions brought it into a clash with the United States, which is both looking to protect its own interests there and responding to appeals for help from its Pacific allies. In recent years, incidents and near-incidents between China and the United States have become more common. These include a June 2016 incident when a Chinese J-10 jet threatened a U.S. reconnaissance plane; a February 2017 encounter between a U.S. P-3C reconnaissance plane and a Chinese KJ-200 military aircraft over the South China Sea;[40] and a March 2017 report that a Chinese submarine commander had carried out an undetected mock attack against U.S. ships in the South China Sea—among other episodes.[41]

"This is militarization," said Greg Poling, director of the Asia Maritime Transparency Initiative, of Beijing's behavior. "The Chinese can argue that it's only for defensive purposes, but if you are building giant anti-aircraft gun and CIWS emplacements, it means that you are prepping for a future conflict."[42] China was seeking "hegemony in East Asia," said U.S. admiral Harry Harris.[43]

A Chinese military and naval buildup has been proceeding for years, but for many Americans, the Chinese have made their impact felt most in recent years in cyberspace. After a 2015 summit between Xi and President Obama, Chinese attacks lessened in number—but they deepened in their sophistication.[44] "China continues to have success in cyber espionage against the U.S. government, our allies, and U.S. companies," said Director of National Intelligence James Clapper. "Beijing also selectively uses cyberattacks against targets it believes threaten Chinese domestic stability or regime legitimacy."[45] In an age of cyber warfare, the United States and other Western democracies can count on authoritarian states like China and Russia remaining aggressive in the realm of hacking and cyber espionage.

While China's recent economic growth has slowed, its record over the last 30 or so years—in which it has doubled living standards about once per decade—is a daunting challenge to Western-style open markets and open societies.[46] "Many developing countries that have introduced Western values and political systems are experiencing disorder and chaos," says Wang Jisi of Beijing University—in contrast to the Chinese model, which has provided sustained growth and stability.[47]

But the broadest and most disturbing threat China poses is, as with Russia, its open challenge to the ideals of democracy itself and its explicit formulation of its own alternative to the Western model of open societies, free markets, and democratic governance. "It has been China's dream for a century to become the world's leading nation," says Colonel Liu Mingfu.[48] Indeed, what Xi in fact calls the China Dream includes China becoming an economic and military power, very much in counterpoint to the power of the Western democracies, especially the United States.

It is a conscious and deliberate challenge to the Western democratic model. Xi's vision differs from that of traditional liberal Western perceptions, notably because Xi prioritizes national identity and "insists on absolute state sovereignty," as Andrew Browne puts it.[49] Indeed, Xi targets Western ideas for eradication in Chinese social thought, including in schoolrooms. "Young teachers and students are key targets of infiltration by enemy forces" attempting to subvert the purity of Chinese education, said Chinese education minister Yuan Guiren.[50]

Under Xi, human rights lawyers, feminists, religious leaders, and activists have faced harassment and threats of imprisonment. "When he first came in he exhibited how much the Gorbachev phenomenon had spooked him," said Harvard's Roderick MacFarquhar, a scholar of Chinese politics. "He is very conscious of long-term threats—and maybe he doesn't see it as long-term. If he is only thinking in terms of 10 years, now is the time to solidify the country and he thinks he knows how to do it."[51] There is simply no room for democratic or pluralistic thought. "We have to unify the thinking and will of the whole Party first in order to unify the thinking and will of the people of all China's ethnic groups," Xi writes in *The Governance of China*.[52]

This prophecy of China's ascendance to military, economic, and cultural power has formed a cornerstone of Xi's political agenda—and to achieve it, he sees it as crucial that he enlist his Asian neighbors, many of them longtime allies of the United States. Xi encourages Asian nations to cooperate economically with China rather than remain in the U.S. orbit, and he has made substantial headway in changing their behavior. In what Bloomberg News calls "potentially the world's biggest free trade block," China and 15 other nations, including India, are working to formalize the Regional Comprehensive Economic Partnership (RCEP), which would strengthen economic integration among the countries—in part by lowering tariffs and other trade barriers—while making no demands, as Western economic deals do, that countries observe principles like labor rights or environmental standards.[53] At present, countries in the RCEP make up 24 percent of global GDP—so they will present a formidable bloc from day one.[54]

And then there's China's One Belt, One Road Initiative, an economic development plan centered on Eurasia that would build out a China-centered trading network with a goal of giving Beijing economic primacy in the region. The initiative is valued at $1 trillion and has the potential to reshape world trade.

"China wishes to integrate its development closer with that of its neighbors," Xi has said, "and China welcomes neighboring countries to take a fast and free ride with China's development so that it can better benefit the neighborhood and allow everyone to enjoy the good life."[55] He warns that Taiwan can either go in the "right direction" (moving closer to Beijing) or follow "outdated perceptions" (its alliance with the United States).

Xi's coercion and the United States' problems have played into this project. Chinese state media used Trump's election to condemn the failures of Western democracy. "Western style democracy used to be a recognized power in history to drive social development," an editorial said shortly after the presidential election. "But now it has reached its limits....Democracy is already kidnapped by the capitalists and has become the weapon for capitalists to chase profits."[56]

"America has lost," Filipino president Rodrigo Duterte said during a visit to China in January 2017. The Philippines, Duterte said, planned to "shift gears" and "realign myself" in China's "ideological flow."[57] He has since walked back from this talk, but he's far from the only one impressed by Xi's efforts: evidence suggests that the strong-leader image has taken hold among millions of Chinese and that Xi enjoys broad support at home for his aggressive efforts at building out China as a world superpower. Many Chinese call Xi "Xi Dada," or "Uncle Xi."[58]

"You get the feeling that President Xi cares about the little guy," says Yang Tianrong, a 75-year-old retired soldier from the Hebei Province of China. "He gives you hope that the government can solve your problems."[59]

"Our president has a stiff spine and will lead China to a brighter place," says Wang Feng, a middle-aged party functionary.[60] That remains to be seen, but the perception is widespread, as the results of a 2014 survey from the Harvard Kennedy School's Ash Center for Democratic Governance and Innovation revealed. The survey asked 26,000 respondents in 30 countries for their impressions of a host of international political leaders. In it, an amazing 94.8 percent of Chinese citizens expressed confidence in how Xi handled domestic affairs; 93.8 percent expressed confidence in how he handled international affairs.[61]

"He has the backing of the whole country," says songwriter Zhang Jingchuan.[62] Zhang wrote a song called "Everyone Praises Xi Dada," reflecting how average Chinese love their leader. "I feel that I can relate to the warmth and the great expectations that the public have for Xi—[the belief] that he will lead the country to a better future and towards national rejuvenation," he said. "That is why I wrote this song."[63]

Not surprisingly, Xi has developed a cult of personality that involves massive displays of Chinese power and his own singular authority. "There is this aristocratic flair which has now become more apparent, particularly after the military parade," said Willy Lam, referring to a grandiose military exhibition in Beijing in 2016. "The word demi-god would be an exaggeration but after the military parade he looked like an emperor."[64] Some of Xi's political allies have referred to him as "helmsman," and a newspaper called him a "great leader"—both terms associated in the past only with Mao.[65]

Xi's—and Putin's—gains are magnified by the spectacle of a decaying, declining West, a West that in substantial measure no longer seems to believe in its own democratic ideals—and, where it does, to lack the will that such conviction requires.

AUTHORITARIAN MOMENTUM

The remarkable irony to all of this is that people around the world continue to indicate a desire for democratic governance, or at least an openness to it. Their sentiments often stand in stark contrast to those of governing elites in the West, who have not been steadfast or enthusiastic in promoting democracy in recent years. Writing for the Center for Strategic and International Studies, Michael J. Green cites polls in Asia indicating that "people are far more likely to identify with democratic norms and rule of law than the so-called 'Beijing consensus' of authoritarian development. Yet authoritarianism is returning in Russia, China, Turkey, Hungary, Cambodia, Thailand, the Philippines, and scores of other countries."[66] Yet while Russia and China "compare notes" on how to suffocate civil society and suppress press freedom, Western elites aren't pushing back. Both Europe and the United States have reduced their spending on democratization initiatives abroad over the last decade; certainly democracy promotion was not a high priority of the Obama administration, which seemed to view it as intrusive at best, imperialistic at worst. Green also cites a 2014 CSIS survey in which American officials were more skeptical about democracy and human rights promotion in Asia than any other nation surveyed, but for one—China.[67]

As I have discussed elsewhere, U.S. democratic legitimacy is suffering not only because of our leaders' lack of conviction but also because of the system's own failures and crises—as reflected in the 2016 presidential race, with its ongoing investigations of Russian interference causing deep-seated concern about the legitimacy of our electoral system, once considered the gold standard for democracies. As president, Trump has exacerbated the public perceptions of a system coming undone with his volatile conduct. His pledges to prosecute Hillary Clinton and later insinuations about how she had committed criminal acts represent a depressing degeneration into a criminalization of political differences— another hallmark of non-democratic governments. Trump's addiction to personal attacks, his reckless use of Twitter, and his contempt for the free press are distressing signals of authoritarian behavior as well. Trump's constant dramas, with firings and instability in his inner circle, also suggest the dynamics of an authoritarian regime—a particularly chaotic one.

And yet, the Trump administration will represent an interesting test case for the comparative power of public perception versus private substantive achievement. In reality, of course, the Trump administration is not authoritarian. It governs within a democratic system; like all previous presidents, Trump is subject to the checks and balances of the American constitutional system, to say nothing of intra-party dynamics, as his struggles with attaining enough Republican support for various initiatives during his first year demonstrated. And in terms of substance, the Trump administration is showing more robust support for democracy as a foundational American foreign policy principle than candidate Trump ever suggested on the campaign trail, though he has not come as far in this regard as I would like to see (I'll have more to say about this in chapter 10). But from a symbolic and perhaps psychological standpoint, the Trump administration's quasi-authoritarian trappings represent a confusing picture of American democracy to the world. In an age when authoritarian leaders are working full-time to present their own undemocratic systems in the best possible light, the American president's indifference to the power of public example is distressing.

CHAPTER FIVE

THE ROGUE MENACE

"Tehran's nuclear menace, especially given the Pyongyang connection, is here now, not 10 years away."

—JOHN BOLTON[1]

"Now, with even relatively inaccurate intercontinental ballistic missile technology, [North Korea] can destroy the better part of a city with this yield."

—VIPIN NARANG, MIT NUCLEAR-PROLIFERATION EXPERT[2]

Even for the most virulent critic of President Trump, the scene at the Capella Hotel on Sentosa Island, Singapore, was a stunner: the president of the United States, the leader of the free world, walking beside the mysterious and megalomaniacal dictator of North Korea, the Hermit Kingdom, and holding talks. A U.S. president and a leader of North Korea had never met in person before, yet here was Trump, as controversial and contentious a figure as has ever occupied the White House, making a historic bid to become the man who brought peace between the Communist dictatorship and the United States, and in the process remove a dread nuclear threat from the Korean peninsula and from the world.

That was the image, anyway: in substance, it is not clear that the Trump-Kim summit will lead to anything like the breakthroughs that the president claimed afterward, and a good many sound analysts find Trump's concessions to Kim deeply troubling. But on one point it was generally agreed: no one would have predicted such a meeting even months earlier.

In fact, the early months of the Trump administration coincided with a ramping up of threats and rhetoric between Washington and

Pyongyang—and this in a climate that had hardly been tranquil beforehand. The threatening environment had been worsening for years, with a series of by-now somewhat predictable events: harsh words, harsh rejoinders, and, eventually, a provocative gesture. In the case of Kim Jong Un, that gesture usually involved a demonstration of his military's nuclear capabilities—or what he wanted the world to believe were its nuclear capabilities. Thus, a series of ballistic missile tests and firings, most failing by wide margins to show North Korea as being anywhere near operational capability.

In 2017, the tenor changed—not only in the frequency of the incidents and tests but in their results as well. Kim started firing missiles that showed greater plausibility. Analysts declared that he would likely be able to reach Alaska and Hawaii soon, and eventually, the mainland United States. The concerns deepened as the war of rhetoric between Kim and President Trump escalated.

Then, on September 3, 2017, North Korea detonated a powerful device underground that it claimed was a hydrogen bomb—words that, among those old enough to remember, conjured images of the fallout shelters and air raid drills of the 1950s. Worse, Kim claimed that the bomb could be put on an intercontinental ballistic missile (ICBM), and that the missile could reach the United States. The blast equaled the magnitude of a 6.3 earthquake, according to the U.S. Geological Survey, and was described as a "city buster" by an MIT nuclear expert, who said of the North Koreans, "Now, with even relatively inaccurate intercontinental ballistic missile technology, they can destroy the better part of a city with this yield."[3]

Though it was far from clear what the true capabilities of the device were—and observers were factoring in the North's usual exaggeration—it was clear that Pyongyang had crossed some kind of threshold in summer 2017 in detonating a nuclear device with seven times the destructive power of the bomb that leveled Hiroshima.[4]

North Korea's 2017 missile tests set off a tense showdown with the United States. As debates raged about how the Trump administration should respond and what its options were—none particularly palatable—observers were reminded of how conflict with North Korea had been postponed, deferred, and avoided over more than two decades, and that, sure enough, delaying a solution to the problem had only made it worse.

The same logic could apply to the problem of rogue regimes themselves, of which North Korea is only the most sensational example. The problem in dealing with rogues for the Western democracies is that taking serious action often poses serious risks with not always evident upsides; for Western societies and governments, muddling through has often seemed the easier bet. For rogues, by contrast, open conflict—short of outright war—often seems to represent opportunity. The result, all too often, is that we have allowed provocation and outright lawless behavior to persist and metastasize. For the West today, three countries that exemplify the dangers of "kicking the can down the road" are North Korea, Syria, and the Islamic Republic of Iran—the last of which, while often overshadowed by Pyongyang's instability, is the more consistent and far-reaching disturber of regional and global stability.

IRAN

"These uprisings have just begun," said one protestor. "People are not at all willing to give up." He spoke in January 2018 from the streets of Tehran, where, a month earlier, demonstrations and protests had broken out in the largest numbers since the 2009 Green Movement, in opposition to the rule of Iran's Supreme Leader Ayatollah Ali Khamenei—and has so far resulted in 21 deaths. The protests represent a reaction to a flagging economy, rising cost of living, and other hardships, and also suggest that the Iranian people are fed up with waiting for the promised economic benefits that were to come their way after the regime finalized its controversial nuclear deal with the Obama administration in 2015. So far, the only benefits seem to be accruing to the mullahs.

In a marked contrast from his predecessor, President Trump has cheered on the protestors while also attacking the regime. Trump said that the Iran deal had "served as a slush fund for weapons, terror and oppression, and to further line the pockets of corrupt regime leaders. The Iranian people know this, which is one reason why so many have taken to the streets to express their outrage."[5]

Vice President Mike Pence echoed those sentiments. "Iran is the leading state sponsor of terrorism in the world," he told Voice of America. "To see the people of Iran rising up, to demand change in their country, should hearten every freedom loving American and people who cherish freedom around the world."[6]

ISIS may have gotten more headlines in recent years, but Pence's words are a reminder of a fact all too often overlooked: Iran remains the world's leading state sponsor of terrorism, according to a State Department report that covered terror attacks through 2016.[7] Iran remains the linchpin for destabilizing the Middle East through its proxies, especially Hezbollah, which has played a role in inflaming conflicts in Iraq and Syria and also, at least as the United States and Saudi Arabia see it, in Yemen, where a bloody civil war has been raging since 2015 between the Saudi- and American-backed government of Abdrabbuh Mansour Hadi and the Houthi rebels, who are Shia. Hezbollah denies supporting the rebels, at least with weapons, and Tehran denies smuggling weapons to them. But a U.N. panel in January 2018 accused Iran of doing just that.[8] The Yemeni civil war has so far caused the deaths of more than 5,000 people (more than 20 percent of them children), caused the world's largest cholera outbreak, displaced millions, and caused what the U.N. calls a "catastrophic" humanitarian crisis.[9]

Iran's support for terrorism has accelerated since it signed the nuclear deal with the Obama administration in July 2015. There is a good case to be made that the nuclear deal has encouraged Iran to get bolder with its destabilizing activities and to support terrorist efforts with more generous financing.[10] Iran bankrolls Hezbollah to the tune of more than $700 million a year.[11] Hezbollah's secretary general, Hassan Nasrallah, bluntly declared that "Hezbollah gets its money and arms from Iran, and as long as Iran has money, so does Hezbollah."[12] "In 2016, Iran remained the primary source of funding for Hezbollah and coordinated closely with Hezbollah in its efforts to create instability in the Middle East," said State Department official Justin Siberell, then serving as Acting Coordinator for Counterterrorism. He pointed out that Hezbollah had "gone full-in on supporting the Assad regime and its war against the Syrian people...and [also] carried out several attacks against Israeli Defense Forces in 2016 along the Lebanese border."[13] Iran's rearming of Hezbollah is in direct violation of U.N. Security Resolution 1701, passed after the end of the 2006 Israeli-Hezbollah war. Iran has even trained Hezbollah fighters at camps in Iran.

Tehran also pumps about $50 million annually into the budget of Hamas and directs about $70 million to Palestinian Islamic Jihad and other groups.[14] These groups have been behind terror attacks in Gaza and the West Bank. Iran remains a devoted ally of Palestinian terrorist groups and a sworn enemy of Israel.

Before ISIS, Iran was long the primary destabilizer of Iraq, and it is still very active there, fomenting terror most recently through its support for Kata'ib Hizbollah, a Shia terrorist organization that has committed human rights abuses against Sunni civilians. Tehran sees the group as a key partner in its battle against ISIS and in supporting the Assad regime in Syria. Iran has fought furiously against ISIS in Iraq, often deploying Shia terrorist groups in efforts that many see as exacerbating sectarian tensions.

Even today, many global analysts don't seem to grasp the importance Iran places on Syria—that is, on a Syria that continues to be ruled by Assad. One analyst who does understand it keenly is Afshon Ostovar, who, in an important essay in *Foreign Policy*, wrote,

> Of the outside backers of the Bashar al-Assad regime, Iran—which has sent hundreds of its troops to Syria and facilitated the involvement of several thousand non-Syrian Shiite militants to prop up Assad—has the most influence in Syria.... Iran and Syria grew even closer during the 1990s over their shared antagonism to Israel. Syria became the conduit for support to Lebanese Hezbollah, which ever since has been used as proxy by Iran to threaten and pressure Israel and to serve as a pillar of Iran's deterrence strategy toward Washington. Losing access to Syrian territory, in other words, would undermine Iranian deterrence and make it more vulnerable to Israeli and U.S. coercion. As one former official with the Islamic Revolutionary Guard Corps (IRGC) put it, Syria is so strategically important that Iran considers it to be its "35th province."[15]

"The Iranian generals run the civil war for the Syrian regime," says retired general Jack Keane. "They direct the ground campaign, and they direct the use of Syrian air power and selected use of Russian air power in support of the ground campaign. They make up the largest forces on the ground. Their generals lead it on the ground."[16] Much of this activity is directed through the IRGC's Qods Force, which has played a direct role in the conflicts in Iraq and Syria.[17]

Iran has been a devoted backer of the Assad regime in Syria, and in this effort it has often teamed up with Russia, with whom it is developing a closer partnership. The two nations would continue to work together in Syria, Iran president Hassan Rouhani said in 2016, "until the ultimate goal of eradicating terrorism and restoring peace and full security to the region is achieved."[18] For both countries, "peace" means victory and perpetual rule for Assad.

In Bahrain, Iran has bankrolled and trained Shia militants in their attacks against security forces.[19] Finally, Iran has even made common cause with the Taliban in Afghanistan and with Sunni al-Qaeda—refusing to bring senior members of the terrorist group detained in the country to justice. Remarkably, Iran has allowed al-Qaeda operate a financial and human trafficking network throughout the country since at least 2009.[20]

Unlike North Korea, Iran is a sophisticated player on the world stage, and recent years have seen it deepening its alliance with powerful new allies—none of them friends to the United States or to the West. The Iranian-Chinese relationship has grown and deepened in recent years. Iran sells Beijing arms and is also an important oil supplier. Its burgeoning trade with Beijing helped Tehran blunt the effect of the long-standing economic sanctions placed on it by the United States and its allies. China plans to increase its trade with Iran by $600 billion over the next decade.[21]

I've noted the deepening Iran-Russia ties above, the key rationale for which remains the Syrian conflict. Iran has even allowed Russian air force planes to fly from Iranian air bases to conduct bombing operations in Syria. Both countries have had a long and difficult history with one another, but both share deep suspicion of U.S. motives in the region and a determination to blunt its influence.

Perhaps Iran's most disturbing relationship is with North Korea. The two have had complementary ties for some years, Iran supplying oil, the North Koreans providing nuclear and missile technology. A 2016 South Korean report suggested that representatives from a blacklisted North Korean company were visiting Iran, presumably to share ideas on illegal weaponry.[22] The South Korean press had reported some years earlier that hundreds of North Korean scientists were working in Iranian nuclear facilities, sharing their knowledge of technologies. It was also reported that Iranian scientists were present at a North Korean nuclear test in 2013. In the years since, delegations have gone and back forth between the two countries, clearly suggestive of some collaborative or at least cooperative relationship in the nuclear area.[23]

And it is the nuclear area that hovers over everything else concerning Iran, since it was the Obama administration's horribly ill-advised decision to enter into a nuclear agreement in 2015 that lifted sanctions against Iran and put the country in the driver's seat to become the world's next major nuclear power. Iran was actively working toward building a nuclear weapon when it signed the Joint Comprehensive Plan of Action (JCPOA) with the United States in July 2015.[24] The deal was designed to delay Iran acquiring a nuclear weapon for the next 10 to 15 years, but implicit in that time frame was an acceptance that Tehran would eventually go nuclear. What minimal gains the United States stood to derive from the deal were purely temporary, while for Tehran, the deal was a boon.

Thankfully, Trump withdrew from the agreement in May 2018, saying, "We cannot prevent an Iranian bomb under the decaying and rotten structure of the current agreement.... Therefore, I am announcing today that the United States will withdraw from the Iran nuclear deal." He announced that he would re-impose sanctions on Iran's oil sector that had been lifted as part of the deal. The deal is not technically dead, since Britain, France, Russia, China, and Germany—the other signatories—have so far not reinstated sanctions, and Iran has hinted that it would stay in the deal if these countries did not pull out. Shortly after Trump's announcement, Secretary of State Mike Pompeo released the administration's aggressive new Iran policy, which looked to apply unprecedented financial pressure on the regime, deter Iranian aggression on all fronts, and push the regime on human rights. By deterring Iranian aggression, Pompeo meant the whole panoply of Tehran's efforts: terrorism, nuclear pursuits, and support for proxy groups, the combination of which makes Iran a formidable adversary. The Heritage Foundation rated Iran a greater menace than ISIS in a 2016 report: "Iran poses a major potential threat to U.S. bases, interests, and allies in the Middle East by virtue of its ballistic missile capabilities, nuclear ambitions, long-standing support for terrorism, and extensive support for Islamist revolutionary groups.... Iran represents by far the most significant security challenge to the United States, its allies, and its interests in the greater Middle East."[25] After the Obama administration signed the nuclear deal, Secretary of State John Kerry even admitted, remarkably, that some of the money made available to Iran by the removal of sanctions would end up in the hands of terrorist groups.[26]

It's remarkable that the Obama administration ever signed the deal in the first place. Some saw it as cynical on Obama's part, an effort merely to stall Iran's eventual attainment of nuclear status until after he left the White House. "Iran got virtually everything that it asked for in return for ostensibly slowing down or deferring portions of its nuclear weapons program for the next decade," wrote Joseph V. Micallef in the *Huffington Post*. "Since it is unlikely that Iran was anywhere close to actually creating useable nuclear weapons, Iran gave up a capability it did not yet have in return for the immediate benefit of sanctions relief."[27] And for this relief, it made no commitments of its own to stop funding, training, and supporting terror groups and proxy actors around the Middle East.

Obama reportedly thought that the Iran deal might open up an avenue between the United States and Iran, but it did no such thing. Iran and Russia only grew closer. Before the Trump administration withdrew from the deal, President Rouhani gleefully threatened to restart his nuclear program within hours if Washington resumed its "threats and sanctions." So much for the Obama administration's new beginning. Listen to Iran's president: "In an hour and a day," Rouhani boasted, "Iran could return to a more advanced [nuclear] level than at the beginning of the negotiations" in 2015.[28] The deal was calamitous.

And finally, there is the matter of recognizing that Iran continues to forge its society on determinedly antidemocratic, even totalitarian lines. While President Rouhani is slightly more moderate than his predecessor, Human Rights Watch states that there have been no significant human rights improvements in Iran since his election. The military, the intelligence services, and the judiciary hold huge power in Iran, and punishment for crimes is harsh. More than 700 state-sponsored executions took place in the first six months of 2015 alone. Restrictions and punishments in the Islamic Republic of Iran that violate international human rights norms include harsh penalties for crimes like homosexuality or insulting the prophet, execution of offenders under 18 years of age, restrictions on freedom of speech and the press (including the imprisonment of journalists), restrictions on freedom of religion, and gender discrimination. Authorities also torture prisoners and dole out punishments like cutting off an arm for stealing. They have cracked down on press and social media use in recent years, even doling out death sentences to bloggers.[29]

It's a bleak picture—no small reason why the Iranian people have, again, taken to the streets, showing enormous bravery and determination. Americans who doubt the appeal of democracy and a better life for citizens outside the West should look closely at the faces at the Tehran protests. They are a reminder of our common humanity.

NORTH KOREA

Under the rule of Kim Jong Un, North Korea remains among the world's most repressive countries. The Kim family's political dynasty has severely restricted all basic freedoms, and it rules with an iron fist. A 2014 U.N. Commission of Inquiry found that abuses in North Korea were without parallel in the contemporary world. They include extermination, murder, enslavement, torture, imprisonment, rape, forced abortions, and other sexual violence. North Korea operates secretive prison camps where perceived opponents of the government are sent to face torture and abuse, starvation rations, and forced labor. Fear of collective punishment is used to silence dissent. There is no independent media, functioning civil society, or religious freedom.[30]

The current crisis has a long background. Over the past few decades, the United States and the international community have tried to negotiate an end to North Korea's nuclear and ballistic missile programs. Those efforts have been replete with periods of crisis, stalemate, and tentative progress toward denuclearization, and North Korea has long been a key challenge for the global nuclear nonproliferation regime.

President George W. Bush labeled North Korea part of the "Axis of Evil," along with Iran and other rogue nations with sophisticated weapons technology that threatens the international community. But he was unable to get North Korea to commit to and then abide by a denuclearization agreement. For eight years, President Obama did little to minimize the dangers that Pyongyang poses to its Asian neighbors or to disentangle the regime from Beijing's embrace. His administration's strategy of "strategic patience" resulted in a North Korea with more sophisticated weapons technology and an escalation in the frequency and size of its nuclear tests.

Since North Korea's 1994 announcement of its desire to withdraw from the Nuclear Non-Proliferation Treaty, the United States has engaged in a series of diplomatic efforts to get North Korea to abandon its nuclear weapons in exchange for aid. But each of these talks has ultimately failed to get North Korea to abide by its commitments. The second of these diplomatic efforts was the Six-Party Talks initiated in August 2003, which involved China, Japan, North Korea, Russia, South Korea, and the United States. The goal of the talks was to reach an agreement for denuclearizing the entire Korean peninsula. In between periods of stalemate and crisis, those talks arrived at critical breakthroughs in 2005, when North Korea pledged to abandon "all nuclear weapons and existing nuclear programs" and return to the Non-Proliferation Treaty, and in 2007, when the parties agreed on a series of steps to implement that 2005 agreement. Those talks, however, broke down in 2009 following disagreements over verification and an internationally condemned North Korean rocket launch.[31] North Korea said that it would never return to the talks and that it was not bound by past agreements. Between 2009 and 2018, there were no real discussions, and North Korea ramped up its missile and nuclear testing.

As the Obama era waned, North Korea escalated its weapons testing and provocations toward South Korea and the United States, conducting 17 missile tests and two nuclear weapons tests in 2016 alone.[32] Trump's first year in the White House was marked by escalating tensions with Pyongyang, as I suggested earlier. The summer of 2017 was a period of mounting fears about a potential conflict, or even nuclear exchange, between Washington and Pyongyang. The July 2017 ballistic missile test prompted Trump's infamous warning to Kim Jong Un that the North would face "fire and fury" if it continued to make threats.

To have gone from this frightening climate to the historic photo ops of a smiling Trump and Kim in June 2018 was more than a little surreal. Yet what the summit actually achieved very much remains in question. By any objective analysis, Kim would appear to have gotten more out of the summit than Trump did. The United States extracted only vague promises of cooperation from the North Koreans on the nuclear question. Sue Mi Terry, Senior Fellow for Korea at the Center for Strategic and International Studies, said that "working towards denuclearization," the wording in the agreement that Trump and Kim signed, was a weaker formulation than previous North Korea regimes had given.[33] Indeed, contrary to Trump's typical boastfulness—"I signed an agreement where we get everything, everything," he said[34]—the United States had made what appeared to be substantial concessions to Pyongyang, which had not given up anything of import. Most troublingly, the United States agreed to suspend military exercises with South Korea while the denuclearization details were being worked out. Agreeing to this seems to be frankly gullible on the president's part. Pyongyang has run previous administrations around on the denuclearization issue, but those earlier administrations didn't give the North such a concession as this. Perhaps, as Trump and his defenders claim, the summit was the first step in remaking the United States–North Korean relationship and bringing peace to a troubled region. For now, however, the United States has made the concessions, while North Korea has reaped the benefits.

The nuclear question, of course, hovers over everything. At present, the exact capability and status of the North's arsenal remains subject to debate. The best analysts struggle to pin it down, since Kim and the regime excel at obfuscation. What seems generally agreed upon is this: North Korea is believed to have about 1,000 missiles of various ranges; these include medium-range missiles thought capable of carrying nuclear warheads to South Korea or Japan. U.S. intelligence believes that the regime has anywhere from 25 to 60 nuclear weapons. The big question, from an American perspective, is whether it has achieved the technological capability to deliver those weapons to the mainland United States. That requires a warhead capable of surviving reentry into the atmosphere, and most experts at the moment doubt that the North has developed one.

Pyongyang is probably "a few more ICBM tests launched in a standard trajectory away from being able to reach the U.S. mainland," says nukes expert Siegfried Hecker of Stanford University. "My estimate is that will require both a few more ICBM tests and another nuclear test—likely another couple of years away."[35] It's this still-nascent capability—though it is ramping up fast—that leads some experts, like Edward

Luttwak, to argue that the time to bomb North Korea is now, to wipe out its nuclear facilities before its long-range missiles become operational.[36]

Perhaps the most disturbing aspect of the entire North Korean nuclear situation is the revelations that have come out regarding the North's close ties to Russia—and the almost certain implication that Pyongyang's sudden and rapid advance in technological capability likely owes to direct assistance and instruction from Moscow.

In late July 2017, North Korea test-fired an ICBM that experts concluded could have the range to hit major U.S. cities—and certainly Alaska. Even more disturbingly, the tests seemed to represent a quantum leap forward for North Korea's missile development efforts; most previous tests, while concerning, were usually marked by failure, sometimes abject failure, suggesting that the North was a long way from missile viability. Now, apparently overnight, Pyongyang had attained a serious missile capability. How?

In early August 2017, an answer emerged, in the opening paragraph of a bombshell *New York Times* report: "North Korea's success in testing an intercontinental ballistic missile that appears able to reach the United States was made possible by black-market purchases of powerful rocket engines probably from a Ukrainian factory with historical ties to Russia's missile program, according to an expert analysis being published Monday and classified assessments by American intelligence agencies." The report went on to detail how U.S. analysts had studied photos of Kim inspecting the new missiles' rocket motors and concluded that the motors derived from old Soviet designs. They are thought to be powerful enough that "a single missile could hurl 10 thermonuclear warheads between continents." The focal point of the activity is thought to be a missile factory in Dnipro, Ukraine, which, in Cold War days, made the deadliest missiles in the Soviet arsenal.[37]

The North Korea/Russia/Ukraine missile story was the strongest sign yet of a phenomenon that remains largely unknown to the general public: the tightening embrace between Russia and North Korea. Most observers continue to associate the Hermit Kingdom with its traditional benefactor, China, but Putin's Russia is moving closer and closer to a meaningful alliance with Pyongyang. Multiple reports in April 2017 indicated that Russia was massing its troops along its border with the Hermit Kingdom in the aftermath of a tense stare-down between the

United States, Pyongyang, and Beijing over North Korea's recent missile test. Putin took no action against Kim when North Korea fired a ballistic missile in February 2017. He has defended the North Korean nuclear program as one of self-defense. And now, with the Ukraine story, we have more insight into why he would take such a position.

Russia has become North Korea's leading fuel supplier; Moscow and Pyongyang are finalizing a labor and immigration agreement. North Korea's state-controlled news agency lists Russia as a top ally of the Democratic People's Republic of Korea. Putin sent "a friendly greeting to your country and your people on the occasion of the 71st anniversary of Korean liberation."[38]

The Trump administration has frequently expressed frustration with China over its failure to rein in the North Koreans, but this betrays ignorance, or naivete, on the president's part about what role China plays in the North Korea imbroglio. China remains Pyongyang's number one ally and protector, though it is often an exasperated benefactor. The relationship has long been close but fraught.

China is the North's biggest trading partner and main source of food, arms, and energy. It has helped sustain Kim Jong Un's regime and has historically opposed harsh international sanctions on North Korea. China views North Korea as an important buffer between itself and U.S. ally and mutual-defense signatory South Korea. For all of its protestations against the North's most reckless behavior, the fact remains that China does not want regime change in Pyongyang; it would prefer that North Korea succeed in its current incarnation, though it would also like to see less provocative behavior. Its attitude toward North Korean nukes is hard to parse, again because, while dangerous, the situation also brings benefits, in keeping the United States and South Korea on the defensive.[39]

On the other hand, Pyongyang's testing of nuclear weapons has caused strains in the relationship—especially because the more the North saber-rattles, the more likely it is to arouse a stronger American presence in the region, in response to America's Asian allies' requests for protection. This thwarts China's goal of becoming the Asian hegemon, a vision that depends on a lessened American presence—something that the Trump administration had sounded, on occasion, like it was willing to acquiesce to. More recently, and especially with the release of its

National Security Strategy (discussed in chapter 10), the administration sounds more hawkish and committed to American leadership in Asia. With Kim firing ballistic missile tests over the Sea of Japan, American commitment is not really optional.

China–North Korea relations have been bumpy under Kim Jong Un. The young leader has purged his government of many of its top officials, consolidating his power and executing anyone he deems a threat. First, he executed his uncle, a high-ranking official in his father's government who had strong connections with China, the economic lifeline of North Korea.[40] This irrational move gave Chinese leaders pause. In May 2015, Kim Jong Un executed the country's defense minister, Hyon Yong Chol, after the regime accused him of treason. Hyon Yong Chol was killed by fire from an anti-aircraft gun at a military school in front of hundreds of people in Pyongyang.[41]

With a dangerous, nuclear-armed regime as an adversary, the United States has generally relied on sanctions to try to rein in the North. Harsh sanctions were imposed after the cyber attack on Sony Pictures Entertainment, and even more were added after the recent nuclear tests. These constitute the most restrictive sanctions on North Korea to date.[42] The North shows every sign of being able to soldier on through these difficulties—especially because it takes no concern for the suffering and dying of its citizens.

For example, in March 2016, North Korea's state-run newspaper— a mouthpiece for the government—instructed the country to brace itself for possible famine and severe economic hardship after the U.N. imposed another round of tough sanctions on the nation for a nuclear test a few months earlier. But the paper told its citizens not to despair about this, because "the road to revolution is long and arduous."[43] Famine is nothing new for this country. In the 1990s, a famine in North Korea is reported to have killed as many as three million people. Though tough sanctions and international isolation are a main reason for the hardships of the North Koreans, the leadership still pursues its nuclear agenda. And Kim himself lives a life of luxury.

SYRIA

Since 2011, Syria has been the epicenter of a reordered Middle East and, to some extent, of the international order. It was in Syria that a civil war—which continues, and which remains a humanitarian disaster—caused the deaths of hundreds of thousands of people and prompted the largest refugee crisis the world has ever seen. It was in Syria (and in Iraq) that the Islamic State set up its caliphate and began exporting its terrorist ideology around the world. And it was in Syria that the United States demonstrated for the world what its "leading from behind" strategy would look like in practice—hesitating to get involved in the conflict, drawing a "red line" on chemical weapons and then backtracking, declaring support for the "moderate," anti-Assad rebels and then not fully committing to their cause, conducting air strikes but not nearly enough to destroy ISIS. Amid American paralysis, Russia reasserted itself as a superpower in the Middle East, and Putin's uncompromising backing of Syria's Bashar al-Assad ensured the survival of one of the world's most brutal dictators and sponsors of state terror. Assad is backed not only by Russia but also by Iran and Shiite terrorist groups like Hezbollah. Syria, on the State Sponsor of Terrorism list since 1979, has become ground zero for training terrorists and exporting the Islamist extremist ideologies that are menacing the world.

All too often, we in the West become inured to disaster in far-off regions, but it's worth remembering how grisly the costs of the Syrian civil war have been in human terms. Estimates of the death toll range from 330,000 to 475,000, with about 100,000 deaths being civilian, including children.[44] Likewise, the refugee crisis is something beyond modern imagining. As of March 2017, it was estimated that 5 million Syrians had fled the country and 6.3 million people were displaced from their homes within the country.[45] This is the largest refugee crisis on record; more people have now been displaced than were after World War II.[46]

The Syrian refugee crisis, of course, has created the migrant crisis in Europe, with more than 1 million refugees crossing into Europe in 2015 alone, many of these from Syria but also from Iraq, Afghanistan, and North Africa.[47] The migrant crisis and the corresponding rise in terrorism in Europe have also helped fuel a wave of anti-immigrant populism on the European continent (as well as in the United States).

It would be foolish to suggest that American leadership, if exerted more effectively, could have entirely prevented a catastrophe on the scale of Syria. But there is no question that American failure (and with it, the failure of the Western alliance) to come to terms with the Syrian crisis in humanitarian and geopolitical terms has led to a monumental disaster. It adds up to more than a half decade of brutality, diplomatic futility, and strategic incoherence, with costs that continue to mount and that, over the long term, are incalculable.

In my view, the Syrian crisis is the Obama administration's greatest failure of leadership, with ramifications that will be felt for years. The template of the American leadership style in Syria was established in August 2013, when President Obama retreated from his self-proclaimed "red line" to take action against Assad if the Syrian dictator ever used chemical weapons on his own people. That month, Assad fired rockets filled with the nerve agent sarin at several suburbs of Damascus. Videos of civilians suffering from the gas caused outrage. The Geneva Convention and the Chemical Weapons Convention outlaw the use of these weapons.

For a brief period afterward, it looked as if the United States was getting ready for military action against Syria. But when Obama backed off from his threat, Russia, the United States, and Assad came to an agreement for Assad to ship out all of his chemical weapons for destruction.[48] Beyond these conditions, Assad would pay no price for his blatant violations of international law and brutality against his own people. A few years later, when Assad used chlorine gas on his own people, Obama did nothing.

If the administration had committed early on to supporting the anti-Assad Free Syrian Army and provided them with heavy weapons and even manpower, the situation would likely look very different. But Obama was willing to give only humanitarian aid and some military gear. "The philosophical discussion at the White House was heated and fierce, leading to stalemate, not resolution," writes Tara McKelvey of the BBC. "For years Obama and his deputies refused to say categorically: we're not doing this. Instead a decision was postponed." Postponing, delaying, believing in "patience"—the Obama administration is a powerful case study of how passivity can be as provocative as power.

The Free Syrian Army showed early promise with some victories, but with only token American assistance, the group began to fall back—especially after the 2014 emergence of ISIS, which grew out of the chaos in Syria and the power vacuum left when the United States withdrew from Iraq. Taking advantage of America's marginalization of Saddam Hussein's ruthless Baathist soldiers and bureaucracy and stoking tensions with Shiites, the Sunni Islamic terrorist group expanded rapidly and began recruiting soldiers from throughout the Middle East, Europe, and even the United States, financing their operations through black-market oil sales and ransom payments. The Obama administration greatly underestimated the power of ISIS, with Obama notoriously referring to them as a "jayvee team."[49] A year and a half after the United States and its allies began confronting the threat of ISIS, Obama admitted to reporters that "we don't have, yet, a complete strategy" to confront the threat posed by the Islamic State.[50] By then, far too much ground had been lost, not only against ISIS but also in Syria generally. ISIS proved to be more or less a death knell for plausible Syrian opposition groups, which could not compete with the group's financing, let alone its brutality.

American timidity in Syria was a major boost not only to Assad but also to Vladimir Putin, who positioned himself as a Syrian power broker. Since then, of course, Russia has been the primary support for Assad and has more or less achieved its goals in Syria. That's quite a story.

Russian military intervention in the Syrian civil war started in September 2015, after Assad cabled Putin asking for his help combating rebel forces and ISIS. Though Russia initially claimed to be fighting "the terrorists," its initial bombing campaigns targeted the more moderate rebel factions almost exclusively.[51] Russia has been a critical force in propping up the Assad regime, and Moscow's entry into the fighting has essentially ensured that Assad will defeat the rebel forces and remain in power. And as a result, Russia has established itself as a superpower in the Middle East, in more or less direct proportion to the diminution of American influence. American inaction left a void; Russia has swooped in to fill it.

The Russian-Syrian alliance has come at great human cost to the Syrian people. In October 2016, Human Rights Watch accused the two nations of committing war crimes during a month-long aerial bombing campaign of opposition-controlled territory in Aleppo. The bombing campaign killed at least 440 civilians, including more than 90 children. Russia has also been accused of deliberately bombing hospitals, and the human rights group also alleges that Russia has used "indiscriminate weapons"—that is, weapons that can't be directed at specific military targets—such as cluster munitions and incendiary devices.[52]

America's failed Iranian policy is also relevant here, since Iran and Syria are historical allies, and Iran, along with Russia, has done the most to help Assad. Tehran has a vested interest in keeping Assad in power as a counterweight to Saudi Arabia and other Sunni-controlled countries, part of a Sunni-Shia civil war within Islam that is threatening the stability of the Middle East. Iranian security and intelligence services are advising and assisting the Syrian military. Iran has deployed its Revolutionary Guard troops in Syria, where it also funds Hezbollah, which is also helping Assad, a longtime backer of the terrorist group.[53]

THE FUTURE

In my view, while these three rogue states all present formidable challenges, the threats they present to international stability tend to run in inverse proportion to the public attention they generate. That is to say, as I see it, the Iran situation is the one that is most potentially serious. It is overshadowed by Syria's grim civil war body count and by North Korea's doomsday posturing. But it is Tehran that holds the most cards and that presents the most formidable overall threat. Iran presents the most plausible threat to the interests of the Western democracies; Iran is the nation among the three that is richest, most stable, and best positioned to thrive; and it is the one among the three with the farthest-reaching tentacles and potential to influence other conflicts. Tehran is the key power player in Syria, for example, and it has ties to North Korean nuclear and ballistic missile development.

This is not to minimize the frankly terrifying threat that North Korea continues to pose. North Korea is dangerous, without question; but it is also a weak and desperate society. Iran, by contrast, is the linchpin of the Middle East and an aspiring world power.

The Middle East is a cauldron that could ignite at any time, with Iran at the center of nearly everything going on there. The Yemeni civil war has been under-covered in the American press, but it is a nightmare approaching Syrian proportions, with butchery and wholesale slaughter on an increasing scale, to say nothing of a cholera epidemic, famine, and water crisis. And Iran, through its support for the Houthis—in tandem with its terrorist client, Hezbollah—is stoking the flames. The prospect of an Iranian–Saudi Arabian war remains real. And Tehran has busily bolstered its allies in the region, from the Houthis to Hezbollah, from Assad in Syria to Shia militias in Iraq.

But the mullahs have two new problems. The first is a reawakened democracy movement in Iran spurred by an unhappy populace that sees none of the economic windfall it was promised from the nuclear deal. "Leave Syria, think of us!" protestors have chanted.[54]

The second is the Trump administration, which seems determined to pursue a substantially different course than its regime-friendly predecessor. I'm heartened by the administration's withdrawal from the nuclear deal. The administration has also reapplied sanctions aimed at squeezing the Iranian economy, and those sanctions are showing signs of impact already, with some European businesses pulling out of Tehran and the country's oil exports being curtailed.

Trump has shown his willingness to risk international condemnation to stand up for democratic principles—as he did in his dramatic recognition of Jerusalem as Israel's capital. He will need this same brazenness to prevail in the struggle with Iran. Trump showed keen timing in his withdrawal from the nuclear deal, with the Iranian democratic movement reborn and with the mullahs' expansionist designs badly in need of containment.

I'm also encouraged by Trump's words in favor of the Iranian democratic advocates. It's true that it has been only words, so far, but that's more than the Obama administration offered in 2009, when, to its shame, it did not utter a word in favor of the brave people struggling (and some dying) in Tehran and elsewhere in favor of democracy. Trump has rightly noted that the Iranian people are separate from the regime and declared that America stands with the Iranian people in their aspirations.

This is precisely the right message—but we shouldn't stop with messages. The United States should offer technological assistance to democratic advocates to help them break through Internet firewalls, for instance. But the best thing we can do for the people of Iran, in my view, is to stand up to the regime's provocative behavior across the region, raising the costs of its incursions and giving it reason to think twice before making them—or even to retreat. For too long now, whether via its terrorist proxies or its Shia allies elsewhere, Iran has had little reason to fear American reprisals. This simply *must* change, and with allies in Riyadh and in Jerusalem, as well as others in the Middle East (who might prefer to remain unidentified), there is no reason why we cannot do so.

My sense is that the Trump administration's Iran policy, in addition to being crucial in itself, will also provide a key to understanding how it will approach other dangerous adversaries. Certainly the situation in Syria will hinge closely on what approach we take to Iran. So far, Trump's Syria policy is a failure, since it doesn't break from the Obama policy in any substantive way. American efforts over the last several years have been almost solely focused on defeating ISIS there, and while that's an understandable effort, it has come at the expense of putting any check on Iran and Russia's adventurism. Let the Americans destroy ISIS, they have calculated; we can spend our time destroying the Syrian opposition and defending Assad. And they have done so, with marked success. Ceasefire agreements and "de-escalation zones" have been mostly a farce because the Russians and Iranians have used them to attack their adversaries in the interests of the regime. The entire diplomatic process in Syria will remain a farce until Russia and Iran learn that they cannot continue making such incursions—because, in other words, the United States will stop them, which it can do through airpower, if it is willing to use it. Otherwise, Moscow and Tehran will continue pushing on toward their main goal, which is to become the power brokers of the Syrian future, an end to which they have made substantial progress. The United States can still prevent such an outcome, but the clock is ticking.

Finally, there is the matter of Pyongyang. Much of the debate about what to do centers around a dispute that is integral to understanding the entire situation—Pyongyang's motives. One school of thought holds that Kim and his predecessors pursue nukes solely out of determination to ward off an American attack, even an invasion on the peninsula. Another view, held by Trump's former national security adviser H.R. McMaster, among others, is that the North's real goal is reunification of the peninsula—conquest of the South, in other words, under the Communist banner—a goal for which nukes are integral, since they will (in this thinking) perhaps deter American intervention. Those holding this view, as McMaster does, are more inclined to hawkish approaches—not necessarily a preemptive strike, let alone an invasion, but far more robust, even provocative, deterrent measures, including, as James Jeffrey writes in *The Atlantic*, "redeployment of battlefield nukes in or near Korea, and encouraging the development of Japanese and South Korean long-range conventional strike capabilities or, in extremis, their own nuclear capabilities."[55] The goal, Jeffrey says, "would be to affect both North Korean and Chinese calculations and introduce automaticity—an almost unstoppable escalation toward a nuclear exchange once any conflict begins—and thus credibility to deterrence."[56]

It seems to me that "credibility to deterrence" is the right approach to take here. We should operate as if the McMaster thesis is true while stopping short, at least for now, of the most dramatic implications of that view (the necessity of a preemptive attack). It is certainly clear that the United States has not put in place the kinds of tough measures that Jeffrey describes; we need to understand whether they might suffice. The approach would involve—somewhat ironically—a tacit acceptance of North Korea's nukes, at least in their current indeterminate capacity, with a focus not on what might be a futile goal of disarmament but on a comprehensive deterrence that prevents catastrophe: a framework that enables clear and specific responses to North Korean provocations. And we need to reassure our Asian allies that we remain committed to their defense. (Trump's spats with South Korea have been distracting and damaging in this regard.)

There is another way to strengthen the American hand here. I agree with Michael Auslin that the "best way to dampen Kim's nuclear threat is to remove his ability to strike American territory or interests"[57]—and that means a serious, comprehensive missile-defense system. It is simple common sense that Kim's calculations could change if he recognizes that he cannot penetrate American defenses. Naturally, the creation of such a shield is a long-range undertaking, but as we have no way of knowing how much longer the Communist dictatorship in Pyongyang will endure, we need plans that take a long view every bit as much as we need immediate strategies.

CHAPTER SIX

THE ISLAMIST CHALLENGE

"There will be more hashtags, more vigils, and more people sitting around singing John Lennon songs. The story will fade until the next Islamist slaughter, where yet more innocent people will die and the cycle will begin again."

—ROBIN SIMCOX, *THE DAILY SIGNAL*[1]

"We all need to recognize the reality that we are not winning this war."

—PETE HOEKSTRA, INVESTIGATIVE PROJECT ON TERRORISM[2]

The caliphate, it turned out, lasted only a few years. In October 2017, U.S.-backed forces in Syria completed a task barely thought possible only a few years earlier: the retaking of Raqqa, the northern Syrian city regarded as the "capital" of the Islamic State, or ISIS. The streets of Raqqa, once the scene of beheadings and other brutalities in which the Islamist fanatics specialized, were now filled with cheering and joy. The only gunfire now was celebratory. Coming on the heels of the retaking of Mosul, in Iraq, in July 2017, the fall of Raqqa completed, in many analysts' eyes, the sacking of ISIS militarily and, at least in a broad military sense, the defeat of the Islamic State and its dream of a long-lasting, region-wide caliphate—a tremendous victory for the United States and a vindication of the Trump administration's ramped-up strategy for fighting the terror group.

Until fairly recently, ISIS had reigned far and wide. At the group's peak, its armed force, tens of thousands strong, controlled portions of Iraq and Syria roughly equivalent in size to Great Britain. Its conquests, over a short period, seemed to suggest a new power center in the Middle East—especially since the group had grown out of the remnants of al-Qaeda in Iraq and had made its greatest gains when the United States had completed withdrawal from that country and was following a policy that put Washington on the sidelines in terms of determining the future of the country. ISIS filled the void quickly. The group first came to prominence in early 2014, when it overran Fallujah—so hard-won, at the cost of so much blood and treasure by the United States—and then parts of Ramadi, before turning to Syria, now functioning essentially as a failed state, in the midst of its civil war. It seized Raqqa and, later in 2014, Mosul, Iraq's largest city after Baghdad. It was after the seizure of Mosul that the ISIS leader, Abu Bakr al-Baghdadi, declared a new Islamic caliphate.

ISIS quickly set to work terrorizing the populations under which it ruled, with mass executions and brutality including kidnapping young girls into sexual slavery, public burnings and beheadings, and wholesale slaughter of Iraq's Yazidi community. The group's uncompromising, utterly fanatical application of sharia law and its evident glee in savagery inspired thousands of foreign Islamists to join the cause on the battle-field. For a time, it seemed that ISIS was unstoppable, the vanguard of radical Islam.

Only when the United States became re-engaged in the region and awoke to the threat that the Islamic State presented did results on the ground begin to change, culminating in the triumphs of 2017. "Our partners have removed ISIS from 87% of territory they once held and liberated over 6.5 million people," said Colonel Ryan Dillon, speaking on behalf of the anti-ISIS coalition.[3] In that course of action, and in its result, lies a lesson for the future about the struggle against radical Islam. But before we sort out that lesson, it is vital to understand what the Islamic State's defeats signify. That understanding can best be summarized in the answers to two questions.

First question: Should the Islamic State's defeat, at least militarily, in Syria and Iraq encourage Westerners as to our ability to combat radical Islam around the world? Answer: Yes, absolutely. And I'll have more to say about this at the end of this chapter.

Second question: Does the Islamic State's defeat, at least militarily, in Syria and Iraq mark a crucial turning point in our battle against radical Islam? Answer: Sadly, no, it does not—it signifies only that the terms of the battle are shifting again, as they have multiple times since 2001, and as they will again. The sobering truth about the decline of ISIS as a military force is that its fighters will remain determined and violent actors in the region, whether as guerrilla forces or as independent terrorists. Moreover, its loyalists will be even more determined to bring the battle to Western countries and Western cities, to bring fear, savagery, and mayhem to the citizens of the countries that have helped destroy the caliphate.

We have seen this already, in the uptick in terror attacks in recent years in Western capitals. These attacks track rather neatly with ISIS's declining fortunes in the Middle East. The sobering truth is that the fall of the Islamic State as a major military player likely makes ISIS *more* dangerous to the West at home than it was in 2014.

In short, the battle against radical Islam isn't even close to being over, especially with the vast Muslim populations now resident in Europe; with the massive demographic advantage Muslim populations are now gaining over Western societies, in terms of birthrates; and also because, far from the battle being confined to ISIS, other Islamist radical groups are growing in power and influence as well. These include al-Qaeda, which, after being nearly debilitated, is now on the rebound, seeing an opening in the troubles of the Islamic State. Most chillingly of all, al-Qaeda—and Islamic radicalism worldwide—might someday soon have a new and powerful leader, one bearing the most famous name in the entire world of terrorism.

RETURN OF AL-QAEDA

On May 1, 2011, when President Barack Obama announced that U.S. forces had killed Osama bin Laden, it was natural for Americans to feel some euphoria. Bin Laden, after all, was the mastermind of the deadliest terror attack in the history of the world, and he had been public enemy number one in the United States for nearly a decade. But it wasn't just American citizens who felt better; U.S. policy makers also felt that the long-running battle against al-Qaeda could be nearing completion. Obama said in September 2011 that al-Qaeda was "on a path to defeat." Defense secretary Leon Panetta said the same year that the United States was "within reach of strategically defeating al Qaeda."[4]

Unfortunately, what they didn't realize was that the terror group was already in the midst of reassessing its mistakes and setbacks over the decade since 9/11, and the death of Bin Laden gave them renewed impetus. Under the direction of Ayman al Zawahiri, Bin Laden's top lieutenant, the group determined to work more under the radar than they had been doing, to avoid direct conflict with the West, and to rebuild relationships with Arab and Muslim populations. They saw opportunity in working with local populations in civil wars, such as in Syria, and in struggles against oppressive governments elsewhere. Instead of subjecting populations to the extremist savagery of ISIS, al-Qaeda focused more on being political and military champions of embattled Muslim populations. In short, al-Qaeda has opted for what Western intelligence operatives would call something like a covert strategy—working behind the scenes in ways not unlike the Americans' counter-insurgency tactics of the past. Working among the masses to raise consciousness and build support, al-Qaeda encourages these citizens to take their own action, while also refraining from the most high-profile and reckless acts of terror, including efforts to topple unfriendly Arab governments.

The strategy received a huge boost with the rise of ISIS, for two reasons: first, because the Islamic State's savage style alienated so many Muslims, including some who might have been in political sympathy but were repelled by the group's tactics; and second, because the Islamic State soon rose to become the top priority of counterterror policy in the United States and the West more generally. With the massive territorial gains that ISIS made in 2014, the focus in Washington, and among European allies, was on fighting ISIS. And that served al-Qaeda's new low-profile style perfectly.

For the last several years, the overwhelming focus of Western counterterror efforts has been on fighting ISIS—understandably. That is changing now, though, as al-Qaeda surges back onto the American counterterror radar screen. Reports suggest a shifting of Washington priorities as intelligence reports reveal that al-Qaeda is pursuing, again, plans involving blowing up jet airliners with sophisticated and hard-to-detect bombs.[5]

And even by April 2015, terror analysts Daveed Gartenstein-Ross and Bridget Moreng were pointing out that "the jihadist group that has won the most territory in the Arab world over the past six months is Al Qaeda." By the fall of 2016, Gartenstein-Ross saw al-Qaeda doing even better. The terror analyst said the territory the group controls is "greater than it has ever been."[6]

Indeed, as Hamza bin Laden, the 28-year-old son of Osama, who had spent time in hiding with his father in Afghanistan, said in the summer of 2016, al-Qaeda operatives now had reached "Sham [Syria], Palestine, Yemen, Egypt, Iraq, Somalia, the Indian subcontinent, Libya, Algeria, Tunisia, Mali, and Central Africa."[7]

Hamza bin Laden might someday soon be the leader of al-Qaeda, the man who takes the group into its next era. Shortly before leaving office, President Obama placed him on a U.S. Specially Designated Global Terrorist list. All signs point to his eventually succeeding Zawahiri—a shrewd leader, it turns out, judging by the success of his under-the-radar strategy, but not a man with a strong following among jihadis from other groups, who see him as an outsider. Hamza won't have that problem: he is the son of Bin Laden, the greatest jihadi in history and a man whom ISIS followers revere. And as Ali Soufan wrote in a powerful portrait in the *Daily Beast*, his is a name Westerners might start hearing regularly.

Hamza lives today in a compound outside Jeddah, Saudi Arabia, where he is watched closely and kept under tight security by Saudi authorities. But that hasn't stopped him from sending out his messages to Islamists around the word—and even calling for regime change in Saudi Arabia. His first message was broadcast in August 2015, when Zawahiri, whose stock was plunging among Islamists, introduced him on a recording as "a lion from the den of al-Qaeda." Hamza invoked his father, praised jihadis around the world, celebrated terrorist attacks in the United States at Fort Hood and at the Boston Marathon, and called for Islamist warriors to bring the fight "from Kabul, Baghdad, and Gaza to Washington, London, Paris, and Tel Aviv."[8] Continued statements from Hamza prompted the Obama administration to put him on its global terrorist list. By May 2017, Hamza's prominence and prestige had grown to the extent that al-Qaeda has begun calling him "sheikh," a title given only to the group's top leaders.

Hamza's messages have several striking themes that should be of grave concern to the West. First, unlike Zawahiri, he has renewed calls for attacks against the West, and on Jewish interests. "Sell your soul cheaply for the pleasure of [God]," he urged listeners on a May 2017 audiotape, encouraging them to commit lone-wolf attacks by any means possible. If guns and bombs weren't available, he said, "stabbing with knives and using vehicles and trucks" would be perfectly suitable. Moreover, he stressed that fighting in the great battlefields in Syria and Iraq and elsewhere was not necessary to achieve martyrdom—jihadis can strike where they are, including in Western countries. "Perhaps you yearn for sacrifice in the battlefields," he said. "Know that inflicting punishment on Jews and Crusaders where you are is more vexing and severe for the enemy."[9] And he urged would-be terrorists to make sure that they had made clear what message they wanted to convey by their attacks, via the media.

In a July 2016 audio message entitled "We Are All Osama," Hamza called for the avenging of his father's death—a theme sure to inspire followers, though he couches it not as a personal crusade but rather as "revenge for those who defended Islam." Addressing the United States and its coalition partners, and sounding very much like his father, Hamza said, "We will continue striking you and targeting you in your country and abroad in response to your oppression of the people of Palestine, Afghanistan, Syria, Iraq, Yemen, Somalia and the rest of the Muslim lands that did not survive your oppression."[10]

More recently, in a January 2018 video, Hamza called for the overthrow of the Saudi monarchy. He argued that "Saudi Arabia's monarchy should be punished for forming strategic historical alliances with the West and uniting with the British Empire against the Ottoman Empire," according to a *Newsweek* report.[11]

Finally, as Ali Soufan notes, Hamza is one of the few al-Qaeda leaders who refrained from criticizing the Islamic State. Tensions between the two groups ran high over the years, as Zawahiri and other al-Qaeda leaders objected to the ISIS tactics of wanton brutality, often against innocent Muslim civilians, as well as the group's seemingly willful cultivation of the West's concentrated efforts to destroy it. Given the setbacks that ISIS has experienced, al-Qaeda's objections look prescient, but ill will between the organizations remains. From the West's perspective, of course, such fragmentation is welcome, but Hamza has taken a less confrontational line, never calling out ISIS leaders, as Zawahiri had done, but instead appealing for unity. Apparently, ISIS has noticed; while it freely lashes out at Zawahiri, it never criticizes Hamza. In Soufan's view, "This is the best evidence that Hamza could be a unifying figure."[12]

JIHAD, INC.

Charismatic and blessed with his famous name, Hamza has the potential, Soufan believes, not only to take al-Qaeda to new heights but also to unite jihadist forces around the globe. That would be a feat of remarkable and unprecedented proportions, presenting a unique new threat to the West. Even if such a goal proves beyond Hamza's conception or his reach, his likely rise to al-Qaeda leadership someday soon will almost certainly inspire jihadis around the world. And even if no such great unification of terror groups is in the offing, the number and reach of such groups worldwide is unprecedented.

As Soufan documents, al-Qaeda-affiliated groups in Afghanistan, Yemen, Somalia, North Africa, and elsewhere have thousands of fighters, at least some of whom are hardened terrorists with experience plotting attacks, both in that area of the world and in the West. Al-Nusra in Syria may have as many as 20,000 militants at its command. Al-Qaeda on the Arabian Peninsula has a major presence in Yemen, where it controls sizable portions of the nation's highways and coastline. And al-Qaeda in the Islamic Maghreb has created what Soufan calls "a jihadi conglomerate" through a merger with other factions; these groups have conducted hundreds of terror attacks in recent years.[13]

The savagery of other Islamist groups should remind Western observers that the threat is not confined to ISIS and al-Qaeda. In Africa, Boko Haram has terrorized Nigeria, the continent's most populous country and largest economy, for years. The group's pitiless tactics—exemplified by its abduction of hundreds of girls in 2014, which became a worldwide story—have displaced more than two million people from the country. The remarkable thing about the group is the way that it has used its tiny $10 million budget to arm itself more effectively than the Nigerian military; its arsenal includes "rocket-propelled grenades, machine guns with anti-aircraft visors, automatic rifles, grenades and explosives."[14] For now, the West can be grateful that the group's focus remains on Nigeria, not on conducting Western attacks—though Boko Haram did pledge allegiance to ISIS in March 2015 and has celebrated news of the group's terror attacks in Western cities.

In Somalia, al-Qaeda-linked al-Shabab hasn't drawn as much media attention as Boko Haram, but recent data compiled by the

Africa Center for Strategic Studies, an institution affiliated with the U.S. Defense Department, suggest that it is inflicting more casualties.[15] It has made a special project of attacking bases run by the African Union Mission in Somalia (AMISOM), a peacekeeping mission that operates with U.N. approval. A January 2016 attack from al-Shabab killed almost 150 Kenyan soldiers on an AMISOM base. The group has also struck hotels and government buildings with suicide bombings. Al-Shabab militants have turned down offers from the Somali government of amnesty in exchange for laying down their weapons. The group's main targets, as these details suggest, are AMISOM and the Somali government that supports it, as well as U.N. forces and Western countries, including the United States, that support these efforts with troops, intelligence officers, and the like.

For now, the battleground remains in Somalia, not on the streets of U.S. cities. The United States considers al-Shabab the deadliest and most dangerous terror group on the African continent, and reports suggest that several Westerners have journeyed to Somalia to join the group. Al-Shabab is making "an active and deliberate attempt" to recruit Americans, the FBI believes. By the end of 2017, the United States had stationed more than 500 troops in Somalia, the largest American military presence there in nearly 25 years.[16]

And despite its recent troubles, ISIS is hardly out of the picture. It may have been pushed back in Iraq and Syria, but its fighters are wreaking havoc in other parts of the globe—especially in the Philippines. There Islamist militants, reportedly funded by ISIS, have overrun the city of Marawi, where more than 500 have died. The fighting has not gone well for the Filipino army, whose deficiencies have been glaringly revealed.[17]

Moreover, ISIS—more than any other Islamist group currently operating—has its sights set on bringing the war to the developed world, especially the West. It is at home that we must worry most about the Islamist challenge, not only because our open societies make it so much easier for outsiders to come and go but also because immigration policies have dramatically altered population demographics, especially in Europe. The simple fact is that the West has more than enough homegrown jihadis to cause continual havoc—as we have seen in recent years.

JIHAD IN THE WEST

As noted at the opening of this chapter, those who cheer the demise, at least militarily, of ISIS in Iraq and Syria are well justified in their sentiments; indeed, we can all take heart in this development. But the sobering fact remains that the strength and presence of radical Islam within Western societies, including the United States but especially in Europe, is worsening year by year. Moreover, it is likely to continue to worsen—again, especially in Europe, where demographic factors now put the Continent's native-born population increasingly on the defensive against a surging Muslim population. Consider this partial list of ISIS attacks on Western targets since 2015:

January 7, 2015: Charlie Hebdo offices, Paris (12 dead)

November 13, 2015: Stade de France, Bataclan, bars/restaurants in Paris (130 dead, hundreds injured, the deadliest assault on French soil since World War II)

March 22, 2016: Brussels Airport and Metro Station suicide bombings (32 dead, more than 300 wounded)

July 14, 2016: Promenade lorry attack, Bastille Day, Nice (84 dead, hundreds injured)

July 18, 2016: Train ax attack, Wurzburg, Germany (19 injured)

July 26, 2016: Normandy church attack, Normandy, France (churchgoers were held hostage and a priest was killed)

December 19, 2016: Berlin Christmas Market attack, Berlin, Germany (12 dead, more than 60 injured)

March 22, 2017: Westminster Bridge attack, London (5 dead, 4 killed on the bridge when the attacker crashed his car into people including a police officer while attempting to escape)

April 7, 2017: Stockholm attack when a failed asylum seeker drove a truck down a busy shopping street (4 dead, at least 15 injured)

April 20, 2017: Champs Elysees attack, Paris (1 dead, 2 wounded; a policeman was killed by an attacker, claimed by ISIS)

May 22, 2017: Ariana Grande concert attack, Manchester (more than 22 dead, 59 injured)

June 3, 2017: London Bridge attack, when knifemen mowed down civilians on the bridge and then proceeded to attack people at pubs and restaurants (8 dead, many injured)

August 17, 2017: Barcelona attacks (13 dead, 130 injured)

September 15, 2017: Parsons Green bombing—an explosion occurred on a District line train at Parsons Green Underground station, in London (30 injured; suspect had undergone ISIS training)

September 30, 2017: Edmonton, Canada—30-year-old Abdulahi Sharif struck a police constable and four pedestrians with a rental truck (5 injuries, no deaths; there was an ISIS flag in the trunk)

October 1, 2017: Marseilles stabbing—a man killed two women at the Saint-Charles Station in France (2 dead)

October 31, 2017: New York City truck attack (8 dead, 12 injured)

December 11, 2017: New York City—attempted Port Authority bombing (4 injured; perpetrator pledged allegiance to ISIS)

March 23, 2018: Carcassonne and Trèbes attack, France—hostage situation in supermarket (5 dead and 15 injured)

May 12, 2018: Paris knife attack (2 dead, 8 injured)

May 29, 2018: Liège attack—a prisoner on temporary leave stabbed two police officers and took their guns (4 dead, 4 injured; ISIS claimed responsibility)

July 22, 2018: Toronto shooting (3 dead, 13 injured; ISIS claimed responsibility; suspect had visited ISIS websites and had lived in Pakistan and Afghanistan but had no apparent direct connection)

The fact is, Islamist attacks are on the rise in the West across the board. Since 2014 alone, in Europe, 15 different countries have been the target of more than 150 attacks.[18] According to a 2016 report from the Investigative Project on Terrorism (IPT), fatalities from terror attacks have increased an incredible 744 percent from the years 2007–2011 to 2014–2015. In total numbers, that's an increase from 3,200 average deaths per year to 27,000. The IPT predicts increased terror attacks in Europe, in part because "Europe's security systems will become more stressed and unable to respond to the rising challenges associated with the mass migration of refugees. Violence in Europe will increase in size and scope as Islamists exploit its nearly unregulated immigration system and Muslim enclaves such as Molenbeek in Brussels become more widespread."[19]

The European continent faces huge problems in this regard, and at the root of it is a changing population. More than 40 years ago, former Algerian president Houari Boumédienne made a prophetic prediction: "One day, millions of men will leave the Southern Hemisphere to go to the Northern Hemisphere," he said. "And they will not go there as friends. Because they will go there to conquer. And they will conquer it with their sons. The wombs of our women will give us victory."[20]

And it's happening. With Europe's low birthrates—below replacement levels in several countries, especially Italy—and rapid rates of immigration, along with the high birthrates of those new arrivals, the designation of Europe as "Eurabia," as some critics call it, is not hyperbole. In 2015, *all* European Union member countries had sub-replacement levels of fertility.[21] In Brussels, headquarters of the EU, 70 percent of residents are immigrants, born elsewhere.[22] That figure is projected to reach 85 percent by 2020. Multiple European cities, including Paris and London, have enclaves that police consider essentially no-go zones, so heavily Muslim has their population become. In these areas, sharia law is applied, against all European custom, and most basic services are not delivered. The areas are ungovernable, and their residents live in strict segregation from the broader society, with radicalization common. In Britain, an estimated 85 sharia courts are in operation. Millions across Europe live in such zones.

It is no wonder, then, seeing such results, that Americans in particular objected to the Obama administration's desire to accept more Syrian refugees for settlement. Americans are a compassionate people, but with no reliable way to vet such a massive population, it was difficult to support the influx. And that support would no doubt be even lower if more Americans knew about the stated goals of Islamist groups like the Muslim Brotherhood, which already operates in North America and which states that its members "must understand that their work in America is a kind of grand Jihad in eliminating and destroying the Western civilization from within and 'sabotaging' its miserable house by their [own] hands and the hands of the believers so that it is eliminated and Allah's religion is made victorious over all other religions."[23]

And if all this isn't bad enough, consider what Robin Wright wrote in the *New Yorker* in October 2017, summarizing the findings of a report cowritten by counterterror consultants the Soufan Group and the Global Strategy Network about where displaced ISIS fighters are headed:

> At least fifty-six hundred people from thirty-three countries have already gone home—and most countries don't yet have a head count. On average, twenty to thirty per cent of the foreign fighters from Europe have already returned there—though it's fifty per cent in Britain, Denmark, and Sweden. Thousands more who fought for *isis* are stuck near the borders of Turkey, Jordan, or Iraq, and are believed to be trying to get back to their home countries.[24]

The problem of the Islamist threat is not going away. The nations of the West, including the United States, need an answer, not only for the ongoing military campaigns around the world against jihadist groups, but also—and ultimately more importantly—to face the challenge at home.

NOW OR NEVER

The year "2017 will most likely go down as the deadliest year in the 'war against terrorism,'" writes Pete Hoekstra of the IPT. "This ought to be a wakeup call to everyone…. We all need to recognize the reality that we are not winning this war. Partisan divides need to be pushed aside. There is plenty of blame to go around."[25]

He's right. We must not allow some military success in the Middle East to divert us from the fundamental reality that in the West, the problem of radical Islam is almost certain to grow, testing the convictions and resolve of secular societies that have been much more comfortable with self-criticism—even self-flagellation—than self-defense or self-assertion in recent years. The Islamists have preyed on this very quality, this lack of confidence and refusal to assert the prerogatives of Western ideals, cultural assumptions, and open political culture. When we have asserted them, however—that is, in the Middle East, in the form of our military power—we have seen success. This should tell us something.

Assertion must begin with honesty—about the problem, its scope, and the need of Western countries to address it (as well as their right to do so). There must be an honest, unswervingly frank discussion about the specifics and goals of radical Islamist theology, both in the Middle East and within Western societies. In Europe, especially, honesty about the scope and scale of the threat could provide the political incentive to expand security monitoring of dangerous individuals and improve the information sharing among intelligence agencies and police. The nations of Europe must get much tougher on their policies of jailing and deporting foreign nationals who present terror threats.

But more than anything else, European countries need to take a long, hard look at where they want to be in the next decade or two. What kind of society do they think they are building? Do they envision that the open, secular, tolerant societies they have enjoyed—societies that represent one of the great successes of humankind, after the carnage of the twentieth century—can endure forever, without maintenance, and in the face of border and immigration policies so destructive of these ends? What will remain most important—to preserve their self-defined credentials for "tolerance," or to preserve their societies? Unless Europe takes a stand on these issues, the Islamization of the Continent will continue in force, and with the demographic math being what it is, it will become extraordinarily difficult to prevent terror attacks.

"How high the body count must go until things change is a question only European leaders can answer," writes Robin Simcox in the *Daily Signal*. "Their policies going forward will help decide the future of an entire continent."[26]

American leadership will, of course, be crucial. The routing of ISIS from its strongholds in Iraq and Syria is the most dramatic demonstration in years for the world of what a difference American power and commitment can make to solving even the most daunting foreign policy challenges. After years of destructive and frankly tragic dithering by the Obama administration, Washington woke up to the ISIS threat in the Middle East. After much delay, the Obama administration implemented a strategy that proved successful—one that combined elements of air power, counterintelligence, and special forces deployment, in tandem with Kurdish and free Syrian troops.

It's important to note, however, that President Trump has good grounds to claim credit for the victory against ISIS, since the group still had broad control of its holdings in Iraq and Syria when he took office, and the most dramatic routing of the group took place on his watch—and after he had made vital changes to the operational plan. The most important change Trump made was to loosen the rules of engagement and give combat commanders more authority to make strategic and tactical decisions in the field. This approach contrasts with that of the Obama administration, which tended to micromanagement and seemed to prioritize avoiding civilian casualties even above making battlefield gains against the enemy. Trump's results speak for themselves.

The results also suggest something else: a return to American leadership. "Make no mistake," the *Wall Street Journal* editorialized. "This is another example of America policing the world. If not for U.S. planes and the Peshmerga, Kirkuk in Iraq would have fallen to ISIS—and maybe Baghdad too."[27] It's true—and we shouldn't shrink from the implications of this observation, both in understanding what has recently been achieved and in recognizing what remains to be done. The *Journal* and others rightly warn that United States evacuation of Syria will leave a vacuum that Iran will be only too happy to fill, and that abandonment of our Kurdish and especially free Syrian allies will drive many into the Syrian branch of al-Qaeda.

What the United States has struggled with throughout the War on Terror is the understanding that this is indeed a long war—generational in scope, if not longer. Our strategic exhaustion is understandable, but as past experience shows, when we walk away, we only ensure that we will need to return again before long, and usually to a situation much worse than it would have been if we had stayed committed to the job.

Finally, the United States and Europe, along with all Western-oriented democracies, should recognize that the War on Terror—as George W. Bush called it—is also a war of ideas. Radical Islam is many things, but above all it is a belief system, one that explains the world to disaffected, mostly younger Muslims around the world, offers a coherent path to salvation, and exalts specific deeds for jihadis to perform to get there. It is vile, fascistic at its core, and deadly—but it is also consistent, compelling, and determined. The West's advocacy for free societies, both in terms of their principles and in terms of their results—higher standards of living, technological advancement, happier citizens, more just and fair societies—must be every bit as committed and determined. We should take a page from the determined way that we fought the Cold War, via Radio Free Europe and other tools that got the word out to the Soviet bloc that a better way of life was possible. We should call out radical Islam as the demented and vicious system that it is and make an unambiguous appeal for the virtues of our open societies.

Do we want to win? Do we believe our societies are worth preserving? In the end, the answers to these fundamental questions will determine how the West fares against the Islamist challenge.

CHAPTER SEVEN

THIRD WORLD IN CRISIS

"The problems Africa faces are completely different and are much different and are 'civilizational.' What are the problems? Failed states, complex democratic transitions and extremely difficult demographic transitions. Multiple trafficking routes that pose severe issues—drugs, human trafficking, weapons. Violent fundamentalism and Islamic terrorism. All these create major issues."

—EMMANUEL MACRON[1]

"The day I don't exist, it's not going to decrease in any way at all.... drug trafficking does not depend on just one person. It depends on a lot of people."

—EL CHAPO[2]

Here's a sobering statistic that you're not likely to come across often: Latin America accounts for about one-third of all the people murdered around the world every year.[3] Further, just seven Latin American countries—Brazil, Colombia, Mexico, El Salvador, Guatemala, Honduras, and Venezuela—account for one in every four homicides around the world.[4] The region is home to at least 43 of the world's 50 deadliest cities; its murder rate is three times the global average.[5]

Crime and homicide are not the only problems in the region, though they shadow everything else. Latin America is awash in political corruption, international criminal gangs and drug cartels, authoritarian leaders, unstable and failing governments, and health and crime crises.

Security and humanitarian crises abound across the African continent, too. The conflict in the region known as Lake Chad Basin, described by Al Jazeera as "the world's most neglected crisis," involves the fate of 17 million people. More than two million people, mostly women and children, have been driven from their homes and face starvation. The root of the crisis is Boko Haram's campaign of destruction, beginning in 2009, which spread into four countries—Cameroon, Chad, Niger, and Nigeria—and has already cost many thousands of lives. The area is rife with jihadists and criminal networks preying on innocent civilians. A similar situation exists in the Greater Sahel, where jihadis, including al-Qaeda in the Islamic Maghreb and al-Mourabitoun, have launched deadly attacks for years. Another treacherous spot is Mali, currently ranked as the U.N.'s most deadly humanitarian mission; 70 personnel have lost their lives there since 2013. Armed groups are spreading across the country as a peace agreement remains shaky and a rebel alliance has fractured.

Then there is South Sudan, where multiple conflicts have led to the displacement of nearly two million people and forced another one million to flee the country. The world's youngest nation, achieving independence in 2011, South Sudan has seen its early history dominated by a brutal civil war driven by ethnic and political conflicts and costing up to 300,000 lives. A peace agreement has not been implemented successfully, and reports persist of mass atrocities.

If there is a common thread running under the dysfunction in both areas, it is pervasive, endemic corruption—corruption that runs so deep, through every fundamental institution, that it has often become either an accepted part of life and culture or a fact of life that people despair of ever changing. It is so bad that it has even spawned industries, like the Sakawa boys in Ghana, who commit Internet fraud and earn lavish livings doing so. Like all corruption, the third world brand has a doubly corrosive effect: first, it impedes the functioning of society by rendering unfit the institutions on which normal life depends; second, it seeps into the consciousness of the people, demoralizing and depressing them until they expect nothing better—leading some to determine, by their own ends, that the best way to succeed in life is to get a piece of this corruption racket for themselves.

AFRICA

Africa spins on an axis of corruption that ensures that the continent's many other issues—war, terrorism, tribal brutalities, educational needs, health crises—don't get solved or alleviated but worsen. Corruption in sub-Saharan Africa is endemic in culture, foreign relations, and government finances. It has repercussions for personal and national security and for regional economic viability, and, again, considering the vulnerability of many African nations—with higher rates of poverty and disease and lower access to clean water and arable land—it has dramatically worse effects than in other regions.

One reason that corruption is so endemic on the continent is that it has roots in key characteristics and the history of African governance. Government spending has never been publicly transparent, making theft easy—and impoverishing areas that most need these funds. Foreign powers, especially China, flood Africa with aid, but this aid, too, is often stolen by African governments.

So deep-seated is corruption in Africa that it has created cultural assumptions, one being that the only way to get ahead is through graft—an assumption that further reinforces the prevailing culture. Working in government becomes synonymous with getting rich, and thus government officials are determined to maintain their grip on power at any cost—and those on the outside looking in are equally determined to stage coups.

In Africa writ large, an economy of corruption reigns. Services that should be free must be paid for. Complex laws and regulation discourage entrepreneurship, though the corruption-friendly climate makes the continent a prime staging ground for shady business dealings involving foreign multinationals.

The culture of corruption is, boiled down, an economy of bribery. A 2015 Transparency International poll showed that 58 percent of Africans saw bribery as increasing.[6] Seven out of ten Liberians said that they had to pay bribes for services including health care and education.[7] In all, the report found, some 75 million people in sub-Saharan Africa paid bribes in 2015.[8] Close to one in five of all Africans pay bribes for needed official documents. The most corrupt institutions of all, by Africans' reckoning, were the police and the courts—the institutions that must operate with integrity, or at least the perception of integrity, for societies to function in any meaningful way.

"Corruption is the single biggest threat to Africa's growth," says Ali Mufuruki, CEO of Tanzania's Infotech Investment Group and member of the IMF Group on Sub-Saharan Africa. "The solution lies in good, ethical leadership, strong and enforceable laws against corruption, severe sanctions for corruption crimes underpinned by a national culture of promoting ethics from family to national level."[9] That's a tall order, though, and few African countries are making any headway cutting down on corruption. The few that are—like, say, Mauritius and Botswana, where citizens report little need to bribe officials—don't rank anywhere near the continent's top economic powers.

On the other hand, one of the continent's top 20 economic powers, Kenya, is awash in corruption and misappropriated government funds, which takes many forms: increasing prices of staple foods, variable and unpredictable tariffs, and currency fluctuation. Once considered a leading nation in Africa, Kenya is volatile and indebted. Corruption reached new heights in 2015, when it was reported that the government was spending $85 each for ballpoint pens and thousands of dollars for condom dispensers.[10]

"This is the biggest bunch of crooks to ever run a government in this part of Africa," said John Githongo, an anticorruption activist. "This is literally the rape of the country, everything from the poaching of our wildlife to the accumulation of debt at an extraordinary level."[11]

Kenyan government corruption puts the United States in an awkward position, because the country is a critical base for counterterrorism operations—but Washington doesn't want to be seen as enabling the graft. In 2015, the United States announced a joint investigative effort with Kenya to battle corruption in the country, especially that stemming from international crime. But activists have claimed the rhetoric is empty and demanded increased action. (In July 2015, not long after President Obama visited the country, Kenya's auditor general announced that he could not account for about one-quarter of the country's $16 billion budget.[12]) The poverty conditions and high unemployment rate in Kenya keep the issue emotionally charged.

In Kenya, corruption is a toxic influence not just in government but across all levels of society. Corruption—especially bribery—runs rampant in the police force.

"The little amount that you are paid as salary cannot get up for you and your family," said a police officer in the neighborhood of Eastleigh. "So, if somebody gives you some amount somewhere, you have to take the money and then you forget about work.... It's right from the junior officer to the higher-most.... A criminal can come, do anything that they want, they go free. You will pay and you go free."[13] One local resident said that police see his neighborhood as an "ATM machine."[14]

Perhaps the bleakest note in Kenya comes from a man named Daniel Mwirigi, who, investigating fraud at Kenya's Postbank in 2000, discovered that bank officers were stealing Western Union transactions. He reported the crime—with the result that, he says, his bosses colluded to frame him for the crimes he had exposed. This launched him on a two-year fight to clear his name, a battle he won, but at the cost of his job, public reputation, and health. Even his family doubted him. "My father was alive at that time," he says. "He has died thinking that I am a thief. My mother was alive. She had died thinking that I'm a thief."

His final judgment is as bleak as it gets: "There's no point of doing a good job in this country. The future generations are doomed."[15]

Ghana's Sakawa Boys

A good example of how deep the culture of corruption runs is the phenomenon of the Sakawa boys of Ghana—Internet fraudsters whose practitioners enjoy high standards of living and flaunt their wealth and fashion to a public that well knows how they earn their money. "Sakawa" is a Ghanaian term describing illegal practices, generally involving Internet fraud but also implying various other elements, such as fetish rituals and coercion. The BBC followed the story of a 25-year-old Sakawa boy who had been defrauding people full-time for two years:

> "I know it's wrong but it gives me a lot of money," he says.
>
> He used to sleep on the streets. Then he saw his friends in internet cafes earning money defrauding people online.
>
> A typical con is pretending to be a woman romantically interested in men from Europe, America or Asia.
>
> He learnt the trade and, with little formal education, earned enough money to rent an apartment, buy a car and have money left over to spend.

But he insists the money isn't earned easily.

"Some say this work is easy but it is not."

"You have to be patient, smart, fast and cultivate trust between you and the white person."

...

It's not just a living, but a lifestyle.

Sakawa boys are so renowned in Ghana that a primary school pupil can point one out—their lavish lifestyle gives them away.

...

A decade ago the term Sakawa was not even used in Ghana. Instead internet fraudsters were called Yahoo boys—a term mostly used for conmen in Nigeria.

The Nigerian singer Olu Maintain released the song Yahooze in 2007. In the song he says "it's all about the Benjamins baby," referring to hundred dollar bills. And at gigs he started spraying money at fans.

He said in an interview with *Modern Ghana* at the time "nobody is interested in how you got to where you are. Everybody is interested in results."[16]

Sakawa has become a glamour industry in Ghana, even spawning films, which make insinuations about the use of black magic. And some claim that the Sakawa boys now have become influential players in politics. Political leaders have complained about public officials who seem to conspire to help Sakawa boys avoid punishment. One minister complained about receiving death threats after he moved to arrest some of the grifters. Even though the Sakawa boys' long-term impact on Ghana will prove hugely destructive—and is already proving so, with the country blacklisted as a money launderer by the Financial Action Task Force, a clear caution to investors—the financial and material success of the Sakawa boys exerts a powerful hold on the public imagination, especially among the young.[17]

In sum, the Sakawa story demonstrates many unique aspects of African corruption: it is endemic in the culture and admired by youth; the young are most concerned with obtaining money and possessions, not with being ethical; the criminal industry has achieved a significant presence in popular culture, much as with gangsta rap in the United

States; and for all its depravity, its appeal is no mystery, since it is one of few options for uneducated, unemployed Africans.

How Corruption Corrodes Education in Africa

Corruption in African education takes many forms. The siphoning of funds meant for education means scarce resources and dissatisfied teachers. Rampant student cheating goes unaddressed. Some argue that students are even taught to take part in the culture of corruption in school. In many cases, professors either shirk their duties or abuse their power. The lack of stable, ethical, and thorough education weakens the economy by not turning out qualified graduates.

In May 2015, South African authorities reportedly shut down several dozen fraudulent colleges and universities that were offering bogus academic programs. They were advertised as being U.S.-based universities and promised degrees in 15 days.[18] One-third of students at three East African universities surveyed in 2012 said that they had engaged in plagiarism or fabrication of personal references; one-quarter admitted that they had colluded with others during tests to communicate answers.[19] American students, by comparison, answered similar questions in the affirmative at much lower rates.

Reflecting on corruption in academia, one Nigerian professor reflected:

> My generation's penchant for corrupt academic practices seems unprecedented as we brazenly and unabashedly demand gratifications of various forms as though such demands enjoy some measure of legitimacy. "If you don't buy my book, you can't pass my course." "If you don't show appreciation by compensating me for my time, you'll carry the course over." "If you, Shade, Amaka or Amina, do not yield to my advances, you can't graduate from this school." "Besides, if you spend money to secure admission, you also need to spend your body for the money spent not to amount to a waste." "Why can you not use what you have to get what you want?" These are among the mantras on the lips of some lecturers in my generation. We in our own uncommon wisdom even announce our birthdays to our students several weeks ahead to enable them get well

prepared to "appreciate" us. And incidentally, we as corrupt lecturers are handling a more morally bankrupt generations of students who are very proficient in the various dialects that constitute the Modern language of corruption.[20]

A 2013 Transparency International report describes other cases of corruption in education, including "the embezzlement of national education funds in Kenya, the selling of fake diplomas in Niger, teacher absenteeism in Cameroon," and "sexual harassment by male lecturers in Nigeria."[21] As Transparency International's Chantal Uwimana puts it, "Africa is way behind other regions as far as education is concerned. We lack good educational structures and basic infrastructures, and there are not enough schools for the growing numbers of children. For those in school, corruption is learnt from a young age, and even accepted as a norm for them and society."[22]

How Corruption Impedes National Defense and Law and Order

National cultures so susceptible to corruption and graft are poorly equipped to administer basic law and order, let alone to guard against more destabilizing threats, from criminal gangs to terror networks.

In 2015, Nigerian national security adviser Sambo Dasuki was arrested for hoarding weapons and accused by newly elected president Muhammadu Buhari of stealing more than $2 billion from the military. The former presidential party spokesman, Olisa Metuh, was also charged.[23] Such charges are serious in any case, but in Nigeria, home base to one of the world's deadliest terror groups, Boko Haram, they carry even graver implications: the military, already in an uphill battle against the murderous terrorist group, often lacks the resources with which to fight them. One Nigerian soldier spoke of military weapons without bullets and trucks without gas. "We had so many casualties," he said. "There wasn't fuel in the vehicles. The commanders came out categorically telling us that there's no fuel and they don't have money." Many were forced to flee from the terror organization's superior firepower, he said. "You will see the Boko Haram, your man will start thinking, can I face them? Or I should find my way out? Because without those supplies we are doing nothing."[24]

In 2015, evaluating 47 African countries on their prevention of graft in the military, Transparency International gave them all failing or near-failing grades. Defense spending is on the rise across the continent, but as in Nigeria, there is little or no public transparency. "Absolutely, corruption is undermining the fight against Boko Haram [in Nigeria]," says Leah Wawro of Transparency International. "When soldiers' salaries are pocketed, when they see their commanders driving fancy cars while they struggle to eat, they are more likely to sell weapons and other supplies. They are more likely to take bribes, and they are more likely to allow arms or drugs to be smuggled across borders." She added that they are also more likely to desert.[25]

Kenya's armed forces have also been accused of corruption. Journalists for Justice, a Nairobi-based, nonpartisan organization, reported that Kenyan soldiers in Somalia have collaborated with al-Shabab to impose what they call "taxes" on profits gained from illegal smuggling of sugar and charcoal through Kismayo, a Somali port. Here is a stark picture of how deep the culture of corruption is in the military forces: the Kenyan military, which has lost more than 100 soldiers to al-Shabab, is supposed to be fighting the terror group, not sharing black-market profits with its jihadis. "What you are seeing is a direct link between the ability of al-Shabab to arm and sustain itself and the corruption within the Kenya defense establishment all the way to the top," says Eléonore Vidal de la Blache, a coauthor of the Transparency International report.[26] The Kenyan government has denied the allegations.

Burkina Faso suffered from a violent hotel siege in early 2016 that killed 30 and wounded at least 56. The country holds one of the worst ranks in the Transparency International report, with accountability basically nonexistent. Public trust in the military and related institutions is nearly zero, and that vacuum is easily filled by terrorist groups. "What you can say about any country that scores an 'F' [as Burkina Faso does] is that there is no one to hold the military to account about what is being done to prevent these attacks, and how the increase in funding we are likely to see after an attack like this will be put to use," says Leah Wawro of Transparency International.[27]

Foreign-aid corruption also plays a role in enabling terrorism, Wawro points out, and she faults France and the United States, the principal financial backers of many of Africa's counterterror efforts, for not stepping up to address these issues—especially since Washington is a major funder of the Kenyan military. "So, if you look through a winding lens, U.S. money is indirectly filtering in to support terrorism." She urges the United States and other foreign backers to push for greater transparency in defense spending.[28]

Water

There may be no area in which the role of corruption is so prominent and so damaging in African life than water. Water stress (economic, social, or environmental problems caused by unmet water needs) and water scarcity in sub-Saharan Africa are acute problems. The U.N. Environment Programme (UNEP) notes that residents of sub-Saharan Africa suffer the worst safe-water access anywhere on the continent: in at least eight sub-Saharan countries, only one-third of the population, at most, enjoys access to safe water.[29] UNEP expects that by 2025, more than two dozen African nations will struggle with water scarcity and "water stress."[30]

Government corruption also plays a large role here. A 2008 report by Transparency International estimated that corruption had played a role in denying 1 billion people access to safe drinking water (worldwide) and kept 2.8 billion from accessing sanitation services. The report also blamed corruption for "[raising] the price for connecting a household to a water network by as much as 30 percent."[31] In Nairobi, for example, poor people pay ten times more for water than the non-poor.[32]

Privatization of water services may be a partial solution and has met with some success in Africa, though corruption remains a major impediment. In Maputo, capital of Mozambique, for instance, delegation of water management to private companies expanded water access, and similar reforms have borne some fruit elsewhere, including in Uganda. But the bribery culture is very powerful. In a study of Uganda's water sector, "private contractors estimated the average bribe related to a contract award to be 10 percent [of the total cost]," said Maria Jacobson of the U.N. Development Programme. "The same study showed that 46 percent of all urban water consumers had paid extra money for connections."[33] Bribery will remain an African cross to bear; privatization alone will not fix it. That's especially true considering that, in some other African countries—including Kenya, Mali, and

Ghana—privatization met with protests after it resulted in increased fees and tariffs.

Corruption in African Health Care

The World Bank created the term "quiet corruption" in 2010 and said it was a major reason why African countries are failing at health care. Quiet corruption can take many forms, including "absenteeism among teachers or doctors, the distribution of fake drugs, or the sale of diluted fertilizers to poor farmers."[34] It can also include medical staff charging mercenary fees to attend to patients, demanding bribes for medication, and prioritizing patients who pay such bribes. A 2010 World Bank report found that 95 percent of resources allocated to the health sector in Ghana were diverted to individuals. Ghana was found to be second to Chad in terms of health sector corruption.[35]

One doctor working in Zimbabwe—ranked 163rd out of 174 countries on Transparency International's Corruption Perceptions Index, where lower is worse[36]—described seeing a family purchase medicine as well as infusion devices, disinfectants, and even scalpels before a surgery.[37] "One can only accuse the system, not the individual doctors," the doctor said. "When doctors and nurses aren't paid regularly but turn up for work anyway, they of course want to ensure a source of income—and they let the patients pay for that." The doctor said that the government siphons off funds meant for health care to use for its own purposes.[38]

Uganda's situation is typical. "The biggest problem there is getting medical care at all," says Widha Moses of Transparency International. "Medical personnel don't provide the services they should."[39] Poorly paid doctors and nurses are often hours late or don't show up at all. When they do come to work, there is no guarantee that they will provide the proper treatment for their patients; looking to make a profit, they often send their patients home with defective drugs.[40]

LATIN AMERICA

Latin America offers a good laboratory test case for those in the West who doubt the value of our inheritance of rule of law, consensual governments, and democratic processes. Historically, Latin America has been dominated by non-ideological authoritarian governments, reliant on military strength. This strongman political style, especially when coupled with destructive economic policies and chaotic political cultures, led to underdeveloped economies throughout the region.

Almost two-thirds (62 percent) of the Latin Americans surveyed by Transparency International for its 2017 Global Corruption Barometer—more than 22,000 respondents, across 20 countries—said that corruption had risen where they lived over the previous year. More than half said their governments were failing to address it. A distressing one-third said they had had to pay a bribe for using a public service. Extrapolating from these data and the proportional responses, Transparency International concluded that "based on the estimated population size of these countries, this means that around 90 million people paid bribes."[41]

The problems run broad and deep. Leftist inclinations in Latin American countries undermine stability and create corruption as much as they empower those in need. Both Brazil's and Venezuela's leftist initiatives to assert state authority over national oil corporations led to bribery scandals in government and economic instability, which in turn led to political instability and insufficient resources for pressing problems, such as fighting the Zika virus. More broadly, hard-left governance, especially in economics, has brought outcomes ranging from hardship to outright ruin—the latter being the only appropriate term to describe the current state of Venezuela.

Even in the struggling Latin American region, no country suffers like Venezuela, a nation blessed with some of the world's most plentiful oil reserves but which has nevertheless become a basket case of dysfunction and looming disaster. The nation's dissolution is a stark illustration of the wages of state socialism, an ideological system that should have been retired from use long ago. Everything in Venezuela is collapsing: incomes, economic output, health standards, sanitation, and the currency. The economy is among the world's worst-performing, shrinking dramatically year by year. Inflation was estimated at 46,000 percent in 2018, and the IMF projected that it could reach 1 million percent.[42] More than 1.5 million have fled the country in 2018 alone. The nation faces potential default on a crushing foreign debt. More than 90 percent of Venezuelans say that they cannot afford to buy enough food. And yet the government of Nicolas Maduro is more concerned with clamping down on street protestors and other political dissidents than with helping the nation's suffering people.

The situation is dire. Close observers continue to call for free elections to choose a new government, but the Maduro government has already invalidated multiple elections, even when overwhelming majorities voted their opposition to his rule. The Trump administration's targeted sanctions against some of Venezuela's leaders have exacted some costs, but they will not be enough. I doubt that sanctions of even aggressive political reform can save Venezuela now. I'm inclined to agree with Ricardo Hausmann, a former minister of planning for Venezuela, that the country's National Assembly should impeach Maduro, appoint a new government, and call for military assistance from a regional coalition of willing partners (which may or may not include the United States). The time has come for dramatic action, because, as Hausmann writes, conditions in Venezuela now "constitute a crime against humanity that must be stopped on moral grounds."[43]

Brazil has recently emerged from the worst-ever recession, in which its GDP growth plummeted from 7.5 percent in 2010 to -3.8 percent in 2015.[44] The country still faces a major pension crisis[45] and may even have to contend with another outbreak of the Zika virus. "There is this idea that Zika is gone, the emergency has been lifted," said Amanda Klasing of Human Rights Watch. "But the risk for another outbreak is there."[46]

As political scandal goes, Brazil's most notable one involves Petrobras, a multinational oil corporation once named the leading ethical enterprise in its field by Geneva-based Covalence Ethical Ranking.[47] The Brazilian government owns more than 50 percent of the common stock and thus maintains voting rights.[48] The investigation into Petrobras, dubbed "Operation Car Wash," looked into allegations that Brazil's biggest construction firms overcharged Petrobras for building contracts, then provided kickbacks to the Petrobras executives and complicit politicians.[49]

In August 2016, the Brazilian Senate impeached President Dilma Rousseff on charges of manipulating the federal budget in an effort to conceal the nation's mounting economic problems.[50] Rousseff was also chairman of Petrobras between 2003 and 2010, the period during which the corruption took place and when the company's state ownership under Lula de Silva was finalized.[51] All told, more than $3 billion was found to be given as bribes to more than 40 high-ranking politicians.

Though Rousseff allegedly had a role in the Petrobras scheme, her impeachment was due to her misrepresentation of economic health during the 2014 campaign. For example, Rousseff's administration effectively borrowed $11 billion from state banks (about 1 percent of Brazil's economy) to fund popular social programs.[52] Rousseff argued that her predecessors had also manipulated the state budget and stated two days before her impeachment, "I am the victim of a process that is rooted in injustice, and legal and political fraud."[53] The contentious proceedings increased social and economic instability. The IMF reported in October 2016 that "confidence appears to have bottomed out in Brazil."[54] The reemergence of modest economic growth in 2017 offers some hope that perhaps the worst of the economic pain has passed. Time will tell.

In Mexico, surveys have shown that citizens place a high priority on fighting the country's endemic and massive problem of political corruption—but also that few have genuine expectations that their politicians will ever reform themselves. President Enrique Peña Nieto's government, deeply unpopular, has been embroiled in a series of scandals, the most prominent one involving Pemex, Mexico's national oil company, and its ties to a Brazilian conglomerate, Odebrecht.[55] The corruption problems make it harder to battle the country's lethal criminal culture. Armed violence in Mexico's Northern Triangle killed 34,000 people in 2016, according to one survey—a higher body count than occurred in Afghanistan during the same time. Much of the violence focuses around the drug trade and is generated by a problem that has Mexico and other Latin American countries deep in its clutches: the phenomenon of international criminal gangs. In Mexico, conflict between the cartels of Los Zetas, Caballeros Templarios, and Sinaloa—headed by the world's most-wanted man, El Chapo, until his 2016 capture—cost 44,000 lives during Nieto's presidency alone (Mexican presidents are limited to one six-year term). The tenure of Nieto's predecessor in office, Felipe Calderón, was even worse, with human rights organizations estimating more than 100,000 deaths.[56]

What makes international criminal gangs so imposing at this point in history is that they have evolved their model of operations; they now operate across vast, increasingly non-hierarchical networks that include public and elected officials as collaborators. These "gray" agents of officialdom—whether in law enforcement, the judiciary, or the government—make cracking down against the criminal organizations even more complicated and difficult. The criminal networks' success at infiltrating official institutions, along with their increasingly dispersed, cross-national scope, explains why El Chapo told Sean Penn in a controversial *Rolling Stone* interview, "The day I don't exist, it's not going to decrease in any way at all.... drug trafficking does not depend on just one person. It depends on a lot of people."[57]

In its July 2018 elections, Mexico handed Andres Manuel Lopez Obrador the presidency in a landslide victory, preparing the country for the most left-wing government in its democratic history. Obrador is a 64-year-old former Mexico City mayor who promises huge increases in spending on social programs and has promised to confront the nation's rampant drug cartels. But Obrador is also a nationalist, with some similarities to Trump, and the two presidents, at least early on, have pledged to work together. Of course, the issues between the two nations remain contentious. Trump campaigned on controlling the United States' southern border and deporting undocumented immigrants, heavily composed of Mexicans fleeing desperate conditions. But any dramatic American effort at large-scale deportation would subject thousands of people to the depredations of criminal gangs. Strengthening the American-Mexican partnership and coming to a mutual understanding on border security is clearly the most constructive approach—challenging as it is to achieve, logistically and politically.

Problems of a very broad nature run across the Latin American region and expand beyond the scope of what I can address here. In keeping with the corruption theme, though, I'd like to call attention to the culture of corruption's special character in Latin America, especially as it pertains to the problem I cited above: the reign of terror of international criminal gangs, which, in turn, both feeds off of and reinforces that culture.

Narco-Crime and Terror and International Criminal Gangs

Narco-crime and corruption is endemic throughout Latin America and exerts power from the lowest municipal levels of government and police to the presidencies. Crime breeds instability and violence, which discourage foreign spending and investment, limiting alternatives to a drug-based economy.

Narco groups act as a sort of totalitarian government supplement. They murder dissidents and engage in cover-ups. Meanwhile, politicians are either threatened by the narco groups or are forced to engage in cover-ups so that their authority is not undermined. Many of these countries rely on the drug economy to support their own, either because they are reliant on a drug crop (coca, as in Peru and Bolivia) or because the illegal money supports their local businesses. Very often prosecutions do not lead to real sentences. A culture of impunity reigns.

That's exemplified in a phrase popular in Brazil that captures the dominance of corruption and the way that citizens accept it. In Portuguese, it is *rouba, mas faz* ("He robs, but he gets things done"). This phrase has enough recognition in the region that, according to urban legend, a well-known congressman and former mayor of the city of Sao Paulo, Paulo Maluf, took maluf@masfaz.com as his email address.[58] In 2000, 47 percent of Brazilian voters surveyed said they would prefer a mayor who was "not totally honest" as long as he "resolved the municipality's problems." In surveys carried out in 2002 and 2007, 40 percent of respondents agreed with the statement that "a politician who carries out a lot of public works, even if he robs a little, is better than a politician who carries out few public works and does not rob at all."[59] This acceptance of corruption is echoed throughout Latin America.

The criminal networks play a huge role in this Latin American corruption and dysfunction. Usually, criminal groups seek control over municipal security forces and the judiciary—the institutions charged with defending against organized crime.[60] But police and anti-narcotics groups are bribed either to act as enforcers or to look the other way. Airport and seaport officials are bribed to ignore trafficking activity. Attorneys and judges are bribed or intimidated to prevent investigation. Gang members run their business from jails, which act as informal networks for criminals.

The reach of criminal organizations in Latin America is such that in Peru, it is widely assumed that the last four elected presidents owe their elections to them. Worse, even when cartel leaders are killed or captured, it often spurs infighting among rival groups and public violence.

With the sway that criminality holds, it should be no surprise that policing in Latin America, as in Africa, is deeply compromised. In Mexico, a 2014 report from the Secretary General of National Public Safety found that in total, 42,214 state and federal police officers were deemed unfit for service—and yet, 17 Mexican states hadn't even dismissed police who failed vetting tests.[61] Many of these states are hotspots for organized crime.[62]

For millions of Mexicans the emblematic case of official corruption, at the governmental and law enforcement level, remains the disappearance of 43 students in Guerrero. In September 2014, municipal police officers shot at three buses of students from a rural teaching college who had reportedly come into town soliciting donations.[63] The college had been linked in the past to anti-cartel protests and resistance of cartel extortion.[64] After the shooting, with six people dead, the police were seen corralling the surviving students into patrol cars. Some of the officers later confessed to turning students over to members of a local drug cartel who, according to the Mexican government, killed them, burned their bodies at a dump in Cocula, and dumped their remains in a river.[65] Mexican authorities claimed that Iguala's then mayor Jose Luis Abarca masterminded the operation. Abarca's wife, Maria de los Angeles Pineda, had ties to drug traffickers.[66] Abarca's ruthlessness and corruption ran deep. He allegedly shot his political rival, Arturo Hernandez. Hernandez's wife, Iguala city councilwoman Sofia Mendoza, said a witness saw the mayor shoot her husband and gave a statement to state prosecutors; they did nothing. Abarca and his wife fled Iguala and were found in Mexico City one month later.[67]

However, the government's official version doesn't square with evidence that the Mexican army was monitoring the movements of the students' buses.[68] Public outrage over the missing students has fed broad discontent with a host of other national issues, such as wealth inequality and federal corruption. The case became a proxy for protest against a corrupt system. The tragedy—and mystery—of the Guerrero students is representative, historian Lorenzo Meyer said, of "the product of decomposition of state structures in Mexico for a long time."[69]

Climate of Fear: The Targeting of Journalists

Targeted killing of journalists, mostly for the uncovering of official corruption, is a scourge in Latin America. It often goes relatively unpunished, with the government declaring cases closed once the hit-men are found, rather than investigating the source of the murders. Between 2006 and 2012, a total of 56 journalists were killed in connection with the drug war in Mexico. In the *Guardian*, Mike O'Connor, a representative for the Committee to Protect Journalists, described just how deep corruption runs in Mexico:

> The silencing of the press and killing of journalists is integral to the reality, the big story, of what is happening here: that the cartels are taking territory.... The inability of the government to really solve hardly any of the crimes against journalists during the four years I've been here is a metaphor for its inability to solve crimes against common citizens. They simply cannot do it. And you wonder: if they can't solve these crimes, why not? Is it because they don't want to?
>
> The government and authorities are ceding territory to the cartels and, for the cartels to take territory, three things have to happen. One is to control the institutions with guns—basically, the police. The second is to control political power. And, for the first two to be effective, you have to control the press....
>
> You can't have a democracy without an informed public.... Mexico has all the structures of a democracy, but it does not have an informed public. It has a public which knows the starting lineup of the Green Bay Packers, but doesn't know who runs the city or the state they live in. It does not know who is in charge. People know it's corrupt, but they don't know what's going on, because the reporters cannot ask: 'Who's in charge?' You cannot find in your newspaper, in most parts of the country, information about the big story—and the big story is that organised crime has taken over, or is working very successfully at taking over, your city, town or village.
>
> And if you report that, you get killed.[70]

According to the Committee to Protect Journalists, about 90 percent of journalist murders in Mexico since 1992 have gone unpunished.[71] Mexico is not unique. In the first six months of 2016, 21 journalists were killed in Latin America: nine in Mexico, five in Guatemala, three in Honduras, two in Brazil, two in Venezuela, and one in El Salvador.[72]

STUBBORN REALITIES

Looking beyond the complexities of the situations in both Latin America and Africa, it's important to remember that no matter what efforts advanced nations, led by the United States, make to help—and they have made many, and should continue trying—the fundamental maladies are broader and deeper than mere policy, embedded not just in specific national cultures but in cultural struggles. French president Emmanuel Macron captured this idea well, I think, when, at a G20 summit in 2017, he was asked by a reporter from Ivory Coast what the world's leading nations were willing to commit in the effort to fight poverty in Africa. The reporter made reference to the Marshall Plan after World War II in Europe, which would cost about $150 billion in today's dollars. Macron's response:

I don't believe in this reasoning, forgive me for my directness. We among the west have been discussing such Marshall plans for Africa for many years.... If it was so simple it would be fixed already. The Marshall plan was a reconstruction plan, a material plan in a region that already had it equilibriums, its borders and its stability. The problem is Africa faces are completely different and are much different and are "civilizational." What are the problems? Failed states, complex democratic transitions and extremely difficult demographic transitions. Multiple trafficking routes that pose severe issues— drugs, human trafficking, weapons. Violent fundamentalism and Islamic terrorism. All these create major issues in a region that at the same time has some examples of excellent growth that prove the continent is a land of opportunity. So if we want a serious answer to African issues and African problems, we must develop a series of politics that are much more sophisticated than a simple Marshall plan or money transfer...As of today, spending billions of dollars out right will stabilize nothing. So the transformation plan that we have to conduct together must be developed according to African interests by and with African leaders. It must be a plan that must take into account the issues I've described.[73]

Macron did not mean to suggest, nor would I, that efforts are futile, only that they needed to be made with a decent respect for the imposing nature of some of these problems, a humility that Western nations have not always shown in their efforts in the developed world. Former British prime minister David Cameron made a similar argument a few years back, again in reference to Africa, when he said that the West needed to focus less on the financial quantity of aid packages and more on what he called "the golden thread" of institutional and societal well-being: stable governments and rule of law, respect for human rights, minimal corruption, and free exchange of information.

Granted, those sound like high bars to set in the developing world, in which some countries seem to lack *all* these things. Yet it is certainly true that no matter how much the world's advanced nations spend, money and aid programs alone cannot lift third world countries out of poverty and dysfunction. The West will remain crucial to their successes, but our efforts must take the long view of visionary (and sometimes tough-minded) diplomatic efforts to support political and institutional reform. And yes, we must remember humility: we must be able to balance, on the one hand, our deep-seated conviction that all people deserve to live in freedom with an understanding, born of hard experience, that national and civilizational cultures exert a gravity of their own. Within such a balance, however, there is much room for sound efforts on the part of advanced nations. Without such efforts, the world's struggling places will face a grim climb.

CHAPTER EIGHT

A GLOBAL ENERGY WAR?

"If the United States opens up the global gas market to unprecedented levels of transparency and competition, which its shale-extracted LNG [liquefied natural gas] exports appear capable of doing, Russian President Vladimir Putin's influence in the region will further diminish."

—ANTHONY FENSOM, *NATIONAL INTEREST*[1]

In November 2017, a ballistic missile attack from Yemen, fired by the country's Houthi militias, was intercepted on its way to Saudi Arabia. Iran had "enabled" the attack, the United States said, warning that such aggression would "threaten regional security and undermine UN efforts to negotiate an end" to the Yemeni civil war. In blaming Iran, Washington was only following the lead of its allies, the Saudis, who had already accused Iran of sponsoring the attack. Tehran is regarded as a key backer of the Houthi rebels and a supplier of their weapons.

The incident was just another in an escalating series of events and rhetoric between the two adversarial Middle East powers—two nations that might well be on a path toward war. (In July 2018, the Saudis announced the suspension of oil shipments through the Bab al-Mandeb strait in the Red Sea after two ships were attacked by Yemen's Iran-backed Houthis.) If a Saudi-Iranian war did break out, the potential consequences would be not only regional but also global, because of the ramifications on energy supplies. Almost 20 percent of the world's oil travels through the Strait of Hormuz, the sea route that connects the Persian Gulf with the global marketplace—and a war between Iran and Saudi Arabia could easily shut it down, causing havoc on world energy markets.

Given the volatile politics of so many countries today—in which domestic social stability seems tenuous at best, political leadership lacks public trust, and regional tensions threaten new or expanded wars—the energy stakes couldn't be higher. The Middle East, unsurprisingly, remains a focal point about concerns regarding world energy markets, especially in regard to political upheaval and war. But the truth is that globally, trouble spots abound; all could have major ramifications for energy prices and supplies.

At the same time, this is also an era of great hope in the energy sector, especially from a Western perspective, because of the emergence of the United States as a global energy power, largely through the transformative fuel potential of shale gas, extracted through hydraulic fracturing, or fracking. My concern, however, is that this very sense of promise—as with past eras of promise—coexists with extraordinary volatility and the potential for disaster. This is not least because what sparks hope in the United States and among its allies is seen as a mortal threat by some of the world's energy powers, which also happen to be among the world's most autocratic regimes.

And at the top of that list is Vladimir Putin's Russia, which has been working tirelessly—and provocatively—to stave off the challenges posed by this new energy landscape and to preserve its dominating, and often coercive, energy advantages.

RUSSIAN ENERGY AGGRESSION

Moscow is moving aggressively against any diminution of its energy influence. Putin is working on multiple fronts, but the key area of operation remains Europe, where Russia remains the main energy player; state-owned Gazprom supplies about one-third of European gas demand.[2] In 2012, the EU accounted for 52 percent of all Russia's exports, and more than two-thirds of those exports were in fuel and energy.[3] In 2015, Russia controlled more than one-quarter of Europe's solid fuels and crude oil and nearly two-thirds of its natural gas.[4]

But with the United States beginning to enter the European market with liquefied natural gas (LNG), Putin senses the importance of strengthening his hand. The main chip in his strategy here is Nord Stream 2, the new export gas pipeline running from Russia to Europe across the Baltic Sea, with a capacity of 55 billion cubic meters of gas per year, planned for finalization in 2019. What Russia is promising with Nord Stream 2 is a bolstered supply of Russian gas to Europe—highly desirable for Europeans, as the Russian company sees it, given that the Continent's gas production is waning, even as demand continues to grow.[5] In April 2017, Gazprom CEO Alexi Miller said that Russian gas exports to Europe will continue to grow until at least 2035 and that Gazprom will provide the bulk of it.

Here is why Nord Stream 2 is crucial: it will make Germany the main hub for gas imports into Europe, via a pipeline that bypasses Ukraine. With the completion of Nord Stream 2, Moscow's reliance on Nord Stream 1 would decline, reducing the importance of any relationship between Russia and Ukraine.[6] Russia would eventually be providing Germany with 50 percent of its oil; German companies have a financial stake in the €9.5 billion contract.[7] Germany welcomes the pipeline due to the large amounts of oil the country consumes—even if, effectively, Nord Stream 2 means that German energy will be in the hands of Moscow. (Indeed, on his July 2018 European trip, President Trump chided Germany for its energy dependence on Moscow. The Germans, the president said, were "captive to Russia," a situation that Trump found particularly galling in that Germany was paying billions for Russian energy that could have been spent on defense—a bill that the United States continues to pay instead.[8])

Nord Stream 2 is becoming a political battle within the EU. Against the backdrop of concern that the new pipeline will make Europe too reliant on Russian fuel, an East-West split is developing. Eastern Europe opposed the project from the beginning, as did the Obama administration. Ukraine is anguished over how Moscow could use the pipeline to strengthen its energy grip on Europe and do so in a way that bypasses Ukraine. Critics pointed out that the original pipeline, Nord Stream 1, was only operating at about half of capacity, leading to questions about Russian ulterior motives—the ulterior motive being, principally, the marginalization of Ukraine's economy. Moreover, the new pipeline would only deepen Western Europe's energy reliance.

"The project is not an economic one," Polish prime minister Beata Szydlo told German chancellor Angela Merkel. "It's a geopolitical one."[9]

That's certainly the way that the Ukrainians see it.

"Russia is moving its traditional Ukraine transit to Nord Stream I," says Andriy Kobolyev, CEO of Naftogaz, Gazprom's supplier in Ukraine. "If you look at the numbers on gas consumption in Europe out to 2020, it is obvious to me that if we get a Nord Stream II and if we get the expansion of Turkish Stream, which is already happening, with two pipelines there now instead of one, then that will mean Ukrainian transit of Russian gas into Europe will equal zero."

That's the key point: right now, Ukraine's economy benefits from the country's role as an energy middleman to Europe; it transports Russian gas through pipelines that traverse the country. Estimates suggest that this commerce accounts for about 10 percent of the Ukraine budget—meaning that losing it would constitute a serious blow. "On one hand, we want to keep Gazprom as a client and they still need us to get into Europe," says Kobolyev, but "if Nord Stream II happens, they will no longer need our pipeline, or will surely use us a lot less."[10] Eastern European countries like Slovakia and Poland also worry about the new pipeline strengthening Russia's leverage, especially given Moscow's past habits of restricting gas flows to its neighbors when it is engaged in political disputes—as it has done to Ukraine in the past.[11]

As for the broader EU, it has expressed its objection to the pipeline as well, seeing it as an obstacle to EU goals to "diversify and secure gas-supply sources, curb dependence on major providers like Gazprom, and prevent a concentration of transit routes."[12] But the EU concedes that it has no legal authority to stop it—and more recently, Western Europe is starting to weaken in its opposition, even criticism, of the project. With greater rates of oil consumption, many Western European nations welcome Nord Stream 2, in part because they believe that it will keep prices low.[13] Sweden initially blocked Russia from using its ports as part of the pipeline's construction. Swedish national leaders still see the new Russian pipeline in the context of Putin's increasingly aggressive moves in the Baltics.[14] Swedish defense minister Peter Hultqvist said, "We are against Nord Stream 2," calling it "a problem from a European perspective."[15] Yet now Sweden has relented, at least at the local level. While political leaders in Stockholm oppose the pipeline, in the tiny town of Karlshamn, local Swedes allowed a Gazprom subcontractor to store pipes for the project. The *Wall Street Journal* saw it as a classic example of Putin's "divide-and-conquer strategy." The Swedish example seems telling—public opposition, practical compromise.

And when the pipeline has a staunch supporter in the Continent's economic and political power, Germany, it has a strong ally indeed. Chancellor Angela Merkel has said the pipeline is no one but Germany's business; Berlin may regard the scheduled completion of the pipeline in 2019 as the moment when the country becomes the energy hub of Europe. Certainly from Germany's perspective, the pipeline offers a means to cut costs and lock in suppliers.[16]

Another factor working in the pipeline's favor is the fear on the Continent about tensions between Moscow and Washington. European officials worry that any escalation of discord between the United States and Russia could result in a Russian energy blockade. Although the United States could provide Europe with LNG and oil, the infrastructure is not yet in place to do a full switch from Russian dependence.[17] Congress is pushing new American sanctions targeting any company that contributes to the development of Nord Stream 2—including European companies—and the EU wants assurances from Washington that the new sanctions will not affect European Union interests in any way.[18]

Russia's European moves aren't confined to Nord Stream: it has also announced its intention to make use of the Trans-Adriatic Pipeline (TAP), a key route on what is known as the Southern Gas Corridor. TAP is vital to Europe because it would be the first non-Russian gas pipeline to the Continent for almost a decade. Through TAP, Europe could begin to lessen its dependence on Gazprom, which currently takes one-third of the European gas market.[19] It's one of the EU's highest priorities in this regard, and American investment has backed the initiative as well.

The plan up to now has been to bring Azerbaijani gas to Europe via the TAP. But Russian entry onto the scene will complicate this goal and potentially change the game entirely. As one EU official puts it, a Russian presence would be "totally contrary to everything we have agreed with partners."[20]

Then there are the Russian moves in the Middle East. In October 2017, Russia and Saudi Arabia announced a $1 billion deal to invest in energy projects—oil, gas, electricity, and renewable energy—a project described as the "tip of the iceberg" between the two countries.[21] Not traditional allies by any means—the two countries back different sides in the Syrian civil war, and the Saudis are traditional American allies— Moscow and Riyadh have nevertheless been moving closer together through the common ground they share on one crucial point: they both wish to blunt the effect of the United States' increased presence in global oil and gas markets, especially with the boom in American shale production, which creates a supply glut and drives down prices, much to the dismay of both countries. The October 2017 story about the energy deal between the two countries wasn't the first news on this front: a month earlier, Bloomberg reported that Russia and Saudi Arabia were colluding on cuts to oil production—again, with the interest being preserving, if not increasing, oil prices in the face of growing supplies. The production cuts will extend to May 2018, at least.[22]

"The Kingdom affirms its readiness to extend the production cut agreement, which proved its feasibility by rebalancing supply and demand," said Saudi Crown Prince Mohammed bin Salman.[23]

Russian energy outreach also extends to the Middle East and North Africa, where Putin is looking to use Russia's state-owned energy companies to get in on the action in Arab nations rich in fossil fuels.[24] Rosneft, the Russian state-owned oil firm run by a close Putin associate, has made serious inroads into Iraq and Libya. In February 2017, Rosneft announced an agreement to buy crude oil from Libya's National Oil Corporation and to extend oil exploration in that country. It also announced that it would buy oil from Iraq's Kurdish region and help the Kurds find new oil markets. Russia is effectively telling the Kurds that it will take care of distributing their oil, which has been a problem for Erbīl for years, due to tensions with Baghdad over oil contracts. For the Kurds, letting Moscow handle distribution ensures that their oil will flow freely, bypassing the strictures imposed by Iraq—which just happens to be a government closely allied with Washington.

Energy-related Russian incursions into the Middle East have been in process for some time. In December 2016, Rosneft bought 30 percent of Egypt's offshore Zohr gas field. In February 2017, the same month that the firm announced its Libyan and Kurdistan deals, it also announced that it would begin drilling in the Block 12 oil field in southern Iraq. The following month, Rosneft bought Egyptian crude oil for the first time and also signed a deal to supply the North African nation with LNG. And Rosneft might also make bids for offshore rights in Lebanon.

Taken together, this dizzying litany of activity represents major progress in Russia's strategic penetration of Middle East energy markets.

Finally, Russia's continued closeness with China also has an energy dimension. In September 2017, CEFC China Energy purchased a minority stake in Rosneft PJSC (the Russian oil company) for $9 billion, deepening the political and energy ties between the countries.[25] With the agreement, CEFC gains access to eastern Russia oilfields, close to the border between the two countries—"the first time a Chinese company has taken a stake in one of the most important businesses controlled by the Kremlin," as the *Financial Times* explained.[26] "We are happy that it was specifically a Chinese corporation," said Rosneft CEO Igor Sechin."[27] Indeed, every sign is that China and Russia are increasing their corporate partnerships in the energy area. Russia has been steadily upping its supply of oil to China, looking to get Beijing's consumption up to one million barrels per day.[28] Russia may soon surpass Saudi Arabia as China's main oil supplier.[29]

THE PUSHBACK: AMERICAN ENERGY PRESENCE

The Russian energy push comes with a crucial context: the American energy revival, a resurgence bordering on a revolution, owing to the transformative impact of shale gas and the technology that extracts it—hydraulic fracturing, or fracking. The United States once produced half the amount of natural gas of Saudi Arabia and Russia but now equals those two nations' output—thanks to fracking. America has become a global force in the energy market, and fracking is largely the reason.

Fracking technology, continuously improving, makes the extraction of the abundant supplies of shale gas relatively cheap. "Just compare an offshore well at $170m with a vertical shale well that costs under $5m, with a five-year payout for a successful deepwater well versus a mere five-month payout for a shale play," the *Financial Times* points out. "And multiply a single, individual shale well by hundreds of wells and hundreds of decisions and you get a new world order."[30]

The impact of fracking can be seen in a simple statistic: in 2017, for the first time in 60 years, the United States became a net exporter of natural gas.[31] In fact, America has become the world's leading gas producer. According to the International Energy Agency, the United States is on track by 2025 to be a net exporter of all fossil fuels, for the first time since 1948.[32] The rise of America as a shale gas power has transformed the world energy market, eroding the power of OPEC, which now shares world leadership with Russia and the United States; among them, the three entities account for 40 percent of "combined liquids production" worldwide. Before the rise of U.S. shale, gas power in the world was held largely by the members of what was known as the Gas Exporting Countries Forum, or GECF, dominated by Russia, Qatar, and Iran. Russian energy minister Sergey Shmatko called it the "gas OPEC."[33]

America's newfound gas leadership is transforming markets—and options—for American allies in Europe, who now have a chance to escape from the clutches of Gazprom and its price gouging. While Western Europe remains tied to Russian energy supplies, nations in the east are more willing to avail themselves of U.S. supplies. In June 2017, Poland received its first shipment of American LNG, to much fanfare. Polish leaders are bullish on American LNG, for understandable reasons: up to now, the country has been nearly totally dependent on Russia for energy imports—meaning, of course, that it has also been consistently vulnerable to Russian bullying and manipulation. "If the United States opens up the global gas market to unprecedented levels of transparency and competition, which its shale-extracted LNG exports appear capable of doing," writes Anthony Fensom in the National Interest, "Russian President Vladimir Putin's influence in the region will further diminish."[34] This is a big deal, because if Fensom is right—and the facts on the ground suggest that he is—Russia's ability to use energy blackmail to intimidate and control countries like Bulgaria, Romania, Poland, and especially Ukraine will be seriously eroded.

The other big factor that could potentially rattle Putin's energy strategy is the growing LNG market. More and more countries are either importers or exporters of the fuel. LNG, natural gas that is cooled into a liquid form, takes up just 1/600 of the volume of regular natural gas—making it transportable on ships. Traditionally, gas had to be moved through pipelines, limiting the geographic scope of a country's energy markets. With LNG, the gas can be transported across long distances, in large quantities, at reasonable cost.[35]

For importers, LNG represents an alternate fuel source to the pipe-lines controlled by Moscow. One key example of such alternate routes is known as the "floating pipeline," a supertanker that taps offshore gas sources at such volumes that they resemble an actual pipeline; unlike a traditional pipeline, however, the floating pipeline can move to new targets, operating at a fraction of the cost of the older arrangements. These new technologies give another edge to LNG in the energy market—and to the United States, which is becoming a key player in the LNG space.

The United States is growing its list of LNG export customers, which now include Brazil, India, the United Arab Emirates, Argentina, Portugal, Kuwait, Chile, Spain, China, Jordan, and the United Kingdom. The Trump administration has announced its intention to move faster on approvals for LNG export terminals—a hopeful sign for the future. With some European countries still deeply dependent on Moscow for gas supplies, the U.S. push into LNG comes at an auspicious time. And the LNG threat to Russian energy dominance doesn't come from the United States alone; other countries are trying to use the fuel to pursue a greater degree of self-sufficiency. In 2014, Lithuania, which had been reliant on Moscow for its entire gas supply, built an LNG import terminal; not long afterward, in negotiations with Gazprom, it managed to secure a 20 percent discount. The dynamic that Gazprom always relied on in the past was a simple and coercive one: the country could play hardball and turn off the energy spigots, or threaten to, if its customers complained too loudly. Now such threats will be less menacing.

Without question, then, the world energy market is changing, and changing in ways that, for the most part, look potentially adverse for Russia. Moscow will retain its strong hand on the European continent for the time being—perhaps even a few more decades—but the long-term future is uncertain, especially in terms of its monopolistic expectations. European countries have been, more or less, captive markets for Russian gas for a long time, but that era is ending, even if slowly. Faced with energy customers that have broadening options, Gazprom will have to learn to compromise on contracts instead of playing its usual game of hardball. This is especially true regarding price, on which Gazprom has preferred to dictate long-term deals with almost no negotiating leverage for its buyers. Crucial, too, could be the lessening of Moscow's ability to use gas supplies as a foreign policy tool.

It's also worth noting that the Obama administration's sanctions against Russia have had some effect. I've been critical of their insufficiency, and I stand by that; Putin has been skillful and determined in working around them. But they are causing some pain, and when taken in tandem with the global drop in crude prices, their bite has been felt in Moscow, where economic indicators are hardly robust. It's little reported that Russia is facing a serious poverty problem, with nearly 20 million people, more than 13 percent of the population according to Rosstat, the government's statistical agency, fitting into that category.[36] The Russian economy contracted in 2015 and 2016 before returning to modest growth in 2017.

Though it's hard to quantify the sanctions' impact, it's likely that they have played a role in the difficulties—as even Putin has acknowledged. "Sanctions are hurting us," he told a 2016 investment forum. "We hear that they are not a problem really, but they are, particularly with technology transfers in oil and gas. We are coping."[37]

Putin's coping abilities are legendary by now; if we can count on anything, it is that he will play Russia's energy hand with as much skill and determination as he can muster, and he'll probably manage a few surprises. Still, we shouldn't lose sight of how transformative the American energy presence has already been. If you doubt it, look no further than the strange-bedfellows alliance between the Russians and the Saudis. On the other hand, as I suggested earlier, America's emergence as a power player is also the element that makes the current global energy situation so volatile: as with so many other instances of major change, whether nationally or globally, turbulence is bound to follow.

I wouldn't trade the United States' new technological powers in the energy field for anything, but at the same time, I'm wary about what the effects could be for tensions and even potential conflict. This worry is further exacerbated when one considers the reduced price of oil since 2014 and what impact that might have, not just on energy markets but on geopolitics as well. Considering the players, such concerns are no trifle.

THE PRICE FAULT LINE AND THE FUTURE

Since 2011, gas prices have dropped by more than $2 per gallon—a by-product of the collapsing price of oil. At the time this chapter was being written, oil stood at $57 per barrel, down from $100 per barrel as late as 2014 (but significantly better than the $27 it had plunged to in early 2016). Politicians like Barack Obama touted the low prices at the pump to their constituents: "Gas under two bucks a gallon ain't bad," Obama told a State of the Union audience, and for Americans, this was certainly true.

But falling energy prices come with all kinds of geopolitical ramifications, many of which have the potential to make an already-tense global environment more so. As I said above, I'm greatly heartened by the United States' progress with shale gas, not only as a step toward energy independence but also as a major new engine of economic growth and job creation—both of which we've seen come to fruition in places like North Dakota. My concern, however, is that considering the players involved in the energy markets—especially authoritarian regimes like Russia, Saudi Arabia, and especially Venezuela—the falling energy prices could lead to further destabilization, both within these countries and outside them, in the form of more aggressive moves.

"Where regime stability rests on a classic 'oil pact' (that is, the provision of economic benefits to key constituencies in exchange for political support or, at least, passivity), low prices create a toxic mix of weak currencies, inflation, growing debt, budget and trade deficits, rising food prices, cuts in essential services and soaring poverty," says Terry Lynn Karl, author of *The Paradox of Plenty: Oil Booms and Petrostates*.[38] That formulation applies to Venezuela more than any other country. By now, Venezuela has more or less achieved the status of a failed state—with an economy in freefall, triple-digit inflation, and humanitarian and constitutional crises—and it has no ability to hedge against the lower oil prices. Oil exports represent more than half of the collapsing socialist country's GDP. Even a recovery of oil prices couldn't pull the country out of its dire situation, especially with a government default on debt looming. Still, the loss in revenue will only worsen a crisis for which a political solution remains unclear; the one dependable conclusion is that millions of Venezuelans are likely to continue suffering.

"Geopolitically," writes Ian Bremner, "the impact of low oil prices is concentrated in the Middle East, where political structures are brittle and based on oil wealth-supported patronage. Across the region, there are immediate and direct security threats without any social, political or economic reform processes in place to address the challenges these regimes face from the inside. What keeps these countries together—as well as those that rely on them for support—when the oil money runs out?"[39]

Much speculation focuses on how Saudi Arabia will proceed. On the one hand, the kingdom has a hedge against falling prices and against the encroachments of the United States into the gas markets: their expanding presence in Asian markets, where countries like China and India are consuming rapidly increasing portions of global imports. On the other, the Saudis are concerned enough about the American natural gas and LNG presence that they have taken the unlikely step of collaborating with Moscow. In 2016, astute observers, such as Dennis Ross, speculated that low oil prices might drive the Russians to work more closely with Iran against Saudi Arabia; the Iranians, too, feel the pinch from lower oil prices, which make economic growth for a nation trying to emerge from American sanctions much more difficult. But Ross spoke in 2016, before the Saudis made common cause with Moscow on reducing oil output. The situation, needless to say, is complicated and unpredictable. Already, we have seen surprises.

As for Moscow itself, the falling oil price is having a blunt-force impact, without question. Lower oil prices will continue to hurt at home, regardless of what success Russia might have with Nord Stream 2, which can be seen both as a means to hedge against American penetration of European markets and as a tool of economic marginalization of Ukraine. Neither goal addresses the price problem. Russia needs those prices to return to $100 a barrel—hence its strange alliance, if alliance it can be called, with the Saudis. The Russian economy is showing the effects of lower oil prices. Wage growth is stagnant, poverty is on the rise, and by some accounts, the average Russian is spending 50 percent of his or her disposable income to cover food costs. Some businesses are late in paying workers; bankruptcies have ticked up. While Moscow has kept a lid on political discontent in the capital, protests in smaller Russian cities have become more commonplace. In the face of what looks to be mounting domestic discontent, Putin will pursue further antidemocratic political consolidation at home, and likely further aggressive action, or at least aggressive provocations and rhetoric, abroad.

My concern is that energy will continue to be the terrain on which broader global battles are waged—especially since, in the European context, any significant transition from dependence on Russian gas will be slow. "Russia will for sure remain Europe's largest gas supplier for at least two more decades," says Vladimir Drebentsov, chief economist for Russia and CIS at BP in Moscow.[40] BP projects that Russia's share of EU gas consumption will rise from about 30 percent today to 40 percent in 2035.

So the obstacles are clear, at least in Europe: an authoritarian Russia that will clearly take every step that it can to preserve the linchpin of its economic vitality—its energy exports, especially to Europe. But Russia needs the European market as much as Europe needs Russian gas—thus underscoring the importance of American policy, especially as regards shale gas. This is why political leadership in the United States will be so crucial. Political opposition to fracking in the United States remains widespread; in some states, especially New York, which has rich shale deposits, fracking has been banned, thus forestalling any chance to extract natural gas in that region of the country. Until the United States fully embraces its shale potential, it will not be playing in this game at full strength. A crucial driver of the future will be how the politics plays out, not just in America but also in Europe: as we have seen, the Continent tends to divide on the issue of Russian gas dependence, by geography—with the west more sanguine about continued reliance on Moscow and central Europe and especially Eastern Europe much more eager to find alternative sources. American leadership will be pivotal.

The bottom line: playing at full strength, America can seriously degrade Russian energy power on the European continent—a development that would have positive economic, political, and strategic ramifications. But we need leadership to make it happen. The same imperative applies to energy tensions elsewhere, whether in Venezuela—where America must play a central role in ensuring some kind of peaceful resolution to the energy-rich nation's political dissolution—or Asia, where China and India are consuming exponentially increasing quantities of energy supplies. The United States has the resources to outflank Russia and other authoritarian energy providers in these markets as well—but again, only if it shows the proper measure of strategic vision and resolve. No other country in the world possesses this kind of dispositive potential.

In short, then, when it comes to the roiling global energy climate, the indispensable nation is, once again, the United States.

PART III

A WAY
FORWARD

CHAPTER NINE

RELIGION AND AMERICAN LEADERSHIP

"We have no government armed with power capable of contending with human passions unbridled by morality and religion."

—JOHN ADAMS[1]

One of the crises of our time is the increasing historical amnesia among the young—a paradox in an information age in which knowledge should theoretically be more available to more people than at any other time in human history. Yet survey after survey shows us that the young generation has less understanding of Western civilization and culture than any generation before them—and less appreciation of the heritage of open societies based on democratic norms and, crucially, on religious tolerance: freedom of worship and conscience. This ignorance, or, if one prefers, naivete, has genuine consequences for how future generations in the West will regard the non-Western world—a world that, by and large, has very different ideas about religious liberty, pluralism, and tolerance.

From the Middle East, where ISIS's reign of terror might be on the wane but Islamic fundamentalism remains brutal and pervasive; to China, where a Communist government continues to repress a broad range of religious communities, whom it sees as a threat to ideological control; to Russia, where a new partnership between Vladimir Putin's government and the Russian Orthodox Church has resulted in diminishing religious liberty for those professing other faiths; to Southeast Asia and Africa, where repression, forced migrations, and religious warfare are all too common, it should be clear to a Western observer that the safest place for religion—all religions—is in the democratic nations of the West, led by the United States, which essentially created religious liberty and pluralism.

And yet, when it comes to religion, and especially the civilization's defining religion—Christianity—the West is troubled. Where elsewhere around the world religion seems to be often put toward authoritarian or terroristic uses, or its free exercise is suppressed, in the West, where Christianity has underpinned democracy and human rights, the faith itself on the wane. Among the more educated, especially, churchgoing and belief in God have shown steady declines over several decades; younger generations seem more and more comfortable with moral relativism, to the point of incoherence. This has implications for Western societies not only in terms of their future, but also in terms of their foreign policy and leadership—and when I say this, I mean America, particularly, the country that has led with a religious impulse since its founding. Many object to the religious underpinnings of U.S. foreign policy, but it is my contention that, warts and all, the Judeo-Christian moralistic quality in modern American foreign policy has been a boon to the world, on balance, even allowing for its missteps, overreaches, and undeniable hubris. We need to reckon with it and make peace with it, lest we cede world leadership to others whose ideas are quite different—and far more adverse to human liberty, human rights, and peace.

In today's climate, perhaps the best way to get a sense of what is at stake in America's religious notions of itself, both at home and abroad, is to consider how religion is deployed as an instrument of authoritarian power elsewhere in the world, or, alternatively, how its free exercise is repressed—in contrast with the West, and especially with the United States, on both counts.

RUSSIA: NATIONALISM AND NIHILISM, WITH RELIGION AS A SUPPORT

In Russia, religious repression is on the rise, though not in a traditional way—that is, it is not so much the free exercise of religion that is suppressed, but the exercise of religions other than that of the Russian Orthodox Church, which has entered into a de facto power alliance with Vladimir Putin's government. "Over time, the Russian government has come to treat the Moscow Patriarchate of the Russian Orthodox Church as a de facto state church, strongly favoring it in various areas of state sponsorship, including subsidies, the education system and military chaplaincies," reports the U.S. Commission on International Religious Freedom. "This favoritism has fostered a climate of hostility toward other religions."[2] This seems like an understatement in light of the current climate.

"President Putin is our leader...given to us by God," says Konstantin Malofeev, owner of Tsargrad TV in Moscow. The network's fastest-growing channel is devoted to the Russian Orthodox faith and hard-line, right-wing views. Alexander Dugin, editor-in-chief of the Orthodox channel, says that the Church is filling the void left by Communism.

Unfortunately, the form that this new devotion has been taking, often in tandem with state encouragement and support, is persecution of other faiths. The 2016 Yarovaya Law (named after one of its sponsors) put new legal restrictions on evangelizing and religious missionary work, defined as "the activity of a religious association, aimed at disseminating information about its beliefs among people who are not participants (members, followers) in that religious association, with the purpose of involving these people as participants (members, followers)." It's a law that seems clearly pointed at faiths other than the Russian Orthodox Church—and that is how it seems to be operating, so far.

No faith has borne the brunt quite as severely as Jehovah's Witnesses. The Russian Supreme Court has labeled the church "extremist" and confiscated its property. Jehovah's Witnesses have had their homes and places of worship attacked. "We run risks when we just talk to someone about the Bible," said one adherent, "let alone about our teachings. Any conversation may raise suspicions—they will go and inform the police."

Others who have simply tried to hold political meetings to discuss the religious atmosphere have also seen their homes or meeting places invaded and ransacked by authorities. Authorities even have a new law on which they can bring charges: it is now illegal in Russia to "insult the feelings of religious believers"—again, it is Russian Orthodox believers, almost certainly, to whom this law refers, to the exclusion of all others.

The change in the fate of the Russian Orthodox Church is a remarkable outgrowth of Putinism. During the Communist era, all religions in the Soviet Union faced persecution. But since the fall of Communism, 25,000 Orthodox churches have been built or restored in Russia, with the backing of the Putin government.[3] It is a truly amazing turnaround from Communist times, when Lenin wrote the words that have been immortalized as a socialist gospel ever since: "Religion is the opium of the people.... All modern religions and churches, all and every kind of religious organisations are always considered by Marxism as the organs of bourgeois reaction, used for the protection of the exploitation and the stupefaction of the working class." But of course, Russia had centuries of devotion to the Orthodox Church, and religious faith was never entirely stamped out by the Communists, no matter how brutal or repressive they became. What changed, after Putin took power in 2000, was the posture of the Kremlin toward the Orthodox Church: Putin increasingly began to see an ally, especially in the Church's spiritual leader, Patriarch Kirill—one that shared his socially conservative views and that could happily align itself with his nationalist, pro-Russia vision. This vision, in the age of globalization, became increasingly anomalous among advanced nations, like the United States and the countries of Western Europe, which prided themselves on their multiculturalist tolerance.

Indeed, it is not multiculturalist tolerance that motivates Russia or the Russian Orthodox Church. As Nicolai N. Petro demonstrated in an important article in the *National Interest,* the Russian social and cultural vision tends to be the inverse of the Western one, both domestically and internationally: whereas the United States and its Western European allies celebrate multiculturalism at home, Russia pushes for greater social and religious homogeneity; but whereas the United States and Western Europe pursue an internationalist vision, with a single standard applied to democracy, human rights, press freedom, and religious liberty, Russia believes that each nation is fully sovereign in these areas and that different national cultures lead to different practices and customs. These practices and customs must be respected, Moscow believes, not threatened with U.N. action or trade retaliation in the form of economic sanctions.

As Petro summarizes:

Russia opposes the adoption of any single set of cultural values as the standard for international behavior. Many in the West counter that Western values are not just a lone cultural standard, but the *de facto* universal standard. Russia labels this unilateralism and advocates a multipolar world order based on pluriculturalism as a better alternative.

Pluriculturalism argues that there is an inherent ("God-given," according to Vladimir Putin) value to diversity among nations. This is distinct from multiculturalism which values diversity within nations. Russia assigns diversity within nations a lower priority than it does diversity among nations. By contrast, Western states more typically prize diversity within nations (the rights of the individual), whereas among nations they seek to subordinate national cultural differences to standards, such as human rights, that express modern Western values.[4]

Russia's impassioned re-embrace of the Orthodox Church, and especially the nexus between the Church and aggressively conservative social, moral, and nationalist views espoused by Putin, has put Russia at the forefront as a standard-bearer of what might be called the global Christian Right. Again, note the irony, considering how Communist Russia for most of the twentieth century was the *bête noire* of all religious communities, liberal and conservative. Not anymore: even in the West, Putin is winning some converts. Franklin Graham lauded the Russian leader for "protecting traditional Christianity,"[5] and Bryan Fischer of the American Family Association called the Russian president the "lion of Christianity."[6]

None of this changes the stubborn fact that the new Russian religious orthodoxy is a far cry from the American vision of religious liberty and pluralism, both within and among nations. With Putin's tightening alliance with the Russian Orthodox Church, and the increasingly troublesome manifestations of that alliance, Russia has become a symbolic anti-example of religious flourishing—its de facto state church enjoying a resurgence with the blessing of the Kremlin, while other faiths face mounting adversity.

And yet, as discouraging as the example of Russia is, China is even worse.

CHINA: THE CLAMPDOWN

"Pope Francis loves China and loves the people of China, its history and population. We hope China can have a great future," said Monsignor Marcelo Sanchez Sorondo, head of the Vatican's Pontifical Academy of Sciences, in August 2017.[7] Speaking in Beijing, where he was attending a conference, the monsignor was trying to reiterate the pope's desire to foster warmer relations with the People's Republic of China, and perhaps someday to visit—despite nearly three-quarters of a century of frosty relations between the Vatican and Beijing, dating back to the victory of the Chinese Communists led by Mao Zedong in 1949. But despite Francis's efforts, it has looked more recently like China and the Vatican will not have a meeting of the minds and that relations will likely remain distant. The main stumbling block between them is symbolic of the issues around freedom of religion, of any faith, in China: in the case of the Catholic Church, Beijing wants control over the naming of bishops in China, the better to vet and control them—and the Vatican cannot acquiesce in that demand.

In a nutshell, that struggle for control underpins the modern story of religious repression in China—the Communist Party cannot cede control of people's hearts, minds, and consciences, and thus, while it allows more religious freedom than under the darkest days of Mao, it is one of the world's more repressive governments when it comes to freedom of conscience and faith.

Freedom of conscience was the life's work of Liu Xiaobo, the long-time democracy advocate, who died in the custody of the Chinese government in July 2017—the "first Nobel Peace Prize winner to die in custody since German pacifist Carl von Ossietzky, the 1935 recipient, who died under surveillance after years confined to Nazi concentration camps," according to the *Guardian*. Liu's long and brave struggle in China included helping to draft a human rights declaration, Charter 08, which declared, among other principles, that "human rights are not bestowed by a state" and that "without freedom China will always remain far from civilized ideals."[8]

This lack of freedom encompasses many areas—political freedom, certainly, as well as freedom from educational indoctrination by the Communist Party. But obstacles to the free exercise of religion have become more and more visible under the rule of Xi Jinping, as the Communist Party takes a hard line on religious faiths that it deems dangerous to Communist ideology and national unity. The Beijing government controls where places of worship can be built and the appointment of religious authorities. It even tries to influence theology. Most of all, it cracks down on sects that it deems a threat, and often brutally.

Five religions are permitted in China—Buddhism, Daoism, Islam, Protestantism, and Catholicism—and Islam and Protestantism seem currently to be getting the worst of it, at least among the official faiths. For adherents of Falun Gong, an officially outlawed spiritual practice in China, things are a good deal worse. Members of the sect have faced persecution for decades. The government considers Falun Gong a "superstition" or "evil cult," and its practitioners have faced jail terms, detention, and torture. And according to a report from the U.S. Commission on International Religious Freedom, the government "has not sufficiently answered accusations of psychiatric experimentation and organ harvesting."[9] The Commission considers China, along with 16 other nations around the world, as being of "particular concern."[10]

More recently, Muslims, particularly Uighurs, have faced intense opposition from the Beijing government. In summer 2017, the government detained hundreds of Uighurs returning to China from a religious pilgrimage. And the PRC is working hard to crack down on Islam more generally, barring teachers and civil servants from worshipping at mosques, fining citizens who study the Koran without permission, and putting Chinese flags in mosques—in the direction of Mecca, so that when worshippers pray, they might just as well be praying to the Communist Party of China as to Allah.[11]

It's worth quoting at length from Alan Dowd's important August 2017 article in *Providence*, in which, citing extensively a Freedom House report, he makes clear the extent of anti-religious repression and brutality that Xi's government is now regularly perpetrating:

> Local government authorities require schools "to completely prohibit teachers and students from participating in Ramadan activities" and require state employees to "pledge to obey political discipline to firmly ensure that families that have party members

and students will not fast and will not participate in any forms of religious activities."

Similarly, national government authorities issued a directive in mid-July declaring, "Party members should not have religious beliefs, which is a redline for all members.... Party members should be firm Marxist atheists, obey party rules and stick to the party's faith.... they are not allowed to seek value and belief in religion."

If you think that affects just a handful of party functionaries, think again: The Communist Party of China numbers nearly 90 million people....

A new Freedom House report details just how backwards the PRC is on religious freedom. Among the lowlights: Christians are barred from celebrating Christmas in groups. Tibetan monks are forced to learn reinterpretations of Buddhist doctrine through "patriotic reeducation." A Uighur Muslim farmer was sentenced to nine years in prison for praying in public. Beijing "devotes significant attention, resources and coercive force to influencing the content of religious teachings, texts and individual believers' thoughts" and has sentenced at least 1,400 Chinese citizens to prison "for exercising their right to religious freedom or rights like free expression, association and information in connection with their faith" since Xi Jinping came to power in 2012.[12]

Indeed, Xi's rise to power has seemed to mark a new chapter in the history of China and religion. In April 2016, Xi gave a speech in which he called for religions in China to follow "the path of Sinicization." What is Sinicization? China Aid, a human rights group, defines it as an attempt to "transform Christian theology into a doctrine that aligns with the core values of socialism and so-called Chinese characteristics."[13] Freedom House reports that this increased religious oppression across society has coincided with Xi's rise to power. The human rights watchdog group chronicles a range of tactics that the government uses to keep a lid on religious activity and the growth of various faiths. "Opportunistic exploitation," for example, is how the Communist Party manipulates religion and religious practice to reflect Communist Party principles and goals. What Freedom House calls "long-term asphyxiation" involves "measures to curb religion's expansion and accelerate its extinction among future generations." And, most chillingly, what Freedom House calls "selective eradication" involves "fiercely suppressing religious groups, beliefs and individuals deemed to threaten party rule or policy priorities, often via extralegal means."[14]

Of course, religious persecution in China goes back a long way. Under Mao Zedong, Christians faced brutal oppression, with as many as half a million Christians "harried to death," as *The Economist* puts it, and many more sent to forced labor camps.[15] Christianity was long regarded in China as a symbol of imperialist oppression—as the bloody Boxer Rebellion of 1900 demonstrated. Since Mao's death, there has been some relaxation of restrictions, it's true, but only in a comparative sense. Christians, Protestants and Catholics together—they number somewhere between 72 million and 92 million, making them China's second-largest religious grouping, after Buddhists—still face a terribly uphill battle for freedom, as do believers of other faiths, especially Muslims.

Beijing's persecutions may yet backfire. Government repression is taking place against the backdrop of what Ian Johnson, author of *The Souls of China: The Return of Religion After Mao*, calls a great spiritual revival. Johnson does not deny that religious repression is escalating, but his point is that the Chinese people, in the face of this adversity, seem more and more determined to practice their faiths: "Protestantism is booming and Chinese cities are full of unregistered (also called 'underground' or 'house') churches. These are known to the government but still allowed to function. They attract some of the best-educated and successful people in China. And they are socially engaged, with outreach programs to the homeless, orphanages, and even families of political prisoners. To me, this is an amazing story."[16]

He's right, though it cannot change the fact that Xi, who continues to consolidate power, is determined to bend all religious worship to the purposes of the state and eliminate challenges to the Party's ideological control. Perhaps China is poised for a great struggle on these matters; perhaps not. In the past, what have often seemed to be percolating social movements have slowly lost momentum and melted away under the pervasive power of the government. What will happen this time remains to be seen—but while the courage and conscience of millions of individual Chinese deserves celebration, no one should doubt that the government in Beijing is one of the globe's great oppressors of religion. China's path is a dead end.

REPRESSION ELSEWHERE

Thus is religion either repressed or used as an instrument of repression in the world's two great authoritarian powers, Russia and China. It's beyond the scope of this chapter to provide a global survey of how religion is faring, but even a cursory review makes clear how the West's norm of religious pluralism and tolerance is an outlier, globally. In sub-Saharan Africa, for instance, by one estimate, eight out of ten armed conflicts have a religious dimension. Consider a few other notable locales, for further contrast with what we take for granted in the West.

The most glaring example, of course, remains the Middle East, where fundamentalist Islam remains the source of most of the world's terrorism while also imposing brutal repression on host populations, especially among those who wish to worship differently. Most readers are well aware of the ongoing global terror threat posed by groups including ISIS, al-Qaeda, and others, as well as the environment of religious absolutism that prevails in many majority-Muslim countries. But what is much less understood, at this point in history, is the grim plight of Christians—and Christianity itself—in the Middle East, especially Iraq and Syria, where believers in Jesus have faced something akin to genocide for about a decade now. The catastrophe has had a long trajectory: it started with the destabilization of Iraq that resulted in the insurgency following the U.S. invasion in 2003, and it metastasized with the rise of ISIS and the onset of the Syrian civil war, developments that happened in tandem and that accelerated in severity during the second term of the Obama administration. Obama was determined not to embroil the United States in Syria and not to re-enter Iraq, after his administration had made a much-touted but clearly premature pullout in 2011.

"Do we want to be the generation that stood by as Christians disappeared almost entirely from the ancient homelands they have occupied since the days of the New Testament?" asked Peter Feaver and Will Inboden in a September 2017 *Foreign Policy* article. "Will the Trump administration and this Congress let this historic and preventable tragedy happen on their watch?"[17]

The situation is indeed dire. In Iraq, for instance, the Christian population, 1.4 million before the U.S. invasion of Iraq in 2003, now numbers roughly 200,000.[18] Their numbers have dwindled dramatically due to a combination of slaughter and flight from the region. When ISIS overran Iraq, its fighters singled out Christians for persecution and brutal treatment. They marked Christian homes with an Arabic letter "N," for "Nazarene," meaning a follower of Jesus. They forced Iraqi Christians to convert to Islam; the only other options were to try to flee or to die as a martyr of the faith. They sold Christian women as sex slaves.

Eventually, even the tender-footed Obama administration could not ignore the singular brutalities of ISIS, nor avoid acknowledging that the terror group (also known as Daesh) was explicitly targeting Christians for genocide, along with adherents of other faiths, such as the Yazidis. "In my judgment, Daesh is responsible for genocide against groups in areas under its control, including Yezidis, Christians, and Shia Muslims," said Obama's secretary of state, John Kerry, a man not known for plain talk, in 2016. He went on to call Daesh "genocidal by self-proclamation, by ideology, and by actions," and accused the group of crimes against humanity and ethnic cleansing, laying out specifics of the barbarism that is the group's defining feature:

> We know, for example, that in August of 2014 Daesh killed hundreds of Yezidi men and older women in the town of Kocho and trapped tens of thousands of Yezidis on Mount Sinjar without allowing access to food, water, or medical care. Without our intervention, it was clear those people would have been slaughtered. Rescue efforts aided by coalition airstrikes ultimately saved many, but not before Daesh captured and enslaved thousands of Yezidi women and girls—selling them at auction, raping them at will, and destroying the communities in which they had lived for countless generations.
>
> We know that in Mosul, Qaraqosh, and elsewhere, Daesh has executed Christians solely because of their faith; that it executed 49 Coptic and Ethiopian Christians in Libya; and that it has also forced Christian women and girls into sexual slavery.
>
> We know that Daesh massacred hundreds of Shia Turkmen and Shabaks at Tal Afar and Mosul; besieged and starved the Turkmen town of Amerli; and kidnapped hundreds of Shia Turkmen women, raping many in front of their own families.
>
> We know that in areas under its control, Daesh has made a systematic effort to destroy the cultural heritage of ancient

communities—destroying Armenian, Syrian Orthodox, and Roman Catholic churches; blowing up monasteries and the tombs of prophets; desecrating cemeteries; and in Palmyra, even beheading the 83-year-old scholar who had spent a lifetime preserving antiquities there.

We know that Daesh's actions are animated by an extreme and intolerant ideology that castigates Yezidis as, quote, "pagans" and "devil-worshippers," and we know that Daesh has threatened Christians by saying that it will, quote, "conquer your Rome, break your crosses, and enslave your women."[19]

Of course, since that time, the region (and the world) has cheered the defeat of ISIS—at least, the defeat of the group in terms of its ambitions for a caliphate, as nearly all its territorial gains have been rolled back due to heroic fighting from Iraqi forces and with significant American assistance, via both weaponry and military assets. This is one of the great victories for freedom and humanity of recent years, but the devastation wrought on Christian communities in the region will take a long time to recover from, and in some cases, recovery may be beyond reach. Small Christian communities in places like Mosul might be lost for good. What the Trump administration and Congress choose to do about it, in terms of providing significant assistance, may prove to be the deciding factor.

Religious freedom isn't faring well in other parts of the world either. Across many countries in Southeast Asia, religious repression has been on the upswing. In a region that is home to 250 million Muslims, 150 million Buddhists, and 120 million Christians, along with a host of other faiths, recent studies reveal a troubling tide of discrimination and intolerance.

In Indonesia, for instance, home to more Muslims than any nation in the world, discrimination against Christians and against a minority Muslim sect, the Ahmadi, has increased in recent years, according to reports by the Asia Centre and the International Panel of Parliamentarians for Freedom of Religion or Belief (IPPFoRB). Incidents of violence have ticked up. And Indonesia enforces a draconian blasphemy law, under which a former mayor of Jakarta, a Christian, was jailed in 2017 for supposedly insulting Islam. Malaysia forces Islamic conversion on an indigenous group, the Orang Asli, prohibits conversion *from* Islam, and imposes broad religious discrimination against women. Vietnam and Laos impose "systematic discrimination and persecution" against religious minorities, including Christians.

The discrimination isn't all in one direction, by any means. Muslims face serious persecution in Burma, Thailand, and the Philippines. More than half a million members of the Rohingya Muslim community have fled persecution in Burma. Rohingyas face discrimination in Thailand as well. In the Catholic Philippines, Muslim women and girls face discrimination, and Filipino officials in the region called Central Luzon proposed a mandatory ID card for Muslims.

In short, if you're interested in freedom of religious worship, religious pluralism, and multicultural, multi-confessional tolerance, your best bet is the nations of the West. And among Western nations, there remains none that stands as such a beacon of liberty and freedom of conscience as the United States. This makes America's current struggles with religious faith, decline of religious conviction—especially Christian—and increasingly hostile attitude toward public religious expression all the more troubling.

AMERICA: AMID FREEDOM OF RELIGION, A LOSS OF FAITH

The steady erosion of religious belief and practice in the United States has been documented in polls for years now. A 2015 Pew survey was illustrative: it reported an eight-point drop in the percentage of adult Americans describing themselves as Christians—from 79 percent to 71 percent—in the span of just seven years. The trend holds among disparate groups: blacks, whites, and Latinos as well as college grads, those with only a high school education, and across gender lines as well.[20] At the same time, numbers continue to spike upward for those identifying themselves as religiously unaffiliated (atheist, agnostic, or "nothing in particular"); that cohort grew more than six points, from 16 percent to nearly 23 percent.[21] White Americans reporting themselves as having no religion reached 24 percent; for Hispanic Americans, that figure reached 20 percent; for blacks, 18 percent.[22]

The sharpest disparities are found along generational lines. More than one-third of both 18- to 24-year-olds and 25- to 33-year-olds describe themselves as religiously unaffiliated. Fewer than 60 percent of millennials identify with *any* branch of Christianity, compared with more than 70 percent among older generations.[23] Just 17 percent of American Catholics today are under the age of 30.

These numbers seem less dramatic to those who note that 70 percent of Americans still identify with some branch of Christianity and that the United States is home to more of the world's Christians than any other country. But the percentage of Christians continues to drop; the nation was 85 percent Christian as recently as 1990. And the percentage of Americans affiliating themselves with non-Christian faiths continues to rise; reaching 5.9 percent in 2014.[24] Belief in God among American adults has dropped from 92 percent to 89 percent.[25]

The decline in religious faith and practice has made those still loyally adhering to Christian faiths feel increasingly unwelcome, even ostracized, especially within elite institutions or in the public sphere. "More and more Christians feel estranged from mainstream culture," David Brooks wrote in 2015. "They fear their colleges will be decertified, their religious institutions will lose their tax-exempt status, their religious liberty will come under greater assault."[26] American public schools have become notorious for their determination to avoid overt mentions of Christianity while increasingly seeking to accommodate Muslim students. "The disapproval and hostility that Christian students have come to experience in our nation's public schools has become epidemic," says Robert Tyler, general counsel for Advocates for Faith and Freedom.[27] Stories of repressed exercises of Christian faith—from commencement addresses to prayers from high school football teams to nativity displays in town squares at Christmastime—have become numbingly familiar to millions of Americans. The decline of religious faith among a large portion of the population has become both reinforced and encouraged by the determination of public officials to shut down expressions of such faith.

I'm focusing on Christianity so much here not only because it is the overwhelmingly majority religion in the United States—and always has been—but also because the decline of religious faith in the United States is largely a Christian story. The truth is, other religions—certainly Islam—are growing in the United States, and public hostility to religious expression is also almost entirely directed against acts of Christian worship, not those of other faiths. In fact, efforts by Muslims to get greater acknowledgment of their faith in public settings have proved success-ful—likely because opposition to such efforts usually results in accusa-tions of bigotry, whereas opposing Christian faith runs no such risks. Many Christian Americans felt that the Obama White House hastened this trend, since the president devoutly sang the praises of Islam—and warned against anti-Islamic bigotry—while often seeming to have only the sparest words to say in defense of Christianity. The Trump admin-istration has reversed this tendency.

There is some evidence from recent polling that Americans are concerned about the waning of religious faith—and not just older Americans. According to Pew, in 2002, 52 percent of Americans believed that religion was losing influence in American life; by 2014, that figure had reached 72 percent.[28] And 56 percent said that this was a negative development, while just 12 percent saw it as a positive.[29] In a 2014 Gallup poll, 75 percent of respondents said that America would be better off if more people were religious.[30]

These numbers are particularly important when taken in context with how Americans view the nation's moral health generally. Survey after survey show that Americans feel that the country is in trouble in terms of morals and ethics, and worry that the future will be worse. A 2016 Gallup poll examining Americans' views of the nation's moral well-being found that most (73 percent) felt moral values were "getting worse," while only 20 percent felt they were "getting better."[31]

What these polling data reflect is a widespread sense among Americans that we are losing the moral bedrock of our nation and civilization. We're a secular republic, founded on religious freedom and rejecting the English idea of a state religion, but we are a Judeo-Christian culture—once a wholly mundane observation, now one that starts arguments. That doesn't change its obvious truth, however. What we're seeing is a generational retreat from the principles and moral underpinnings of that culture. That's a big deal in every way—socially, culturally, politically.

Certainly the American civic and even political heritage is grounded not just in religious faith but also in the notion that religious morality was essential to a free society. "Of all the dispositions and habits which lead to political prosperity, Religion and morality are indispensable sup-ports," George Washington reminded his countrymen in his Farewell

Address.[32] Washington's successor in the White House, John Adams, wrote, "We have no government armed with power capable of contending with human passions unbridled by morality and religion. Avarice, ambition, revenge, or gallantry would break the strongest cords of our Constitution as a whale goes through a net. Our Constitution was made only for a moral and religious people. It is wholly inadequate to the government of any other."[33]

It's not at all clear in the United States, however, that these notions even enjoy majority support anymore. And the decline of religion within the United States has an impact not only on notions of morality, both personal and social, but also on broader cultural vigor—and indeed, on the survival of our civilization. In most Western countries, birthrates have been declining for decades. Europe as we know it is essentially dying out. With its open-borders policy and the influx of migrants from the Middle East, Africa, and Asia—a substantial portion of them radical Islamists determined to perpetrate attacks or pursue sharia law, or both—Europe faces a crisis of cultural survival. The situation is not as dire in the United States, but our birthrates are dropping, too: the fertility rate in the United States fell to a record-low 62 births per 1,000 women aged 15 to 44 in 2016.[34] Holding aside immigration—which accounts for America's rising population—the American birthrate is now below replacement rate.

Many factors have gone into this, but one is certainly the loss of religion. "A people's religion, their faith, creates their culture, and their culture creates their civilization," Pat Buchanan has written. "And when faith dies, the culture dies, the civilization dies, and the people begin to die. Is this not the recent history of the West?"[35]

• • •

For all of this, the United States remains a bastion of religious pluralism, freedom, and tolerance—still the world's shining light of individual liberty and freedom of conscience. And yet, in an increasingly post-religious country, we lack a common anchor to root us. "All human societies have to respond to two fundamental questions," Irving Kristol wrote in 1968. "The first is: 'Why?' The second is: 'Why not?'...It is religion that, traditionally, has supplied the answers to these questions. In our ever more secularized society, it is still religion that has supplied the answer to the second." But, Kristol continued, "on an ever-larger scale, 'why not' is ceasing to be a question.... It is becoming a kind of answer."[36]

Those words have a very contemporary ring, 50 years later.

If the founders and others are right, we will struggle to hold on to the blessings of liberty and democratic self-government as our religious heritage ebbs. A people uncomfortable with making ethical judgments is a people ill-equipped to tackle the fundamental issues facing the United States: family breakdown, the proper education and training of children, the duties we hold to our neighbors and country, and the nature of our country's commitments in the world.

It is this last issue—America's role in the world—that is often overlooked in discussions about waning religious faith in the United States. For U.S. foreign policy has always been imbued with morality and religious overtones, and these impulses have frequently fueled American actions, for better and for worse. The crisis of religious belief in America today seems to mirror the crisis of conviction in America itself, both at home and abroad. Abroad, it takes the shape of confusion and despair about what role America should play in global affairs. The past two administrations, before Trump, had radically different answers to that question: the United States, steeped in its religious and moral heritage, should democratize the world, the George W. Bush administration believed; or the United States, with sins aplenty to atone for, many committed in the mistaken notion that it possessed a superior moral compass to other nations, should stand aside more often, "leading from behind"—if leading at all—in the Obama administration's formulation. Neither of these views has proved sustainable or constructive, as results have shown.

The United States needs a foreign policy that captures what is best in our heritage—which unavoidably contains a moral component—while avoiding the excesses and ambiguities of the recent past. This is a matter not just of national interest but of global concern since, for all its problems, the United States quite simply remains the hope of the world, and the only nation that can serve as a guarantor of security and liberty for others. How an American foreign policy might deliver more promisingly on this hope is the subject of my closing chapter.

CHAPTER TEN

ASSERTIVE DEMOCRATIC IDEALISM

"Trump's victory at the polls falsifies the very idea of American exceptionalism. Whatever American exceptionalism was, it was not a powerful enough force to stop the transnational tides sweeping over the rest of the globe's democracies.... A Trump administration will not be leading the charge on democracy, free trade, or human rights promotion. Trump's America looks just like a normal nation-state."

—DANIEL W. DREZNER[1]

"Our new strategy is based on a principled realism, guided by our vital national interests, and rooted in our timeless values."

—PRESIDENT DONALD TRUMP[2]

Zbigniew Brzezinski was upset. Writing in the *New York Times* in February 2017, just one month after Donald Trump took office as president, Jimmy Carter's former national security adviser saw no sign that the new president had devised, or had any interest in devising, a national security policy, let alone a foreign policy vision that might be identifiable as a "Trump doctrine." Instead, he saw an administration that had recorded an "abysmal performance so far in installing a leadership capable of strategic decision making." The president had "failed to formulate any significant, relevant statements about the global condition," leaving the world to "interpret the sometimes irresponsible, uncoordinated and ignorant statements of his team." Brzezinski then laid out a host of challenges and trouble spots around the world, describing an international order fraying at the seams—not unlike the picture I have drawn in this book—and which could only be made stable through strong, coherent, and strategic American guidance. In conclusion, Brzezinski offered, almost despairingly, "A Trump Doctrine, any doctrine more or less, is sorely needed."[3]

Fast-forward to a few days before Christmas 2017. Another former national security adviser, Susan Rice, who served in that capacity under Trump's predecessor, Barack Obama, lit into the president in another *New York Times* op-ed. Unlike Brzezinski, she wasn't calling for the formulation of a Trump doctrine—she was lamenting the one now in place. President Trump's foreign policy vision, in Rice's view, constituted nothing less than a rejection of American leadership in the world. "There is no common good" in the Trump vision, Rice bemoaned, "no international community, no universal values, only American values. America is no longer 'a global force for good,' as in President Obama's last strategy, or a 'shining city on a hill,' as in President Reagan's vision." Instead, Rice said, there was only a "self-serving, confrontational vision of the world" that relinquished American moral authority.[4]

What had happened in between these two op-eds from distinguished members of the American foreign policy elite was the public unveiling of the administration's 60-page National Security Strategy and the major speech that President Trump gave at the Reagan Building, laying out its highlights. It turned out that what the president had to say, and what he had put his political weight behind—at least rhetorically—constituted something quite different from the chaotic, visionless outlook that Brzezinski saw or the cynical, self-interested approach that Rice lamented. Instead, it was, on paper, the most assertive American foreign policy leadership vision since the Reagan years, and it blended muscular American affirmation of national interests—and warnings to foes that the United States will defend them—with a time-honored championing of American ideals and a commitment to stand for them in the world, to back our allies, and to spread the blessings of democracy, where plausible, around the globe. In my view, it did not go far enough in articulating this last, crucial point—one fundamental to the American idea abroad—but it was a far cry from the worst fears many critics had about Trump's internationalist vision. On the whole, it is a tough, encouraging, and in parts even inspiring formulation.

Since the release of his National Security Strategy at the end of 2017, however, Trump has disheartened allies, supporters, and critics with his mixed messages about democracy, the Western alliance, and especially Russia—most notoriously in his Helsinki press conference with Vladimir Putin in July 2018, in which the American president appeared to take the Russian president's word over that of his own intelligence agencies that Russia had not meddled in the 2016 American presidential election. Trump's administration has enacted policies that are much tougher on Moscow than his predecessor's, yet the president in his own public words continually downplays the outrage of Russia's cyber warfare generally and attempts at election sabotage specifically. And his apparent comfort level with authoritarian rulers, from Putin to Kim Jong Un, especially when juxtaposed to his turbulent relationships with the leaders of many of America's traditional allies, is demoralizing. Trump's diplomatic skills, at least with the leaders of other democracies, are abysmal.

The bottom line: on substance, many of the Trump administration's policies are sound, but all too often the public words and deeds of the president himself are disappointing at best and counterproductive at worst. With such a volatile president, one cannot be overly optimistic. When I began writing this book, Donald Trump had just been elected president. Like many others, I heard his calls for "America First" with some trepidation—not because I didn't recognize the political and practical appeal of that slogan, or the well-founded sentiments that went into it, in a nation that had seen too many costs from globalism with not enough benefits. On the contrary: "America First," properly understood, is a statement of national self-interest and renewal—for which there are no substitutes. Rather, what worried me about candidate Trump was that he seemed to see America First to the exclusion of an American role in the world. As a committed internationalist—one who unabashedly believes that the United States is a force for good, and that, yes, we do have things to teach the world—I didn't want to see the best parts of America's internationalist legacy fall by the wayside under the weight of a new isolationism.

When I wrote the outline for this book, I called my concluding chapter "Assertive Democratic Idealism," by which I meant to argue that the United States could look out both for itself and for the world. Moreover,

I believed, any hopes for a more stable international climate could come to fruition only if the United States pursued such a strategy. I still believe this, devoutly, but my enthusiasm about what Trump might achieve toward these ends is tempered by a volatile dynamic: an administration staffed by some excellent and talented people, from Defense Secretary James Mattis to national security adviser John Bolton, who are tough, determined, and principled advocates of an American role in the world, and who do excellent work when they are allowed to, but whose efforts are often undercut by the repeated undermining and contradicting done by the president himself. Whether Trump's undermining statements reflect merely his temperamental volatility or a more deep-seated rejection of the program that, on paper, his administration committed to, I cannot presume to say. I can only say that the National Security Strategy published by the Trump administration reflected, on balance, a vision that I could get behind, in the pursuit of what I call assertive democratic idealism. But whether this vision can be achieved with the instability of Trump's executive leadership is an open question.

By way of analyzing Trump's *published* national security vision, however, I can offer, in tandem, my views on the posture America should take internationally—and why a strong and active United States is essential to forging a hopeful global future.

THE BURDEN OF RECENT HISTORY

In my view, the history of the last century demonstrates that there is no substitute for American global leadership—missteps and all, failures and all. In the previous chapter, I examined how religion, in the non-Western world, is often either repressed as a free choice or used as an instrument of oppression and violence. Only the West, led by America, has achieved the kind of religious freedom and multicultural tolerance that the rest of the world sorely lacks. This democratic, tolerant, secular, and progress-oriented vision underpins the broader American idea as well: a free, open, and secular society, governed by the rule of law, in which individuals can advance as far as their abilities take them. In our own time, it is fashionable to say that we don't want to foist our values upon others, because, after all, how can we say we're any better? And yet, the evidence is clear that the American idea *is* better—even if it often fumbles in practice. I happen to agree with, of all people, the Irish rock singer Bono, who said in 2016 that America was "the best idea the world ever came up with." He's right.

Thus, America must lead—and its leadership depends not only on the revival of its institutions and the faith and confidence of its people but also on an approach and a vision that, put into practice, will deliver constructive results for the country, its allies, and the world at large.

I call it assertive democratic idealism. As I see it, the United States *must* embrace its role as the leader of the free world and bastion of democratic ideals—there is no other candidate for this job. But without judiciousness, strategic acuity, and an ability to balance ambitions with limitations, we will wind up repeating the mistakes of the past—in particular, of the last two presidential administrations, which, respectively, overreached and underreached.

In 2016, I wrote a book about Richard Nixon's presidency, *The Nixon Effect*, and devoted several chapters to what I saw as the broad-ranging success of Nixon's foreign policy. Key to the Nixon vision was a devotion to the national interest. This is what led to Nixon's notion of "realism," or what Henry Kissinger called *realpolitik*: that the balance of power between states was vital to a stable international environment, and that the United States used its power most effectively when pressing its case in efforts that didn't drain its power and prestige. I admire Nixon's achievements, which I believe put the United States on stronger footing internationally through the prudential use of American power. I believe that they set the stage for the more ambitious—and idealistic—goals of Ronald Reagan, who set out not to manage the Cold War but to win it.

However, Nixonian realism is not enough. America was not founded on "realism" but on aspiration, idealism, and morality: a belief, fundamentally, in individual rights and liberty, and a conviction that democratic government could best protect its people. Jimmy Carter admirably put human rights at the center of his foreign policy—but not with the requisite strategic intelligence that could make such commitments deliver genuine progress. Reagan, in his more muscular way, honored the humanistic Carter vision: one of his principal arguments against the Soviet Union was moral, based on human rights, and on the contrast between Soviet and American visions of the good life.

Today, the United States should stand up for these ideals every bit as boldly as Reagan did—but in such an anarchic international climate, we need to assert our power in measured and prudent ways. We cannot serve our own ends or those of our allies by being expansively interventionist, with no coherent vision; nor can we be reflexively isolationist or passive. In both those cases, in my view, we would exercise our power recklessly—either by dissipating it through excessive use or by eviscerating it through passivity and weakness, leading our adversaries to conclude that American power is not worth respecting (which then leads to further provocation). The history of the Obama and Bush administrations offers compelling evidence of the effects of these errors.

This is not to say that "idealism," in my formulation, should get short shrift. On the contrary, I believe that morality must remain the foundation of American foreign policy. Thus I do not want to see us give up on the promotion or facilitation of democracy abroad. At the same time, draconian "regime change" efforts—whether in Baghdad in 2003 or Tripoli in 2012—are not just counterproductive but destructive, discrediting the moral underpinnings of the American enterprise internationally.

In the end, it comes down to believing in something often derided: American exceptionalism. I do believe in it, as do the vast majority of Americans. The trick is how to put it to work in the world in an effective and sustainable way that strengthens our country first—without which, any hope for serving in a larger role around the world is beside the point.

It is this crucial qualifier, I believe, that has been lacking in the foreign policy practiced over the last several presidencies. If one looks at the world's other two military superpowers—Russia and China, both authoritarian countries that explicitly reject the Western/American vision of liberty and democracy—one sees a steady advance, whether it's Russian expansionism and aggression in Ukraine, Chinese expansionism in Africa, or both regimes' assistance to and support for rogue regimes, such as Pyongyang and Tehran. The advance of China has proceeded across a generation of presidential administrations, with the constant refrain being that integrating China into the international system and finding grounds for commonality was more important than standing up to Beijing on human rights abuses, trade violations, its neocolonialist behavior in Africa, and its enabling of North Korean nuclear blackmail. Russia's advances have come despite different approaches taken by various U.S. administrations: after the end of the Cold War, Bill Clinton planted the seeds for a rebirth of Russian nationalism by welcoming former Soviet satellites into NATO; George W. Bush continued that effort, while being naïve to how American triumphalism was alienating Vladimir Putin, whom he continued to view as an ally until near the end of his presidency; and Barack Obama combined the worst of all worlds, slapping economic sanctions on Moscow and condemning its behavior internationally while doing nothing tangible to stop it—thus closing doors to Putin diplomatically while emboldening him politically and strategically.

Donald Trump won the presidency for many reasons, all coming back, in one way or another, to the idea that enough Americans were willing to take a chance on a man with no military or political experience because they were so troubled about the direction of the country—whether domestically or internationally. We hear often that the United States is losing its good reputation overseas because of Trump's bad character and foul behavior, and these habits are certainly damaging, but from where I stand, the United States lost plenty of its reputational luster under President Obama. American power was mocked and ignored around the world during his tenure—not just in Beijing and Moscow but also in Tehran, Havana, and even Saudi Arabia (which largely ignored Obama when he visited). All too often, Obama's stated desire to "lead from behind" meant, in practice, not leading at all—as was shown most glaringly, and damagingly, in Syria, when the president walked back from his soon-to-be-infamous red line, refusing to punish Bashar al-Assad, as he had promised he would, when the Syrian dictator used chemical weapons. One can make a good argument that American troops were better off not intervening in Syria, but Obama's nonintervention couldn't have happened in a more damaging way, costing the United States precious credibility with allies and adversaries alike.

The Obama foreign policy was defined by lack of conviction about the role of American power in the world—and to the extent that there was conviction, it was that there was too much American power and that the United States needed to stand down more often. This approach helped give birth to ISIS in Iraq, enabled Putin's aggression in Ukraine, alienated and antagonized our allies, and made the United States less secure. Obama's defenders argued that the president was pursuing, in fact, a "realist" course for the national interest, but if that's the case, then his administration had a strange notion of the national interest: its policies unambiguously diminished the power and influence of the United States.

Yet to be fair to Obama, consider where he started from, as president, in 2009: he was inheriting the foreign policy shambles left behind by his extraordinarily ambitious, interventionist predecessor, George W. Bush. I won't rehash the Bush administration's foreign policy record here, except to say that it managed to take an admirable core vision—that American freedom and democracy was a blessing that all the world's people deserved—and to implement it in ways untempered by the restraint and recognition of limitations that is at the core of foreign policy realism. Instead, the Bush team almost seemed to look at "realism" itself as a dirty word, associating it with Nixonian *realpolitik*, without recognizing how realism can often serve the long-range goals of idealism. And of course, in its post-invasion management of the Iraq War, Bush and his team compounded errors of vision with administrative and strategic malpractice. Bush deserves credit, though, for not abandoning Iraq—with the Surge of 2007, his administration made a brave and largely successful effort to stabilize the country. Still, by the end of his presidency, few would call his foreign policy a success. He had launched a hugely ambitious and hugely expensive war—in blood and in treasure—that had fatally wounded his party, turned the White House over to the Democrats and Obama, and, by 2016, left the neoconservative consensus in shambles, paving the way for Trump.

Where Bush was far more successful than Obama, however, was in confronting Islamist terrorism, both domestically and around the world, with every tool available in the American arsenal. After 9/11, no terror attacks followed on American soil during the Bush administration, whereas under Obama, attacks occurred with increasing frequency. Trump, in taking a hard line on radical Islam and on terror generally, was more or less reviving Bush's playbook, only with even tougher rhetoric and, in some areas, even tougher policies. The Obama approach, both in counterterror and in broader foreign policy, was dead on arrival the moment Trump took office in January 2017.

WHAT THE TRUMP NATIONAL SECURITY POLICY GETS RIGHT—FOR THE UNITED STATES AND FOR THE WORLD

The Trump administration's release of the National Security Strategy and his speech announcing it in December 2017 came at the end of a debut year in the White House in which Trump didn't always give a clear idea of where his foreign policy was tending. He opened his presidency seemingly more focused on squabbling with American allies, from Great Britain and France to Germany and Australia, while sounding often more conciliatory toward authoritarian regimes, especially those in Moscow and Beijing. Critics wondered whether Trump's nationalist instincts, and those of some of his advisers, such as Steve Bannon (who departed in August 2017), would fundamentally remake American foreign policy—or whether his campaign rhetoric would prove to be more symbolic than real, obscuring an American presidency that would largely run along established foreign policy lines.

But the unveiling of the National Security Strategy—by which time Bannon had left the administration—draws lines in the sand and commits the administration to concrete principles. To the extent that it does represent a break with previous presidencies, and with many of the establishment impulses of career employees at the Departments of State and Defense, the national defense strategy, as articulated, is *more* idealistic and principled, not less. These strategy documents, as many commentators noted, are often formulaic, with no genuine expectation that they will be implemented—but the Trump strategy has not been greeted that way. There is the sense that we're getting a genuine change of course here, so the president's speech laying out the highlights took on heightened importance.

Consider some of what the president said at the Reagan Building about the nation's national security policy. For starters, the president unabashedly championed American exceptionalism:

Throughout our history, the American people have always been the true source of American greatness. Our people have promoted our culture and promoted our values. Americans have fought and sacrificed on the battlefields all over the world. We have liberated captive nations, transformed former enemies into the best of friends, and lifted entire regions of the planet from poverty to prosperity.

Because of our people, America has been among the greatest forces for peace and justice in the history of the world.[5]

The National Security Strategy (NSS) document itself is even more explicit in its endorsement of the idea that America is a nation set apart:

The extraordinary trajectory of the United States from a group of colonies to a thriving, industrialized, sovereign republic—the world's lone superpower—is a testimony to the strength of the idea on which our nation is founded, namely that each of our citizens is born free and equal under the law. America's core principles, enshrined in the Declaration of Independence, are secured by the Bill of Rights.... Liberty, free enterprise, equal justice under the law, and the dignity of every human life are central to who we are as a people.[6]

"For many years, our citizens watched as Washington politicians presided over one disappointment after another," Trump said. "On top of everything else, our leaders drifted from American principles. They lost sight of America's destiny. And they lost their belief in American greatness."[7]

Under that bill of indictment, Trump included the nation's permission of porous borders; its pursuit of nation-building abroad at the expense of remotely equivalent interest in nation-building at home; its broad-ranging surrender of sovereignty to international and globalist institutions; its ill-considered deal-making with Iran on nuclear energy, craven tolerance of North Korea's nuclear program, and reckless abandonment of Iraq to the savagery of ISIS; its burdening of American taxpayers with the excessive price tag of American security commitments abroad, when many of our wealthier allies could clearly have paid more for the benefits they were enjoying; and its pursuit of an "immigration policy that Americans never voted for, never asked for, and never approved—a policy where the wrong people are allowed into our country and the right people are rejected."[8]

The Trump NSS is admirably clear-eyed about the global environment that the United States finds itself in—a world where challenges to U.S. power, whether economic, military, or political, are more numerous and robust than ever before: rogue regimes, terrorist organizations, transnational criminal networks, and the challenges posed by Russia and China—Trump made clear that all are direct threats to the American way of life. And while he pledged to seek partnerships where possible, conciliation where plausible, he promised to do so "in a manner that always protects our national interest."

To do that, Trump pledged four key areas of focus: defending the American homeland—a project that includes building a wall on the U.S. southern border, as well as vigorous immigration enforcement and efforts against Islamist radicalism at home; "promoting American prosperity," a recognition that American well-being, to say nothing of American global leadership, will depend crucially on economic growth—which Trump looks to secure through tax and regulatory reform, energy independence (including an expansion of shale exploration), and a focus on trade "based on the principles of fairness and reciprocity"; preserving peace through strength, by which Trump means an ambitious reinvestment in U.S. military modernization, an end for the budget sequester of defense spending, and a "multilayered missile defense"; and finally, the advancement of American influence around the world, though Trump hastened to add that this goal "begins with building up our wealth and power at home." Anyone wondering whether the Trump administration planned to abandon American leadership should linger over that fourth pillar: it clearly sets out the vital importance of American leadership in the world, though it does so in a way that underlines the benefits not to the world but to America itself.

DEALING WITH A WORLD OF ADVERSARIES

The most important aspects of the new NSS are the parts dealing with China and Russia, in which the administration makes clear that it sees both as global adversaries that stand in direct opposition to the United States. (And here again, we can—and must—contrast what has been written in the NSS with the chief executive's long record of public statements that seem to undercut a tougher posture toward Russia.) Russia and China, the NSS states bluntly, "want to shape a world antithetical to U.S. values and interests." The administration's answer? In short: a revival of the old Reagan motto, "peace through strength."

I'm encouraged by the NSS's calling out of Russia, though it is thin on specifics for how to respond. Still, it is important to hear that the administration takes issue with Russia's use of "information tools in an attempt to undermine the legitimacy of democracies," referring to its cyber warfare; and the NSS document links these practices with broader "information operations" on Moscow's part that have sought to influence public opinion and even political outcomes around the world. This is notable, considering that the administration has often been languid, at best, in condemning Russia's many provocations, including Russian efforts to influence the 2016 U.S. presidential campaign—appalling conduct from Moscow that most Americans feel appropriately outraged about. And the NSS condemns Russia's "willingness to violate the sovereignty of states" with its "invasions of Georgia and Ukraine."

I'm also gratified that the Trump administration's NSS reflects a much more clear-eyed view of China than previous administrations have held. When Susan Rice, for example, complained in her op-ed that "China is a competitor, not an avowed opponent, and has not illegally occupied its neighbors," she was sounding the elite consensus on Beijing—one very much at odds with the views, and experiences, of China's neighbors, which have been on the receiving end of Chinese aggression for decades. As Gordon Chang has written, Rice should know better than most how wrongheaded her words are, when, shortly before she assumed her post as national security adviser, "China took a chunk out of a neighbor, seizing strategic Scarborough Shoal from the Philippines."[9] Chang goes on to describe an incident in 2012 in which China and the Philippines both crowded the shoal with boats, refusing to back down, until the State Department brokered a deal in which both agreed to withdraw their crafts—but only the Philippines complied. China seized the shoal, with no penalty, and from there, it accelerated its expansionist activities, seeking to seize more territory, in both the South China and East China Seas (incidents I have written about in earlier books). Beijing had an expansionist picnic on the Obama administration's watch. Thus Chang believes, and I concur, that "Trump's assessment of Chinese intentions, as evidenced in his national security strategy, is a needed corrective and that American policies must change."[10]

The NSS pledges to continue the United States' long-running support for Taiwan, but it breaks from earlier articulations in sketching what looks to be a determination to challenge China's growing aggression and expansion in Asia. (Beijing's project has included infrastructure projects, trade policies, militarization of the seas, and threats to the sovereignty of its neighbors.) I'm heartened by the plan to "expand defense and security cooperation with India" to "re-energize our alliances with the Philippines and Thailand" and to "strengthen our partnerships with Singapore, Vietnam, Indonesia, Malaysia, and others, and help them become cooperative maritime partners." India and Japan have proposed a $30 billion Asia-Africa Growth Corridor, and the Trump administration has joined forces with Japanese president Shinzo Abe to maximize this effort and present their countries as alternatives to China for infrastructure investment—but it's only a start, and compared with Beijing's efforts, it's the proverbial pea on the mountain. China's One Belt, One Road Initiative, as I've noted earlier, is valued at $1 trillion. Beijing is throwing its considerable economic clout around via infrastructure, in both Asia and Africa, and U.S. allies have much catching up to do. But it is encouraging that the NSS document recognizes these realities.

The NSS document is admirably blunt, too, in its identification of jihadist terror as an ongoing global menace that threatens not just the United States and its Western allies but also any hope of a peaceful or stable Middle East. Candidate Trump made much of the Obama administration's unwillingness to call radical Islamist terror by its name, favoring instead vague euphemisms such as "violent extremism," but George W. Bush's administration wasn't always much more blunt. Trump signaled early on, with his speech in Saudi Arabia in May 2017, that he would speak plainly about the murderous adversaries of free societies everywhere. And in the NSS document, that trend continues: "Jihadist terrorist organizations present the most dangerous terrorist threat to the Nation. America, alongside our allies and partners, is fighting a long war against these fanatics who advance a totalitarian vision for a global Islamist caliphate that justifies murder and slavery, promotes repression, and seeks to undermine the American way of life."

The language is bracing, but as always, the proof will be not in the words but in the actions that the administration takes. Promising "direct action," the NSS report pledges not only to root out terrorist groups and disrupt their funding sources—familiar policies, though signaled with a new vigor—but also to "deter and disrupt other foreign terrorist groups that threaten the homeland," a description under which it includes "Iranian-backed groups such as Lebanese Hizballah."[11]

The calling out of Iran is no accident. Trump's National Security Strategy here is breaking with two administrations' policies of engagement with Iran, especially Obama's. President Obama was the architect of the now-defunct Iranian nuclear deal, which was negotiated in considerable secrecy. The NSS document rightly calls out Tehran as the world's leading sponsor of terrorism, yet it also takes aim at the heart of the Obama administration's Iran legacy: the nuclear deal, which, in 2018, Trump formally abandoned. Iran, the document states, "is developing more capable ballistic missiles and has the potential to resume its work on nuclear weapons that could threaten the United States and our partners."[12]

That Iran is being put on notice takes on added weight with Trump's monumental gesture in recognizing Jerusalem as Israel's capital, putting the United States even more dramatically in the corner of the Middle East's only democracy, with which we also share deep cultural and religious ties as well as a military alliance. In tandem with this, and with the hard line on Iran, Trump's NSS document makes a point that American policy makers have all too often refrained from making, out of misguided deference to regional sensibilities: "Israel is not the cause of the region's problems. States have increasingly found common interests with Israel in confronting common threats."[13] To that end, the administration is working to facilitate deeper partnerships between Israel and some major regional players, such as Saudi Arabia and Egypt.

Time will tell what the fruits of such a new beginning prove to be, and whether the administration has the courage of its convictions to take concrete action where needed and to stand firm on its principles more generally. Unknown, too, as yet, is to what extent Iran sees these moves as direct provocation to which it needs to respond. Needless to say, a regional war is not the goal, but neither is acquiescence to Iranian designs and quietude toward Islamist terror more broadly.

WHY IDEALISM TRUMPS REALISM

Much road lies ahead. There is no question that the Trump administration's talk must be matched by its walk, and that policy documents, in this administration particularly, are not the same thing as policy in action—especially in the hands of a commander in chief like Trump, who has been known to make adjustments without consultation and whose Twitter feed remains a one-stop shop for subverting the best-laid plans of his senior aides. Trump the man is simply too much of a wild card for policy stability to be taken for granted. Even when his administration is making good policy, and his top-notch aides are pursuing a strategic vision that makes sense, they are susceptible, daily, to sabotage from their commander in chief, via Twitter or his own public statements. In the Trump presidency, every day is unpredictable.

It's also important to note the deficiencies of the NSS document and Trump's speech—namely, not enough emphasis on the idealism part of the ledger, not enough of an endorsement of championing democracy abroad and of the need for America to take an active role in fostering democratic values and reforms around the world—without getting bogged down in self-destructive overreach. I'm pleased that Trump sounded the clarion on American values, but more than words are needed: we need a foreign policy that brings the values of *realpolitik* and realism to an approach that focuses on assertiveness, democratic idealism, and democracy promotion, to counter and eventually even defeat the cause of autocracy—which has, in one form or another, champions in Moscow, Beijing, and around the Middle East.

However, it's instructive here to consider the difference between President Obama's response to the 2009 democratic protests in Iran and President Trump's reaction to the protests that broke out at the end of 2017 and spilled into 2018. Obama said nothing on behalf of the protestors of Iran's Green Movement—a remarkable abandonment of American principle, when mere words from the U.S. president would have sent, at minimum, a message of support to brave Iranians risking their lives for democracy. Years later, even former Obama appointees acknowledge that the president's silence is a blot on his legacy. "I do think that was an appropriate time for the United States to have sent a clearer message that we stand by those who try to represent the rights of people," said Leon Panetta, who served first as CIA director and later as defense secretary under Obama. "That's what the United States is all about. And it would have been important to have sent that message at the time."[14]

That's what the United States is all about. Exactly.

No, Trump did not *do* anything tangible or specific, but he did write, in a tweet, "The people of Iran are finally acting against the brutal and corrupt Iranian regime. All of the money that President Obama so foolishly gave them went into terrorism and into their 'pockets.' The people have little food, big inflation and no human rights. The U.S. is watching!"[15] Presidential tweets won't win a revolution for the Iranian people, needless to say; only Iranians can do that. But at least we're *saying* some of the things that need saying, at long last.

"America will lead again," the president promised in his December 2017 address. "We do not seek to impose our way of life on anyone, but we will champion the values without apology. We want strong alliances and partnerships based on cooperation and reciprocity. We will make new partnerships with those who share our goals, and make common interests into a common cause. We will not allow inflexible ideology to become an obstacle to peace."[16]

The years ahead will reveal how committed President Trump is to the vision he has described. In my view, everything hinges on strong and well-considered presidential leadership. American ideals *are* our strength: freedom of speech, liberty and freedom, the rule of law, human rights. Internationally, we need to stand for and uphold a rules-based international order. No one else will do it.

Yes, the United States faces monumental challenges at home—economically, culturally, demographically, and probably spiritually. And yes, the international climate, as I have tried to emphasize in this book, is as dangerous and volatile as it has been in a generation, at least. But if the United States truly commits, under Trump's leadership, to the vision that it describes as practical realism and I call assertive democratic idealism, a more stable and promising future may yet be in the offing. It is my fervent hope that the United States will get the leaders it needs to steer a course of American leadership that, in my view, remains the last, best hope for the world.

NOTES

INTRODUCTION: WHEN THE WORLD KNEW

1 Melanie Arter, "Panetta: 'Biggest National Security Threat' to U.S. Is 'Total Dysfunction in Washington,'" CNS News, February 16, 2015, http://www .cnsnews.com/news/article/melanie-hunter/panetta-biggest-national-security -threat-us-total-dysfunction-washington.

2 Julia Glum, "The Moment Liberals Knew Trump Won: 24 Horrified Quotes, Pictures and Tweets That Capture Election 2017," *Newsweek*, November 8, 2016, http://www.newsweek.com/trump-election-anniversary-liberal-reactions -clinton-loss-704777.

3 Glum, "Moment."

4 Douglas E. Schoen, *The End of Authority: How a Loss of Legitimacy and Broken Trust Are Endangering Our Future* (Lanham, MD: Rowman and Littlefield, 2013), 26.

5 Peggy Noonan, "How Global Elites Forsake Their Countrymen," *Wall Street Journal*, August 11, 2016, http://www.wsj.com/articles/how-global-elites-forsake -their-countrymen-1470959258.

6 Noonan, "Global Elites."

7 Noonan, "Global Elites."

8 Glenn Harlan Reynolds, "When Rulers Despise the Ruled: Glenn Reynolds," *USA Today*, August 15, 2016, http://www.usatoday.com/story/opinion/2016/08/15 /elite-populist-uprising-populist-trump-brexit-merkel-immigrants-glenn -reynolds/88718374/.

9 Chris Buckley and Keith Bradsher, "Xi Jinping's Marathon Speech: Five Takeaways," *New York Times*, October 18, 2017, https://www.nytimes .com/2017/10/18/world/asia/china-xi-jinping-party-congress.html.

10 "Assessing Threats to U.S. Vital Interests: Middle East," in *2016 Index of U.S. Military Strength: Assessing America's Ability to Provide for the Common Defense*, edited by Dakota L. Wood (Washington, D.C.: Heritage Foundation, 2015), 175, http://index.heritage.org/military/2016/assessments/threats/middle-east/.

11 Jessica Dillinger, "The Most Dangerous Cities in the World," *World Atlas*, October 2, 2017, https://www.worldatlas.com/articles/most-dangerous-cities-in -the-world.html.

12 Milena Veselinovic, "Why Corruption Is Holding Africa Back," *CNN*, January 8, 2016, https://www.cnn.com/2015/12/24/africa/africa-corruption-transparency -international/index.html.

13 Peter S. Goodman, "Every One of the World's Big Economies Is Now Growing," *New York Times*, January 27, 2018, https://www.nytimes

.com/2018/01/27/business/its-not-a-roar-but-the-global-economy-is-finally
-making-noise.html.

14 Goodman, "World's Big Economies."

CHAPTER ONE: THE COLLAPSE OF INSTITUTIONAL LEGITIMACY

1 Hortense Goulard, "Alexis Tsipras: Europe Is Sleepwalking Towards a Cliff,"
   Politico, September 8, 2016, http://www.politico.eu/article/alexis-tsipras-europe
   -is-sleepwalking-towards-a-cliff.

2 "2016 Edelman Trust Barometer Finds Global Trust Inequality Is Growing,"
   Edelman, January 17, 2016, https://www.edelman.com/news/2016-edelman
   -trust-barometer-release/.

3 Gerald F. Seib, "Behind the Rise of Populism, Economic Angst," *Wall Street
   Journal*, January 20, 2016, http://www.wsj.com/articles/behind-the-rise-of
   -populism-economic-angst-1453199402.

4 "Executive Summary," Edelman Trust Barometer 2018 Annual Global Survey,
   https://cms.edelman.com/sites/default/files/2018-01/2018%20Edelman%20
   Trust%20Barometer%20Executive%20Summary.pdf.

5 John Harris, "If You've Got Money, You Vote In...If You Haven't Got Money,
   You Vote Out," *Guardian*, June 24, 2016, https://www.theguardian.com/politics
   /commentisfree/2016/jun/24/divided-britain-brexit-money-class-inequality
   -westminster.

6 "2016 Edelman Trust Barometer."

7 Dana Blanton, "Fox News Poll: 64 Percent Say U.S. Still in Recession, yet 58
   Percent Optimistic About Economy," *Fox News*, January 15, 2015, http://www
   .foxnews.com/politics/2015/01/15/fox-news-poll-64-say-us-still-in-recession-yet
   -58-optimistic-about-economy.html.

8 Vincent Bevins, "No One Asked Me, But Here Are My Thoughts on the
   Tragedy of the Brexit Vote," Facebook, June 24, 2016, https://www.facebook
   .com/vincent.bevins/posts/10105426634702363.

9 Guy Randolph, "Trump Appeals to Voters Who Feel Unheard," *Wall Street
   Journal*, August 19, 2016, http://www.wsj.com/articles/trump-appeals-to-voters
   -who-feel-unheard-1471642207.

10 Harris, "Money."

11 "Inaugural Address: Trump's Full Speech," *CNN*, January 21, 2017, http://www
   .cnn.com/2017/01/20/politics/trump-inaugural-address.

12 "A Majority of Americans Liked Trump's Inaugural Address, Poll Finds," *The
   Week*, January 23, 2017, http://theweek.com/speedreads/675281/majority
   -americans-liked-trumps-inaugural-address-poll-finds.

13 Ali Meyer, "Obama Economy: 9.9 Million More Employed, but 14.6 Million
   Left Labor Force," *Washington Free Beacon*, January 9, 2017, http://freebeacon
   .com/issues/obama-economy-9-9-million-employed-14-6-million-left-labor
   -force.

14 Nick Timiraos, "Health of the U.S. Economy Is a Matter of Debate," *Wall Street
   Journal*, September 27, 2016, http://www.wsj.com/articles/health-of-the-u-s
   -economy-is-a-matter-of-debate-1475019311.

15 Eduardo Porter, "America's Inequality Problem: Real Income Gains Are Brief
   and Hard to Find," *New York Times*, September 13, 2016, https://www.nytimes

.com/2016/09/14/business/economy/americas-inequality-problem-real-income
-gains-are-brief-and-hard-to-find.html.

16 Mark J. Perry, "As Tax Day Approaches, Let's Thank Top 20% for Shouldering
84% of the Income Tax Burden with Only 51% of U.S. Income," *AEIdeas*, April
10, 2015, https://www.aei.org/publication/as-tax-day-approaches-lets-thank-top
-20-for-shouldering-84-of-the-income-tax-burden-with-only-50-of-us-income.

17 Perry, "Tax Day."

18 Timiraos, "Health."

19 Andrew Dugan, "U.S. Economic Confidence Index Lingers at -12," *Gallup News*,
September 27, 2016, http://news.gallup.com/poll/195815/economic-confidence
-index-lingers.aspx.

20 Roland G. Fryer Jr., "Learning from the Successes and Failures of Charter
Schools," *The Hamilton Project*, September 2012, http://scholar.harvard.edu/files
/fryer/files/hamilton_project_paper_2012.pdf.

21 Dan Lips, Shanea Watkins, and John Fleming, "Does Spending More on
Education Improve Academic Achievement?" *The Heritage Foundation*,
September 8, 2008, http://www.heritage.org/research/reports/2008/09/does
-spending-more-on-education-improve-academic-achievement.

22 "Pisa Tests: Top 40 for Maths and Reading," *BBC News*, October 14, 2015, http://
www.bbc.com/news/business-26249042.

23 Laurence Steinberg, "What's Holding Back American Teenagers?" *Slate
Magazine*, February 11, 2014, http://www.slate.com/articles/life
/education/2014/02/high_school_in_america_a_complete_disaster.html.

24 Kaitlyn Schallhorn, "Cost-Sharing Reduction Payments: What Are the
Subsidies Trump Cut?" *Fox News*, October 13, 2017, http://www.foxnews.com
/politics/2017/10/13/cost-sharing-reduction-payments-what-are-subsidies
-trump-cut.html.

25 Jeffrey M. Jones, "Americans Again Opposed to Taking In Refugees," *Gallup
News*, November 23, 2015, http://www.gallup.com/poll/186866/americans-again
-opposed-taking-refugees.aspx.

26 Jerry Markon, "Senior Obama Officials Have Warned of Challenges in
Screening Refugees from Syria," *Washington Post*, November 17, 2015, https://
www.washingtonpost.com/news/federal-eye/wp/2015/11/17/senior-obama
-officials-have-warned-of-challenges-in-screening-refugees-from-syria.

27 "Confidence About America's Safety from Terrorism Remains Low," *Rasmussen
Reports*, September 12, 2016, http://www.rasmussenreports.com
/public_content/politics/general_politics/september_2016/confidence_about
_america_s_safety_from_terrorism_remains_low.

28 Goulard, "Europe Is Sleepwalking."

29 Eurostat, "Unemployment Statistics," June 2018, http://ec.europa.eu/eurostat
/statistics-explained/index.php/Unemployment_statistics.

30 Eurostat, "Unemployment Statistics," June 2018.

31 Kerry Kolasa-Sikiaridi, "MRB Survey: Majority of Greeks Anticipate Snap
Elections in 2017," *Greek Reporter*, December 27, 2016, http://greece
.greekreporter.com/2016/12/27/mrb-survey-majority-of-greeks-anticipate-snap
-elections-in-2017.

32 Philip Chrysopoulos, "Almost 1.5 Million Greeks Live in Extreme Poverty,"

Greek Reporter, May 2, 2017, http://greece.greekreporter.com/2017/05/02/almost
-1-5-million-greeks-live-in-extreme-poverty.

33 Christopher Adam, "Poverty in Hungary Skyrockets—Government to
Stop Publishing Statistics," *Hungarian Free Press*, June 25, 2015, http://
hungarianfreepress.com/2015/06/25/poverty-in-hungary-skyrockets
-government-to-stop-publishing-statistics.

34 Adam, "Poverty in Hungary."

35 Adrienn Sain, "The Frightening Reality of Poverty in Hungary," *Daily News
Hungary*, January 8, 2016, http://dailynewshungary.com/the-frightening-reality
-of-poverty-in-hungary.

36 National Institute of Statistics, "Italy Unemployment Rate 1983–2018," *Trading
Economics*, accessed January 30, 2018, https://tradingeconomics.com/italy
/unemployment-rate.

37 Roger Bootle, "Italy's Failure to Thrive Puts the Boot into Eurozone Goal," *The
Telegraph*, June 12, 2016, http://www.telegraph.co.uk/business/2016/06/12/italys
-failure-to-thrive-puts-the-boot-into-eurozone-goal.

38 Bootle, "Italy's Failure."

39 James Politi and Jim Brunsden, "Italian Minister Warns Against Efforts to
Tighten EU Banking Rules," *Financial Times*, December 18, 2017, https://www
.ft.com/content/3b32f1d4-e403-11e7-97e2-916d4fbacoda.

40 Eurostat, "France Youth Unemployment Rate 1983–2018," *Trading Economics*,
accessed January 30, 2018, https://tradingeconomics.com/france/youth
-unemployment-rate.

41 Madeline Chambers, "Merkel Braced for More Misery in Berlin Vote in Anti-
Immigrant Backlash," *Reuters*, September 15, 2016, http://www.reuters.com
/article/us-germany-election-idUSKCN11L1B0.

42 Arne Delfs, "Merkel's Frenemies Give Stage to EU Critic of Her Refugee
Policy," *Bloomberg*, January 5, 2018, https://www.bloomberg.com/news
/articles/2018-01-05/merkel-s-frenemies-give-stage-to-eu-critic-of-her-refugee
-policy.

43 Palko Karasz, "Voices from Europe's Far Right," *New York Times*, July 12, 2016,
http://www.nytimes.com/2016/07/13/world/europe/voices-from-europes-far
-right.html.

44 David Zucchino, "'I've Become a Racist': Migrant Wave Unleashes Danish
Tensions Over Identity," *New York Times*, September 5, 2016, https://www
.nytimes.com/2016/09/06/world/europe/denmark-migrants-refugees-racism
.html.

45 Zucchino, "Migrant Wave."

46 Adam Taylor, "Map: France's Growing Muslim Population," *Washington Post*,
January 9, 2015, https://www.washingtonpost.com/news/worldviews
/wp/2015/01/09/map-frances-growing-muslim-population.

47 Richard Wike, Bruce Stokes, and Katie Simmons, "Europeans Fear Wave of
Refugees Will Mean More Terrorism, Fewer Jobs," *Pew Research Center*, July 11,
2016, http://www.pewglobal.org/2016/07/11/europeans-fear-wave-of-refugees
-will-mean-more-terrorism-fewer-jobs.

48 Steve Crabtree and Sofia Kluch, "Terrorism, Migration Trouble Many in
Europe," *Gallup News*, June 15, 2017, http://news.gallup.com/poll/212405
/terrorism-migration-trouble-europe.aspx.

49 Wike, Stokes, and Simmons, "Wave of Refugees."

50 Harry Cooper, "Migration, Terrorism Biggest Concerns for EU Citizens: Poll," *Politico*, July 4, 2016, http://www.politico.eu/article/migration-terrorism -biggest-concerns-for-eu-citizens-poll-muslims-europe.

51 Noonan, "Elites Forsake Their Countrymen,"

52 "2017 Edelman Trust Barometer Reveals Global Implosion of Trust," *Business Journals*, January 16, 2017, http://www.bizjournals.com/prnewswire/press _releases/2017/01/16/NY88176.

53 "Edelman Trust Barometer 2016 Executive Summary," *Edelman*, January 15, 2016, https://www.edelman.com/research/2016-trust-barometer-executive -summary.

54 "Edelman Trust Barometer 2016 Executive Summary."

55 "2016 Edelman Trust Barometer."

56 "2016 Edelman Trust Barometer."

57 Scott Clement, "What's Wrong with the 'Right or Wrong Track' Polling Numbers," *Washington Post*, October 28, 2016, https://www.washingtonpost .com/opinions/whats-wrong-with-the-right-or-wrong-track-polling -numbers/2016/10/28/ccb0a14a-9c76-11e6-b3c9-f662adaa0048_story.html.

58 Frank Newport, "Americans' Confidence in Institutions Edges Up," *Gallup News*, June 26, 2017, http://news.gallup.com/poll/212840/americans-confidence -institutions-edges.aspx.

59 "Public Trust in Government: 1958–2017," *Pew Research Center*, December 14, 2017, http://www.people-press.org/2017/05/03/public-trust-in-government -1958–2017.

60 Samantha Smith, "6 Key Takeaways About How Americans View Their Government," *Pew Research Center*, November 23, 2015, http://www .pewresearch.org/fact-tank/2015/11/23/6-key-takeaways-about-how-americans -view-their-government.

61 Smith, "6 Key Takeaways."

62 Smith, "6 Key Takeaways."

63 Art Swift, "In U.S., Confidence in Newspapers Still Low but Rising," *Pew Research Center*, June 28, 2017, http://news.gallup.com/poll/212852/confidence -newspapers-low-rising.aspx.

64 "Voters Don't Trust Media Fact-Checking," *Rasmussen Reports*, September 30, 2017, http://www.rasmussenreports.com/public_content/politics/general _politics/september_2016/voters_don_t_trust_media_fact_checking.

65 Fraser Nelson, "Brexit: A Very British Revolution," *Wall Street Journal*, June 24, 2016, http://www.wsj.com/articles/brexit-a-very-british-revolution-1466800383.

66 "Press Release: Edelman Trust Barometer 2016—Trust in Government," *Edelman UK*, January 18, 2016, http://www.edelman.co.uk/wp-content/uploads /Edelman-Trust-Barometer-2016-Politics-Release-UK.pdf.

67 "Press Release: Edelman Trust Barometer 2016."

68 Nelson, "Very British Revolution."

69 "Edelman Trust Barometer 2016—UK Findings," *Edelman UK*, January 18, 2016, http://www.edelman.co.uk/magazine/posts/trust-barometer-2016.

70 Ashley Kirk and Daniel Dunford, "EU Referendum: Leave Supporters Trust Ordinary 'Common Sense' More Than Academics and Experts," *Telegraph*,

June 22, 2016, http://www.telegraph.co.uk/news/2016/06/16/eu-referendum-leave-supporters-trust-ordinary-common-sense-than.

71 Kirk and Dunford, "EU Referendum."

72 Sam Burne James, "Trust in Media and Government Rising—But Less So Among Lower Demographics, Finds Edelman Trust Barometer," PR Week, January 18, 2016, http://www.prweek.com/article/1379781/trust-media-government-rising-less-so-among-lower-demographics-finds-edelman-trust-barometer.

73 Iain Martin, "Ukip's Great Success Will Be the Death of It," The Times, February 16, 2017, http://www.thetimes.co.uk/article/ukip-s-great-success-will-be-the-death-of-it-3phtzx0x2.

74 "EU Referendum Results," BBC News, accessed January 31, 2018, http://www.bbc.com/news/politics/eu_referendum/results.

75 "Standard Eurobarometer Survey of Spring 2016 (EB85)," European Commission Public Opinion, July 2016, http://ec.europa.eu/COMMFrontOffice/publicopinion/index.cfm/Survey/getSurveyDetail/instruments/STANDARD/surveyKy/2130.

76 "Standard Eurobarometer Survey of Spring 2016."

77 "Standard Eurobarometer Survey of Spring 2016."

78 "Autumn 2017 Economic Forecast," European Commission, October 23, 2017, https://ec.europa.eu/info/business-economy-euro/economic-performance-and-forecasts/economic-forecasts/autumn-2017-economic-forecast_en.

79 Daniel Larison, "The Decline of Popular Trust in Political Leaders," American Conservative, June 15, 2016, http://www.theamericanconservative.com/larison/the-decline-of-popular-trust-in-political-leaders.

80 "2017 Edelman Trust Barometer Reveals Global Implosion of Trust."

CHAPTER TWO: A WORLDWIDE MOVEMENT AGAINST ELITES

1 Seib, "Populism, Economic Angst."

2 Jeremy Ashkenas and Gregor Aisch, "European Populism in the Age of Donald Trump," New York Times, December 5, 2016, https://www.nytimes.com/interactive/2016/12/05/world/europe/populism-in-age-of-trump.html.

3 Oli Smith, "'I Will Not Submit!' Marine Le Pen REFUSES to Grovel to Merkel and EU in Swipe at Elite," Express, February 19, 2017, http://www.express.co.uk/news/world/769025/Marine-Le-Pen-Angela-Merkel-French-presidential-elections.

4 Lizzie Stromme, "France Next: Le Pen Hails Donald Trump's US Election Triumph as 'Victory for Freedom,'" Express, November 9, 2016, http://www.express.co.uk/news/world/730592/Le-Pen-HAILS-Donald-Trump-US-election-triumph-victory-freedom.

5 Lizzie Dearden, "Marine Le Pen's Front National Issues Chilling Warning over Donald Trump Win: 'Their World Is Collapsing. Ours Is Being Built,'" Independent, November 9, 2016, http://www.independent.co.uk/news/world/americas/us-elections/donald-trump-president-us-election-result-front-national-marine-le-pen-jean-marie-far-right-world-a7406426.html.

6 Matthew Goodwin, "European Populism Is Here to Stay," New York Times, October 20, 2017, https://www.nytimes.com/2017/10/20/opinion/european-populism-is-here-to-stay.html.

7 "Finns Party Gains Popularity, Blue Reform Slides Further Down in Poll," *Helsinki Times*, July 5, 2018, http://www.helsinkitimes.fi/finland/finland-news /politics/15662-yle-finns-party-gains-popularity-blue-reform-slides-further -down-in-poll.html.

8 Cécile Alduy, "France's National Front Is Dead, but Its Politics Are Alive and Well," *The Nation*, July 20, 2018, https://www.thenation.com/article/frances -national-front-dead-politics-alive-well/.

9 Seán Clarke, "German Elections 2017: Full Results," *Guardian*, September 25, 2017, https://www.theguardian.com/world/ng-interactive/2017/sep/24/german -elections-2017-latest-results-live-merkel-bundestag-afd.

10 Theo Ioannou, "New Poll: New Democracy Leads, Greeks Reject 'Macedonia' in FYROM Name," *Greek Reporter*, January 20, 2018, http://greece. greekreporter.com/2018/01/20/new-poll-new-democracy-leads-greeks-reject -macedonia-in-fyrom-name/.

11 "Party Popularities Changing Among Committed Voters," *Budapest Business Journal*, January 22, 2018, https://bbj.hu/analysis/party-popularities-changing -among-committed-voters_144284.

12 "Partisympatiundersökningen November 2017," *SCB*, December 5, 2017, https:// www.scb.se/hitta-statistik/statistik-efter-amne/demokrati/partisympatier /partisympatiundersokningen-psu/pong/statistiknyhet /partisympatiundersokningen-psu-i-november-2017--val-i-dag/.

13 "Dutch Election Results," *The Economist*, March 16, 2017, https://www .economist.com/blogs/graphicdetail/2017/03/daily-chart-10.

14 "A Hot Summer Is Giving Europe's Populists a Boost," *The Economist*, July 26, 2018, https://www.economist.com/europe/2018/07/26/a-hot-summer-is-giving -europes-populists-a-boost.

15 Gregor Aisch, Adam Pearce, and Bryant Rousseau, "How Far Is Europe Swinging to the Right?" *New York Times*, October 23, 2017, http://www.nytimes .com/interactive/2016/05/22/world/europe/europe-right-wing-austria-hungary .html.

16 Karasz, "Voices from Europe's Far Right."

17 "The March of Europe's Little Trumps," *The Economist*, December 10, 2015, http://www.economist.com/news/europe/21679855-xenophobic-parties-have -long-been-ostracised-mainstream-politicians-may-no-longer-be.

18 Tobias Buck, "Discontent from Germany's Eastern States Boosts AfD," *Financial Times*, September 29, 2017, https://www.ft.com/content/758344d0-a4fa -11e7-9e4f-7f5e6a7c98a2.

19 Josh Lowe, Owen Matthews, and Matt McAllester, "Why Europe's Populist Revolt Is Spreading," *Newsweek*, November 23, 2016, http://www.newsweek .com/2016/12/02/europe-right-wing-nationalism-populist-revolt-trump-putin -524119.html.

20 "Europe's Little Trumps."

21 David Frum, "The Great Republican Revolt," *The Atlantic*, January/February 2016, http://www.theatlantic.com/magazine/archive/2016/01/the-great -republican-revolt/419118/.

22 "Voter General Election Preferences," *Pew Research Center*, July 7, 2016, http:// www.people-press.org/2016/07/07/2-voter-general-election-preferences/7-7 -2016-2-30-10-pm-2/.

23 Donald J. Trump For President, "Donald Trump Presidential Announcement Full Speech 6/16/15," *YouTube*, June 16, 2015, https://www.youtube.com /watch?v=q_q61B-DyPk.

24 Donald J. Trump For President, "Presidential Announcement."

25 Vicki Needham, "Trump Says He Will Renegotiate or Withdraw from NAFTA," *The Hill*, June 28, 2016 http://thehill.com/policy/finance/285189-trump-says-he -will-renegotiate-or-withdraw-from-nafta-without-changes.

26 "Views on Economy, Government Services, Trade," *Pew Research Center*, March 31, 2016, http://www.people-press.org/2016/03/31/3-views-on-economy -government-services-trade/#free-trade-agreements-viewed-positively-by -democratic-voters.

27 "Voters Like Trump's Proposed Muslim Ban," *Rasmussen Reports*, December 10, 2015, http://www.rasmussenreports.com/public_content/politics/current _events/immigration/december_2015/voters_like_trump_s_proposed _muslim_ban.

28 Pamela Engel, "Trump on Syrian Refugees: 'Lock Your Doors, Folks,'" *Business Insider*, April 25, 2016, http://www.businessinsider.com/trump-syrian-refugees -isis-2016-4.

29 Betsy Cooper, Daniel Cox, Rachel Lienesch, and Robert P. Jones, "Anxiety, Nostalgia, and Mistrust: Findings from the 2015 American Values Survey," *PRRI*, November 17, 2015, http://www.prri.org/research/survey-anxiety -nostalgia-and-mistrust-findings-from-the-2015-american-values-survey/.

30 Frum, "Great Republican Revolt."

31 Donald J. Trump For President, "Donald Trump Presidential Announcement."

32 Peter Hasson, "Politico Co-Founder: Media's Anti-Trump Bias 'Scary,'" *Daily Caller*, September 9, 2016, http://dailycaller.com/2016/09/09/politico-co-founder -medias-anti-trump-bias-scary/.

33 Donald J. Trump For President, "Donald Trump Presidential Announcement."

34 Jenna Johnson and Jose A. DelReal, "Here's Who Supports Trump—and Why," *Washington Post*, March 3, 2016, https://www.washingtonpost.com/politics /heres-who-supports-donald-trump--and-why/2016/03/03/7674b578-e088-11e5 -846c-10191d1fc4ec_story.html.

35 Heather Horn, "'Little Trumps Are in Every European Country,'" *The Atlantic*, March 3, 2016, https://www.theatlantic.com/international/archive/2016/03 /donald-trump-europe-election/472113/.

36 Steve Visser and Elizabeth Roberts, "Angela Merkel Admits Immigration Policy Hurt Party in Elections," *CNN*, September 5, 2016, http://www.cnn.com /2016/09/04/europe/germany-alternative-fur-deutschland-afd-angela -merkel/.

37 Aisch, Pearce, and Rousseau, "How Far Is Europe Swinging?"

38 Manasi Gopalakrishnan, "Arsonists Increasingly Target Refugee Shelters in Germany," *DW*, September 12, 2016, http://www.dw.com/en/arsonists -increasingly-target-refugee-shelters-in-germany/a-19545693.

39 "Germany Records Over 900 Assaults on Refugees in 2016, Number of Arrivals Drops," *RT*, December 30, 2016, https://www.rt.com/news/372275-germany -refugees-attacks-rise/.

40 Gopalakrishnan, "Arsonists Increasingly Target."

41 Kate Connolly, "Frauke Petry: The Acceptable Face of Germany's New Right?," *Guardian*, June 19, 2016, https://www.theguardian.com/world/2016/jun/19 /frauke-petry-acceptable-face-of-germany-new-right-interview.

42 Nicholas Vinocur, "Marine Le Pen Makes Globalization the Enemy," *Politico*, February 5, 2017, http://www.politico.eu/article/marine-le-pen-globalization -campaign-launch-french-politics-news-lyon-islam/.

43 William Horobin, "Marine Le Pen Centers Presidential Run on Getting France Out of Eurozone," *Wall Street Journal*, January 18, 2017, https://www.wsj.com /articles/marine-le-pen-centers-presidential-run-on-getting-france-out-of -eurozone-1484735580.

44 Vinocur, "Marine Le Pen Makes Globalization the Enemy."

45 Ros Taylor, "Cameron Refuses to Apologise to Ukip," *Guardian*, April 4, 2016, https://www.theguardian.com/politics/2006/apr/04/conservatives.uk.

46 Nigel Farage, "Donald Trump Calls Himself 'Mr. Brexit.' Here's Why He's Right," *Washington Post*, September 6, 2016, https://www.washingtonpost.com /posteverything/wp/2016/09/06/nigel-farage-donald-trump-calls-himself-mr -brexit-heres-why-hes-right/.

47 Susanne Koelbl, "Why Dutch Populists Want to Leave the EU," *Spiegel Online*, July 1, 2016, http://www.spiegel.de/international/europe/dutch-populist-geert -wilders-wants-to-leave-the-eu-a-1100931.html.

48 Mike Corder, "'Behave Normally or Go Away'; Dutch Prime Minister Mark Rutte Says Integrate or Leave," *Toronto Sun*, January 23, 2017, http://www .torontosun.com/2017/01/23/behave-normally-or-go-away-dutch-prime -minister-mark-rutte-says-integrate-or-leave.

49 Ian Buruma, "Why Geert Wilders Is Taking Over Dutch Politics," *The Spectator*, January 28, 2017, http://www.spectator.co.uk/2017/01/why-geert-wilders-is -taking-over-dutch-politics/.

50 "Dutch Politician Slammed for Calling Moroccan Immigrants 'Scum,'" *NBC News*, February 19, 2017, http://www.nbcnews.com/news/world/dutch -politician-slammed-calling-moroccan-immigrants-scum-n722966.

51 Karasz, "Voices from Europe's Far Right."

52 Ishaan Tharoor, "The Stunning Success of Austria's Anti-Immigrant Far-Right, in One Map," *Washington Post*, April 25, 2016, https://www.washingtonpost .com/news/worldviews/wp/2016/04/25/the-stunning-success-of-austrias-anti -immigrant-far-right-in-one-map/.

53 Karasz, "Voices from Europe's Far Right."

54 Csaba Tóth, "Full Text of Viktor Orbán's Speech at Băile Tuşnad (Tusnádfürdő) of 26 July 2014," *Budapest Beacon*, July 29, 2014, http://budapestbeacon.com /public-policy/full-text-of-viktor-orbans-speech-at-baile-tusnad-tusnadfurdo -of-26-july-2014/10592.

55 Krisztina Than, "Orban's Ratings Rise As Hungarian Fence Deters Migrant 'Invasion,'" *Reuters*, November 6, 2015, http://www.reuters.com/article /hungary-orban-idUSL8N1304UB20151106.

56 Ian Traynor, "Hungary Party to Follow European Extremism's Move Away from Fringes," *Guardian*, April 8, 2010, http://www.guardian.co.uk/world/2010 /apr/08/jobbik-hungary-move-from-fringes.

57 "Old and Nasty," *The Economist*, July 28, 2012, http://www.economist.com /node/21559677.

58 Ishaan Tharoor, "8 Ridiculous, Racist Things Actually Said by Far-Right EU Politicians," *Washington Post*, May 24, 2014, https://www.washingtonpost.com /news/worldviews/wp/2014/05/24/8-ridiculous-racist-things-actually-said-by -far-right-eu-politicians/.

59 "Hungarian Extremist Sentenced to 13 Years in Prison for Terrorism," *Hungarian Free Press*, August 30, 2016, http://hungarianfreepress. com/2016/08/30/hungarian-extremist-sentenced-to-13-years-in-prison-for -terrorism/.

60 Takis Pappas, "Distinguishing Liberal Democracy's Challengers," *Journal of Democracy* 27, no. 4 (October 2016): 22–36, http://www.journalofdemocracy.org /sites/default/files/Pappas-27-4.pdf.

61 Than, "Orban's Ratings Rise."

62 Karasz, "Voices from Europe's Far Right."

63 Ishaan Tharoor, "In a First, E.U. Foreign Minister Calls for a Member State to Be Kicked Out," *Washington Post*, September 14, 2016, https://www .washingtonpost.com/news/worldviews/wp/2016/09/14/in-a-first-e-u-foreign -minister-calls-for-a-member-state-to-be-kicked-out/.

64 Reiss Smith, "Italy Referendum Explained: What Was the Vote About and Could the Result Destroy the EU?" *Express*, December 5, 2016, http://www .express.co.uk/news/world/711044/italy-referendum-explained-result-tear-eu -apart-exit.

65 "Matteo Renzi's Referendum Defeat Risks Italy Political Crisis," *BBC News*, December 5, 2016, http://www.bbc.com/news/world-europe-38204189.

66 Thomas Colson, "'Italy's Trump': This Is What the Five Star Movement Is All About," *Business Insider*, December 5, 2016, http://www.businessinsider.com /what-is-italy-five-star-movement-beppe-grillo-trump-farage-2016-12.

67 Nektaria Stamouli and Marcus Walker, "Greece's Alexis Tsipras Seeks to Revive His Political Fortunes on Economic Promises," *Wall Street Journal*, September 11, 2016, http://www.wsj.com/articles/greeces-alexis-tsipras-seeks-to-revive-his -political-fortunes-on-economic-promises-1473617747.

68 William Wheeler, "Europe's New Fascists," *New York Times*, November 17, 2012, https://www.nytimes.com/2012/11/18/opinion/sunday/europes-new-fascists.html.

69 Aisch, Pearce, and Rousseau, "How Far Is Europe Swinging?"

70 Wheeler, "Europe's New Fascists."

71 "Better Days Forecast for Greek Economy with Credit Rating Upgraded," *Neos Kosmos*, January 22, 2018, http://neoskosmos.com/news/en/Better-days-forecast -for-Greek-economy-with-credit-rating-upgraded.

72 Horn, "Little Trumps."

73 Lowe, Matthews, and McAllester, "Europe's Populist Revolt."

CHAPTER THREE: THE BREAKDOWN OF ALLIANCES

1 Dominic Waghorn, "America Needs To Be the World's Policeman, Former NATO Chief Says," *Sky News*, November 3, 2016, http://news.sky.com/story /america-needs-to-be-the-worlds-policeman-former-nato-chief-says-10642541.

2 "Trump's Speech in Warsaw (Full Transcript, Video)," *CNN*, July 6, 2017, http://

www.cnn.com/2017/07/06/politics/trump-speech-poland-transcript
/index.html.

3 "Trump's Speech in Warsaw."

4 Sean D. Carberry, "Clapper: Presidential Transition 'Will Be OK,'" *FCW*,
September 7, 2016, https://fcw.com/articles/2016/09/07/clapper-carberry.aspx.

5 Carberry, "Clapper: Presidential Transition."

6 Michael R. Gordon and Niraj Chokshi, "Trump Criticizes NATO and Hopes
for 'Good Deals' with Russia," *New York Times*, January 15, 2017, https://www
.nytimes.com/2017/01/15/world/europe/donald-trump-nato.html.

7 Kedar Pavgi, "NATO Members' Defense Spending, in Two Charts," *Defense
One*, June 22, 2015, http://www.defenseone.com/politics/2015/06/nato-members
-defense-spending-two-charts/116008/.

8 Ivana Kottasova, "These NATO Countries Are Not Spending Their Fair Share
on Defense," *CNN*, July 8, 2016, http://money.cnn.com/2016/07/08/news/nato
-summit-spending-countries/index.html.

9 Jeremy Diamond, "Trump Opens NATO Summit with Blistering Criticism of
Germany, Labels Allies 'Delinquent,'" *CNN*, July 11, 2018, https://www.cnn
.com/2018/07/10/politics/donald-trump-nato-summit-2018/index.html.

10 Anne Applebaum, "'What Happens to Us?' Why Sweden Is So Worried About
the Trump Administration," *Washington Post*, February 8, 2017, https://www
.washingtonpost.com/opinions/global-opinions/what-happens-to-us-why
-sweden-is-so-worried-about-the-trump-administration/2017/02/08/59ce0ca6
-ee17-11e6-9973-c5efb7ccfb0d_story.html.

11 "Funding NATO," North Atlantic Treaty Organization, June 2, 2017, https://
www.nato.int/cps/en/natohq/topics_67655.htm; Michael Birnbaum and Thomas
Gibbons-Neff, "NATO Allies Boost Defense Spending in the Wake of Trump
Criticism," *Washington Post*, January 28, 2017, https://www.washingtonpost
.com/world/nato-allies-boost-defense-spending-in-the-wake-of-trump
-criticism/2017/06/28/153584de-5a8c-11e7-aa69-3964a7d55207_story.html.

12 Jonathan Stearns, "NATO Allies Inch Toward Defense Budget Goal
Championed by Trump," *Bloomberg Politics*, June 29, 2017, https://www
.bloomberg.com/news/articles/2017-06-29/nato-allies-inch-toward-defense
-budget-goal-championed-by-trump.

13 Uri Friedman, "How Geography Explains Donald Trump and Hillary Clinton,"
The Atlantic, October 13, 2016, http://www.theatlantic.com/international
/archive/2016/10/anders-fogh-rasmussen-trump/503468/.

14 Paul D. Miller, "How World War III Could Begin in Latvia," *Foreign Policy*,
November 16, 2016, https://foreignpolicy.com/2016/11/16/how-world-war-iii
-could-begin-in-latvia/.

15 "'Very Aggressive': Trump Suggests Montenegro Could Cause World War
Three," *Guardian*, July 19, 2018, https://www.theguardian.com/us-news/2018
/jul/19/very-aggressive-trump-suggests-montenegro-could-cause-world-war
-three.

16 Pamela Engel, "Trump's Nominee for Secretary of State Breaks with President-
Elect on Defending America's NATO Allies," *Business Insider*, January 11, 2017,
http://www.businessinsider.com/tillerson-trump-nato-article-5-2017-1.

17 Engel, "Trump's Nominee."

18 Choe Sang-Hun, "Allies for 67 Years, U.S. and South Korea Split over North Korea," *New York Times*, September 4, 2017, https://www.nytimes.com/2017/09/04/world/asia/north-korea-nuclear-south-us-alliance.html.

19 Donald J. Trump, *Twitter*, January 4, 2018, https://twitter.com/realDonaldTrump/status/948879774277128197?ref_src=twsrc%255Etfw&ref_url=http%253A%252F%252Fwww.newsweek.com%252Fnorth-korea-talks-aim-divide-us-and-south-korea-top-us-commander-says-770649.

20 J. Berkshire Miller, "How Trump Can Reassure Asian Allies," *Foreign Affairs*, February 8, 2017, https://www.foreignaffairs.com/articles/asia/2017-02-08/how-trump-can-reassure-asian-allies.

21 Oliver Holmes, "Rodrigo Duterte Vows to Kill 3 Million Drug Addicts and Likens Himself to Hitler," *Guardian*, September 30, 2016, https://www.theguardian.com/world/2016/sep/30/rodrigo-duterte-vows-to-kill-3-million-drug-addicts-and-likens-himself-to-hitler.

22 "Philippine President Declares 'America Has Lost' and Pledges Allegiance with China," *VICE*, October 20, 2016, https://www.vice.com/en_us/article/3b4a78/rodrigo-duterte-says-america-has-lost.

23 Robert Kagan, "The Twilight of the Liberal World Order," Brookings, January 24, 2017, https://www.brookings.edu/research/the-twilight-of-the-liberal-world-order/.

24 Michael J. Green, "Is the Foundation of the U.S.-Led Order Crumbling?" CSIS, December 15, 2016, https://www.csis.org/analysis/foundation-us-led-order-crumbling.

25 Waghorn, "World's Policeman."

CHAPTER FOUR: AUTHORITARIANISM RISING, DEMOCRACY DECLINING

1 Andrew Jacobs and Chris Buckley, "Move Over Mao: Beloved 'Papa Xi' Awes China," *New York Times*, March 7, 2015, http://www.nytimes.com/2015/03/08/world/move-over-mao-beloved-papa-xi-awes-china.html.

2 Anna Nemtsova, "Is Putin As Popular as Trump Says?" *Daily Beast*, September 9, 2016, http://www.thedailybeast.com/articles/2016/09/09/is-putin-as-popular-as-trump-says.html.

3 "Freedom in the World 2018," *Freedom House*, https://freedomhouse.org/report/freedom-world/freedom-world-2018.

4 "Freedom in the World 2018."

5 Amnesty International, "UN: Inaction on Syria Is Not an Option," December 1, 2016, https://www.amnesty.org/en/latest/news/2016/12/un-inaction-on-syria-is-not-an-option/.

6 Marc F. Plattner, "Is Democracy in Decline?" *Journal of Democracy* 26, no. 1 (January 2015): 5–10, http://www.journalofdemocracy.org/sites/default/files/Plattner-26-1.pdf.

7 Thomas C. Frolich, "10 Countries with the Fastest Growing Militaries," *Huffington Post*, April 15, 2016, http://www.huffingtonpost.com/entry/countries-fastest-growing-militaries_us_57110cebe4b0018f9cb9d472; Ira Iosebashvili, "Putin Pledges More Defense Spending," *Wall Street Journal*, February 20, 2012, http://www.wsj.com/articles/SB10001424052970203358704577234960796991408.

8 "World Values Survey," http://www.worldvaluessurvey.org/WVSContents.jsp?CMSID=Findings.

9 Pippa Norris, "It's Not Just Trump. Authoritarian Populism Is Rising Across the West. Here's Why," *Washington Post*, March 11, 2016, https://www.washingtonpost.com/news/monkey-cage/wp/2016/03/11/its-not-just-trump-authoritarian-populism-is-rising-across-the-west-heres-why/.

10 Shaun Walker, "What Does Russia Really Think About Vladimir Putin?" *Independent*, December 17, 2011, http://www.independent.co.uk/news/world/europe/what-does-russia-really-think-about-vladimir-putin-6277086.html.

11 Bridget Kendall, "Russian Propaganda Machine 'Worse Than Soviet Union,'" *BBC News*, June 6, 2014, http://www.bbc.com/news/magazine-27713847.

12 Jim Heintz, "Putin's Popularity: The Envy of Other Politicians," *US News*, September 8, 2016, http://www.usnews.com/news/world/articles/2016-09-08/putins-popularity-the-envy-of-other-politicians.

13 Heintz, "Putin's Popularity."

14 Adam Taylor, "Russians View U.S. More Favorably After Trump-Putin Summit, Poll Finds," *Atlanta Journal-Constitution*, August 3, 2018, https://www.myajc.com/news/russians-view-more-favorably-after-trump-putin-summit-poll-finds/vPhHMrfM3qXesl7SUAxMMN/.

15 Michael Crowley, "Putin's Revenge," *Politico*, December 16, 2016, http://www.politico.com/magazine/story/2016/12/russia-putin-hack-dnc-clinton-election-2016-cold-war-214532.

16 Crowley, "Putin's Revenge."

17 Julian E. Barnes, "Putin and the Doctrinal Definition of Threat," *Wall Street Journal*, June 6, 2015, https://www.wsj.com/articles/putin-and-the-doctrinal-definition-of-threat-1433596833.

18 "Repression Ahead," *The Economist*, June 1, 2013, http://www.economist.com/news/europe/21578716-vladimir-putins-crackdown-opponents-protesters-and-activist-groups-may-be-sign-fragility.

19 Maxim Trudolyubov, "Putin's Assault on Russia's Free Press Continues Apace," *Newsweek*, May 20, 2016, http://www.newsweek.com/putin-assault-russia-free-press-continues-apace-461571.

20 Anna Arutunyan, "Russia Crackdown on Anti-Putin Media Worsens," *USA Today*, May 20, 2016, http://www.usatoday.com/story/news/world/2016/05/20/russia-crackdown-anti-putin-media-worsens/84583080/.

21 Delphine D'Amora, "Duma Approves Abrupt Advertising Ban for Paid Television," *Moscow Times*, July 6, 2014, https://themoscowtimes.com/articles/duma-approves-abrupt-advertising-ban-for-paid-television-37057.

22 Alec Luhn, "15 Years of Vladimir Putin: 15 Ways He Has Changed Russia and the World," *Guardian*, May 6, 2015, https://www.theguardian.com/world/2015/may/06/vladimir-putin-15-ways-he-changed-russia-world.

23 Priyanka Boghani, "Putin's Legal Crackdown on Civil Society," PBS, January 13, 2015, http://www.pbs.org/wgbh/frontline/article/putins-legal-crackdown-on-civil-society/.

24 Nemtsova, "Is Putin as Popular as Trump Says?"

25 Nemtsova, "Is Putin as Popular as Trump Says?"

26 Nick Bayer, "Vladimir Putin's Popularity Is Skyrocketing Among Republicans," *Huffington Post*, December 14, 2016, http://www.huffingtonpost.com/entry/vladimir-putin-popularity-republicans_us_58518a3ce4b092f08686bd6e.

27 Aaron Zitner and Julia Wolfe, "Trump and Clinton's Popularity Problem," *Wall*

Street Journal, May 24, 2016, http://graphics.wsj.com/elections/2016/donald
-trump-and-hillary-clintons-popularity-problem/.

28 Howard LaFranchi, "Why Putin Is Suddenly Gaining Popularity Among
Conservatives," *Christian Science Monitor*, December 16, 2016, http://www
.csmonitor.com/USA/Politics/2016/1216/Why-Putin-is-suddenly-gaining
-popularity-among-conservatives.

29 LaFranchi, "Putin Is Suddenly Gaining."

30 William M. Arkin, Ken Dilanian, and Cynthia McFadden, "U.S. Officials: Putin
Personally Involved in U.S. Election Hack," *NBC News*, December 15, 2016,
http://www.nbcnews.com/news/us-news/u-s-officials-putin-personally
-involved-u-s-election-hack-n696146.

31 Raymond Li, "Seven Subjects Off Limits for Teaching, Chinese Universities
Told," *South China Morning Post*, May 10, 2013, http://www.scmp.com/news
/china/article/1234453/seven-subjects-limits-teaching-chinese-universities-told.

32 Chris Buckley and Andrew Jacobs, "Maoists in China, Given New Life, Attack
Dissent," *New York Times*, January 4, 2015, http://www.nytimes.com/2015/01/05
/world/chinas-maoists-are-revived-as-thought-police.html.

33 Kristian McGuire, "Xi Jinping as 'Authoritarian Reformer,'" *Freedom House*,
March 3, 2015, https://freedomhouse.org/blog/xi-jinping-authoritarian-reformer.

34 Chris Buckley, "China Enshrines 'Xi Jinping Thought,' Elevating Leader to
Mao-Like Status," *New York Times*, October 24, 2017, https://www.nytimes
.com/2017/10/24/world/asia/china-xi-jinping-communist-party.html.

35 John Simpson, "Critics Fear Beijing's Sharp Turn to Authoritarianism," *BBC
News*, March 3, 2016, http://www.bbc.com/news/world-35714031.

36 Chris Buckley, "China Suggests It Has Placed Weapons on Disputed Spratly
Islands in South China Sea," *New York Times*, December 15, 2016, https://www
.nytimes.com/2016/12/15/world/asia/china-spratly-islands.html.

37 "South China Sea: China Media Warn US Over 'Confrontation,'" *BBC News*,
January 13, 2017, http://www.bbc.com/news/world-asia-china-38607235.

38 Edward Wong, "Xi Again Defends China's Claim to South China Sea Islands,"
New York Times, November 7, 2015, https://www.nytimes.com/2015/11/08/world
/asia/xi-jinping-china-south-china-sea-singapore.html.

39 Shi Jiangtao and Jun Mai, "China's Xi Jinping Rejects Any Action Based on
International Court's South China Sea Ruling," *South China Morning Post*, July
12, 2016, http://www.scmp.com/news/china/diplomacy-defence/article/1988990
/chinas-xi-jinping-rejects-any-action-based.

40 Jesse Johnson, "U.S., Chinese Military Planes in 'Unsafe' Encounter Over
Disputed South China Sea," *Japan Times*, February 10, 2017, http://www
.japantimes.co.jp/news/2017/02/10/asia-pacific/u-s-chinese-military-planes
-unsafe-encounter-disputed-south-china-sea/.

41 Bill Gertz, "China's Military in 2016: Missiles, Intelligence and the SCS," *Asia
Times*, December 28, 2016, http://www.atimes.com/chinas-military-2016
-missiles-intelligence-scs/.

42 David Brunnstrom, "China Appears to Have Installed Weapons Systems on
Artificial Islands, US Think Tank Says," *Business Insider*, December 14, 2016,
http://www.businessinsider.com/r-exclusive-china-installs-weapons-systems
-on-artificial-islands-us-think-tank-2016-12.

43 Karen DeYoung, "Beijing's Actions in South China Sea Aimed at 'Hegemony,'

U.S. Admiral Says," *Washington Post*, February 23, 2016, https://www
.washingtonpost.com/world/national-security/beijings-actions-in-south-china
-sea-aimed-at-hegemony-us-admiral-says/2016/02/23/a669a0d2-da65-11e5-925f
-1d10062cc82d_story.html.

44 David E. Sanger, "Chinese Curb Cyberattacks on U.S. Interests, Report Finds,"
New York Times, June 20, 2016, http://www.nytimes.com/2016/06/21/us/politics
/china-us-cyber-spying.html.

45 Franz-Stefan Gady, "Top US Spy Chief: China Still Successful in Cyber
Espionage Against US," *Diplomat*, February 16, 2016, http://thediplomat
.com/2016/02/top-us-spy-chief-china-still-successful-in-cyber-espionage
-against-us/.

46 "What's Gone Wrong with Democracy," *The Economist*, http://www.economist
.com/news/essays/21596796-democracy-was-most-successful-political-idea-20th
-century-why-has-it-run-trouble-and-what-can-be-do.

47 "What's Gone Wrong With Democracy."

48 Liu Mingfu, "'The World Is Too Important to Be Left to America,'" *The Atlantic*,
June 4, 2015, https://www.theatlantic.com/international/archive/2015/06/china
-dream-liu-mingfu-power/394748/.

49 Camila Domonoske, "China's Xi Jinping Defends Globalization in First-Ever
Speech at World Economic Forum," *NPR*, January 17, 2017, http://www.npr
.org/sections/thetwo-way/2017/01/17/510219078/chinas-xi-jinping-defends
-globalization-in-first-ever-speech-at-world-economic-f.

50 Dan Levin, "China Tells Schools to Suppress Western Ideas, with One Big
Exception," *New York Times*, February 9, 2015, https://www.nytimes.com
/2015/02/10/world/asia/china-tells-schools-to-suppress-western-ideas-with-one
-big-exception.html.

51 Tom Phillips, "Xi Jinping: Does China Truly Love 'Big Daddy Xi'—Or Fear
Him?," *Guardian*, September 19, 2015, https://www.theguardian.com/world/2015
/sep/19/xi-jinping-does-china-truly-love-big-daddy-xi-or-fear-him.

52 Benjamin Carlson, "The World According to Xi Jinping," *The Atlantic*,
September 21, 2015, https://www.theatlantic.com/international/archive/2015/09
/xi-jinping-china-book-chinese-dream/406387/.

53 Enda Curran and Laurence Arnold, "China's Free-Trade Opening in a World
without TPP: QuickTake Q&A," *Bloomberg*, November 22, 2016, https://www
.bloomberg.com/news/articles/2016-11-22/china-s-free-trade-opening-in-a
-world-without-tpp-quicktake-q-a.

54 Emiko Jozuka, "TPP vs RCEP? Trade Deals Explained," *CNN*, January 26, 2017,
http://www.cnn.com/2017/01/24/asia/tpp-rcep-nafta-explained/.

55 Edward Wong, "Xi Again Defends China's Claim to South China Sea Islands,"
New York Times, November 7, 2015, https://www.nytimes.com/2015/11/08/world
/asia/xi-jinping-china-south-china-sea-singapore.html.

56 "China Slams Western Democracy as Flawed," *Bloomberg*, January 22, 2017,
https://www.bloomberg.com/politics/articles/2017-01-22/china-slams-western
-democracy-as-flawed-as-trump-takes-office.

57 Nathan Vanderklippe, "In 'Failure of U.S. Democracy,' China's Strongmen See
a Chance to Get Stronger," *Globe and Mail*, October 28, 2016, http://www
.theglobeandmail.com/news/world/in-failure-of-us-democracy-chinas
-strongmen-see-a-chance-to-get-stronger/article32562518/.

58 Stephen McDonell, "The Ever-Growing Power of China's Xi Jinping," *BBC News*, October 29, 2016, http://www.bbc.com/news/blogs-china-blog-37800062.

59 Jacobs and Buckley, "Move Over Mao."

60 McGuire, "Xi Jinping as 'Authoritarian Reformer.'"

61 Dexter Roberts, "Xi Jinping Is the World's Most Popular Leader, Says Survey," *Bloomberg*, December 18, 2014, https://www.bloomberg.com/news/articles /2014-12-18/xi-jinping-wins-the-popularity-conest.

62 Phillips, "Xi Jinping."

63 Phillips, "Xi Jinping."

64 Phillips, "Xi Jinping."

65 Chun Han Wong, "China Celebrates Xi Jinping with Fervor Not Seen Since Mao," *Wall Street Journal*, December 10, 2017, https://www.wsj.com/articles /china-celebrates-xi-jinping-with-fervor-not-seen-since-mao-1512907201.

66 Michael J. Green, "Is the Foundation of the U.S.-Led Order Crumbling?" *CSIS*, December 15, 2016, https://www.csis.org/analysis/foundation-us-led-order -crumbling.

67 Green, "Foundation."

CHAPTER FIVE: THE ROGUE MENACE

1 John Bolton, "Beyond the Iran Nuclear Deal," *Wall Street Journal*, January 15, 2018, https://www.wsj.com/articles/beyond-the-iran-nuclear-deal-1516044178.

2 Anna Fifield, "In Latest Test, North Korea Detonates Its Most Powerful Nuclear Device Yet," *Washington Post*, September 3, 2017, https://www.washingtonpost .com/world/north-korea-apparently-conducts-another-nuclear-test-south-korea -says/2017/09/03/7bce3ff6-905b-11e7-8df5-c2e5cf46c1e2_story.html.

3 Fifield, "In Latest Test."

4 Fifield, "In Latest Test."

5 Eric Shawn, "Iran Protesters Thank Trump, Call for Stronger Sanctions," *Fox News*, January 13, 2018, http://www.foxnews.com/world/2018/01/13/iran -protesters-thank-trump-call-for-stronger-sanctions.html.

6 Shawn, "Iran Protestors."

7 Matthew Lee, "Iran Still Top State Sponsor of Terrorism, U.S. Report Says," *PBS NewsHour*, July 19, 2017, http://www.pbs.org/newshour/rundown/iran-still -top-state-sponsor-terrorism-u-s-report-says.

8 "UN Report Accuses Iran of Providing Weapons to Yemen's Houthis," *Middle East Eye*, January 12, 2018, http://www.middleeasteye.net/news/un-report -accuses-iran-providing-weapons-yemens-houthis-732396788.

9 "Yemen Crisis: Who Is Fighting Whom?" *BBC News*, January 30, 2017, http:// www.bbc.com/news/world-middle-east-29319423.

10 "State Sponsorship of Terrorism," *American Coalition Against Nuclear Iran*, accessed January 31, 2018, https://www.unitedagainstnucleariran.com/terrorism.

11 Joyce Karam, "Iran Pays Hezbollah $700 Million a Year, US Official Says," *The National*, June 5, 2018, https://www.thenational.ae/world/the-americas/iran -pays-hezbollah-700-million-a-year-us-official-says-1.737347.

12 Matthew Levitt, "Iran's Support for Terrorism Under the JCPOA," Washington Institute for Near East Policy, July 8, 2016, http://www.washingtoninstitute.org /policy-analysis/view/irans-support-for-terrorism-under-the-jcpoa.

13 "Iran Still Number One State Terror Sponsor," *Voice of America*, July 31, 2017, https://editorials.voa.gov/a/iran-still-number-one-state-terror-sponsor/3966281 .html.

14 Yonah Jeremy Bob, "Massive Iranian Funding for Anti-Israel Terror Groups Revealed," *Jerusalem Post*, June 23, 2017, http://www.jpost.com/Middle -East/Iran-News/Massive-Iranian-funding-for-anti-Israel-terror-groups -revealed-497703.

15 Afshon Ostovar, "It's Time to Negotiate with Iran Over Syria," *Foreign Policy*, October 12, 2016, http://foreignpolicy.com/2016/10/12/its-time-to-negotiate -with-iran-over-syria-war-russia-rouhani-united-states.

16 Jack Keane, "Iran Cannot Be Permitted to Threaten World Peace," *Washington Times*, July 17, 2017, http://www.washingtontimes.com/news/2017/jul/17/iran -cannot-be-permitted-to-threaten-world-peace.

17 "Iran Still Number One State Terror Sponsor."

18 L. Todd Wood, "Iran, Russia Reaffirm Middle Eastern Axis," *Washington Times*, December 4, 2016, http://www.washingtontimes.com/news/2016/dec/4/iran -russia-reaffirm-middle-eastern-axis.

19 "Iran Still Number One State Terror Sponsor."

20 "Iran Still Number One State Terror Sponsor."

21 Sara Hsu, "China's Relations with Iran: A Threat to the West?" *The Diplomat*, January 27, 2016, http://thediplomat.com/2016/01/chinas-relations-with-iran-a -threat-to-the-west.

22 "Officials of Blacklisted NK Firm Visit Iran After U.N. Slaps Sanctions: Source," *Yonhap News Agency*, March 28, 2016, http://english.yonhapnews.co.kr /news/2016/03/28/0200000000AEN20160328009400315.html.

23 Samuel Ramani, "The Iran-North Korea Connection," *The Diplomat*, April 20, 2016, http://thediplomat.com/2016/04/the-iran-north-korea-connection.

24 "A History of Iran's Nuclear Program," Iran Watch, *Wisconsin Project on Nuclear Arms Control*, August 9, 2016, http://www.iranwatch.org/our-publications /weapon-program-background-report/history-irans-nuclear-program.

25 "Assessing Threats to U.S. Vital Interests: Middle East," in *2016 Index of U.S. Military Strength: Assessing America's Ability to Provide for the Common Defense*, edited by Dakota L. Wood (Washington, D.C.: Heritage Foundation, 2015), 175, http://index.heritage.org/military/2016/assessments/threats/middle-east.

26 Ryan Browne, "State Department Report Finds Iran Is Top State Sponsor of Terror," *CNN*, modified June 2, 2016, http://www.cnn.com/2016/06/02/politics /state-department-report-terrorism.

27 Joseph V. Micallef, "A Legacy of Failure: Obama's Mideast Foreign Policy," *Huffington Post*, October 18, 2015, http://www.huffingtonpost.com/joseph-v -micallef/a-legacy-of-failure-obama_b_8324094.html.

28 "Iran's President Hassan Rouhani Threatens to Restart Nuclear Program," *CBS News*, August 15, 2017, https://www.cbsnews.com/news/iran-president-hassan -rouhani-threatens-to-restart-nuclear-program.

29 "Iran: Events of 2015," in *World Report 2016*, Human Rights Watch, accessed February 1, 2018, https://www.hrw.org/world-report/2016/country-chapters /iran.

30　"North Korea," Human Rights Watch, accessed February 1, 2018, https://www
.hrw.org/asia/north-korea.

31　"Chronology of U.S.–North Korean Nuclear and Missile Diplomacy," *Arms
Control Association*, modified January 22, 2018, https://www.armscontrol.org
/factsheets/dprkchron.

32　Joel S. Wit, "How the Next President Can Stop North Korea," *New York Times*,
September 13, 2016, http://www.nytimes.com/2016/09/13/opinion/how-the-next
-president-can-stop-north-korea.html.

33　Jonathan Marcus, "Trump Kim Summit: What Did It Actually Achieve?," *BBC
News*, June 14, 2018, https://www.bbc.com/news/world-us-canada-44484322.

34　Marcus, "Trump Kim Summit."

35　John Haltiwanger, "What Kind of Bombs Does North Korea Have? A Guide to
Kim Jong Un's Nuclear Weapons," *Newsweek*, November 22, 2017, http://www
.newsweek.com/north-korea-guide-kim-jong-un-nuclear-weapons-718980.

36　Edward Luttwak, "It's Time to Bomb North Korea," *Foreign Policy*, January 8,
2018, http://foreignpolicy.com/2018/01/08/its-time-to-bomb-north-korea.

37　William J. Broad and David E. Sangar, "North Korea's Missile Success Is
Linked to Ukrainian Plant, Investigators Say," *New York Times*, August 14, 2017,
https://www.nytimes.com/2017/08/14/world/asia/north-korea-missiles-ukraine
-factory.html.

38　Elizabeth Shim, "North Korea: Russia's Putin Sent Kim Jong Un
Congratulatory Message," *United Press International*, August 15, 2016, https://
www.upi.com/Top_News/World-News/2016/08/15/North-Korea-Russias-Putin
-sent-Kim-Jong-Un-congratulatory-message/4891471272780.

39　Katie Hunt, "Is China Totally Impotent on North Korea?" *CNN*, September 9,
2016, http://www.cnn.com/2016/09/09/asia/china-impotent-north-korea.

40　Mike Rogers, "US Must Not Overlook North Korea Threat," *CNN*, December 2,
2016, http://www.cnn.com/2016/12/02/opinions/us-must-not-overlook-north
-korea-threat-rogers.

41　K.J. Kwon and Hilary Whiteman, "North Korea Publicly Executes Defense
Chief, Say South Korean Reports," *CNN*, May 14, 2015, http://www.cnn.com
/2015/05/13/asia/north-korea-executes-defense-chief/index.html.

42　"U.S. Relations with North Korea," Bureau of Public Affairs, *U.S. Department of
State*, October 18, 2016, http://www.state.gov/r/pa/ei/bgn/2792.htm.

43　Nash Jenkins, "North Korea Tells Citizens to Prepare Themselves for Famine,"
Time, March 29, 2016, http://time.com/4274666/arduous-march-north-korea
-famine.

44　Zvi Bar'el, "As Syrian Death Toll Dips, So Does World's Attention," *Haaretz*,
August 19, 2017, https://www.haaretz.com/middle-east-news/syria
/.premium-1.807065.

45　"Syrian Civil War Fast Facts," *CNN*, modified October 17, 2017, http://www
.cnn.com/2013/08/27/world/meast/syria-civil-war-fast-facts.

46　Euan McKirdy, "UNHCR Report: More Displaced Now Than After WWII,"
CNN, June 20, 2016, http://www.cnn.com/2016/06/20/world/unhcr-displaced
-peoples-report.

47　"Migrant Crisis: Migration to Europe Explained in Seven Charts," *BBC News*,
March 4, 2016, http://www.bbc.com/news/world-europe-34131911.

48 Nahal Toosi, "U.N. Report: Assad Again Used Chemical Weapons, Defying Obama," *Politico*, August 24, 2016, http://www.politico.com/story/2016/08/syria -assad-obama-united-nations-227385.

49 David Remnick, "Going the Distance," *New Yorker*, January 27, 2014, http:// www.newyorker.com/magazine/2014/01/27/going-the-distance-david-remnick.

50 Shreeya Sinha, "Obama's Evolution on ISIS," *New York Times*, June 9, 2015, http://www.nytimes.com/interactive/2015/06/09/world/middleeast/obama-isis -strategy.html.

51 "Russia Joins War in Syria: Five Key Points," *BBC*, October 1, 2015, http://www .bbc.com/news/world-middle-east-34416519.

52 "Russia/Syria: War Crimes in Month of Bombing Aleppo," *Human Rights Watch*, December 1, 2016, https://www.hrw.org/news/2016/12/01/russia/syria-war -crimes-month-bombing-aleppo.

53 Will Fulton, Joseph Holliday, and Sam Wyer, "Iranian Strategy in Syria," *Institute for the Study of War*, accessed February 1, 2018, http://www .understandingwar.org/report/iranian-strategy-syria.

54 Editorial Board, "Busting Illusions About Iran," *Wall Street Journal*, January 2, 2018, https://www.wsj.com/articles/busting-illusions-about-iran-1514940007.

55 James Jeffrey, "What If H.R. McMaster Is Right About North Korea?" *The Atlantic*, January 18, 2018, https://www.theatlantic.com/international /archive/2018/01/hr-mcmaster-might-be-right-about-north-korea/550799.

56 Jeffrey, "H.R. McMaster."

57 Michael Auslin, "Land of No Good Options," *City Journal*, September 14, 2017, https://www.city-journal.org/html/land-no-good-options-15441.html.

CHAPTER SIX: THE ISLAMIST CHALLENGE

1 Robin Simcox, "What Europe Should Be Doing to Prevent Another Terrorist Attack Like Barcelona," *Daily Signal*, August 18, 2017, http://dailysignal.com /2017/08/18/europe-prevent-another-terrorist-attack-like-barcelona/.

2 Pete Hoekstra, "Time for Honesty About London: We Are Losing the Fight Against Radical Islam," *Fox News*, June 5, 2017, http://www.foxnews.com /opinion/2017/06/05/time-for-honesty-about-london-are-losing-fight-against -radical-islam.html.

3 "After Victory in Raqqa," *Wall Street Journal*, October 20, 2017, https://www.wsj .com/articles/after-victory-in-raqqa-1508539304.

4 Sean Durns, "Al Qaeda Is Back," *Washington Examiner*, February 4, 2017, http:// www.washingtonexaminer.com/al-qaeda-is-back/article/2613929.

5 Rowan Scarborough, "With ISIS in Crosshairs, al Qaeda Makes Comeback," *Washington Times*, April 2, 2017, http://www.washingtontimes.com/news/2017 /apr/2/al-qaeda-comeback-widens-terror-war-for-donald-tru/.

6 Durns, "Al Qaeda Is Back."

7 Durns, "Al Qaeda Is Back."

8 Ali Soufan, "Bin Laden's Son Is Poised to Unify Terrorists Worldwide," *Daily Beast*, September 13, 2017, http://www.thedailybeast.com/bin-ladens-son-is -poised-to-unify-terrorists-worldwide.

9 Soufan, "Bin Laden's Son Is Poised to Unify Terrorists Worldwide."

10 "Bin Laden's Son Threatens Revenge for Father's Assassination," *Reuters*, July

10, 2016, https://www.reuters.com/article/us-usa-security-qaeda/bin-ladens
-son-threatens-revenge-for-fathers-assassination-monitor-idUSKCN0ZQ0AA.

11 Cristina Maza, "Hamza Bin Laden, Osama's Son, Denounces Saudi Arabia,
Calls for Overthrow of Monarchy in New al-Qaeda Video," *Newsweek*, January
19, 2018, https://www.newsweek.com/hamza-bin-laden-osama-saudi-785121.

12 Soufan, "Bin Laden's Son Is Poised to Unify Terrorists Worldwide."

13 Soufan, "Bin Laden's Son Is Poised to Unify Terrorists Worldwide."

14 Mirren Gidda, "Boko Haram Is Growing Stronger in Nigeria Thanks to
Corruption in the Military," *Newsweek*, May 19, 2017, http://www.newsweek
.com/nigeria-defense-spending-corruption-boko-haram-611685.

15 Conor Gaffey, "How Al-Shabab Overtook Boko Haram to Become Africa's
Deadliest Militants," *Newsweek*, June 2, 2017, http://www.newsweek.com/isis
-africa-al-shabaab-boko-haram-619010.

16 Jack Moore, "Trump Doubles U.S. Forces in Somalia to Fight ISIS and al-
Shabab, Most Since Black Hawk Down," *Newsweek*, November 20, 2017, https://
www.newsweek.com/trump-doubles-us-forces-somalia-fight-isis-and
-al-shabab-most-black-hawk-down-716923.

17 Joseph Hincks, "Rodrigo Duterte Says He Can 'Wait For One Year' to Clear
ISIS Militants from Marawi," *Time*, July 24, 2017, http://time.com/4870485
/marawi-duterte-isis/.

18 Simcox, "What Europe Should Be Doing."

19 Hoekstra, "Time for Honesty About London."

20 Joseph A. Kechichian, "Houari Boumedienne: Guardian of Freedom," *Gulf
News*, April 11, 2008, http://gulfnews.com/houari-boumedienne-guardian-of
-freedom-1.40394.

21 "Total Fertility Rate," *Eurostat*, https://ec.europa.eu/eurostat/web/products
-datasets/-/TPS00199.

22 Laurent Dubois, "What Is Brussels?" *Slate*, March 23, 2016, http://www.slate
.com/articles/news_and_politics/foreigners/2016/03/how_brussels_is
_different_than_paris_the_history_of_a_diverse_city.html.

23 Mike Scruggs, "The Muslim Brotherhood Plan to Dominate North America,"
Tribune Papers, November 22, 2016, http://www.thetribunepapers.com
/2016/11/22/the-muslim-brotherhood-plan-to-dominate-north-america/.

24 Robin Wright, "ISIS Jihadis Have Returned Home by the Thousands," *New
Yorker*, October 23, 2017, https://www.newyorker.com/news/news-desk/isis
-jihadis-have-returned-home-by-the-thousands.

25 Hoekstra, "Time for Honesty About London."

26 Simcox, "What Europe Should Be Doing."

27 "After Victory in Raqqa."

CHAPTER SEVEN: THIRD WORLD IN CRISIS

1 Rupert Darwall, "Europe's Energy Crack-Up," *National Review*, January 22,
2018, http://www.nationalreview.com/article/455628/europe-bogus-clean
-energy-schemes-european-union-coal.

2 Hoekstra, "Time for Honesty About London."

3 David Luhnow, "Latin America Is World's Most Violent Region," *Wall Street
Journal*, April 11, 2014, https://www.wsj.com/articles/latin-america-is-worlds
-most-violent-region-1397248932.

4 Robert Muggah, "How to Fix Latin America's Homicide Problem," *The Conversation*, June 28, 2017, https://theconversation.com/how-to-fix-latin -americas-homicide-problem-79731.

5 Muggah, "How to Fix Latin America's Homicide Problem."

6 Milena Veselinovic, "Why Corruption Is Holding Africa Back," *CNN*, January 8, 2016, http://www.cnn.com/2015/12/24/africa/africa-corruption-transparency -international/.

7 Veselinovic, "Corruption."

8 Veselinovic, "Corruption."

9 Veselinovic, "Corruption."

10 Jeffrey Gettleman, "An Anticorruption Plea in Kenya: 'Please, Just Steal a Little,'" *New York Times*, November 4, 2015, https://www.nytimes .com/2015/11/05/world/africa/kenya-government-corruption.html.

11 Gettleman, "Anticorruption Plea."

12 Beenish Ahmed, "Kenyan Officials Bite Back After a Report Reveals Purchase of $85 Pens," *ThinkProgress*, November 6, 2015, https://thinkprogress.org /kenyan-officials-bite-back-after-a-report-reveals-purchase-of-85-pens -220f489552cf#.lu7f4ogx2

13 *PBS NewsHour*, "How Widespread Corruption Is Hurting Kenya," PBS, April 11, 2016, https://www.pbs.org/newshour/show/how-widespread-corruption-is -hurting-kenya.

14 *PBS NewsHour*, "Widespread Corruption."

15 *PBS NewsHour*, "Widespread Corruption."

16 Sammy Darko, "Inside the World of Ghana's Internet Fraudsters," *BBC News*, May 10, 2015, http://www.bbc.com/news/world-africa-32583161.

17 Darko, "Ghana's Internet Fraudsters."

18 Goolam Mohamedbhai, "Higher Education: A Hotbed of Corruption?," *Inside Higher Ed*, July 26, 2015, https://www.insidehighered.com/blogs/world-view /higher-education-hotbed-corruption.

19 Mohamedbhai, "Higher Education."

20 Saheed Ahmad Rufai, "NNOM, Bamgbose and Institutionalisation of Academic Corruption in Nigeria," *Guardian* (Nigeria), January 1, 2016, http://guardian.ng /features/nnom-bamgbose-and-institutionalisation-of-academic-corruption-in -nigeria/

21 "Corruption in Education Threatens Children's Prospects in Africa and Must Be Tackled," *Transparency International*, http://www.transparency.org/news /pressrelease/corruption_in_education_threatens_childrens_prospects_in _africa_and_must_be.

22 "Corruption in Education."

23 Nick Schifrin, "Did Corruption in Nigeria Hamper Its Fight Against Boko Haram?," *NPR*, December 27, 2015, http://www.npr.org/sections /parallels/2015/12/27/461038854/did-corruption-in-nigeria-hamper-its-fight -against-boko-haram.

24 Schifrin, "Corruption in Nigeria."

25 Aryn Baker, "Corruption in Military Defense Spending Could Be Behind Rise in Africa Terror Attacks," *Time*, January 19, 2016, http://time.com/4184472 /military-corruption-africa-terror-attacks/.

26 Baker, "Military Defense Spending."

27 Baker, "Military Defense Spending."

28 Baker, "Military Defense Spending."

29 Christopher W. Tatlock, "Water Stress in Sub-Saharan Africa," *Council on Foreign Relations*, August 7, 2006, http://www.cfr.org/world/water-stress-sub -saharan-africa/p11240.

30 Tatlock, "Water Stress."

31 Kenneth Odiwuor, "In Africa, Corruption Dirties the Water," *Irin News*, March 14, 2013, http://www.irinnews.org/analysis/2013/03/14.

32 Odiwuor, "Corruption Dirties the Water."

33 Odiwuor, "Corruption Dirties the Water."

34 Pius Agbenorku, "Corruption in Ghanaian Healthcare System: The Consequences," *Journal of Medicine and Medical Sciences* 3, no. 10 (2012): 622–630, https://www.interesjournals.org/articles/corruption-in-ghanaian -healthcare-system-the-consequences.pdf.

35 Agbenorku, "Ghanaian Healthcare."

36 Carla Bleiker, "High Doses of Medical Corruption Worldwide," *Deutsche Welle*, June 1, 2013, http://www.dw.com/en/high-doses-of-medical-corruption -worldwide/a-16501875.

37 Bleiker, "Medical Corruption."

38 Bleiker, "Medical Corruption."

39 Bleiker, "Medical Corruption."

40 Bleiker, "Medical Corruption."

41 "Corruption on the Rise in Latin America and the Caribbean," *Transparency International*, October 9, 2017, https://www.transparency.org/news/feature /corruption_on_the_rise_in_latin_america_and_the_caribbean.

42 "Venezuelan Opposition Legislator Flees After 'Secret Police Threat,'" *BBC News*, July 28, 2018, https://www.bbc.com/news/world-latin-america-44988890.

43 Ricardo Hausmann, "D-Day Venezuela," *Project Syndicate*, January 2, 2018, https://www.project-syndicate.org/commentary/venezuela-catastrophe -military-intervention-by-ricardo-hausmann-2018-01.

44 Ian Bremmer, "The 5 Countries That Illustrate the Decline of the Latin American Left," *Time*, March 5, 2017, http://time.com/4719076/ecuador -venezuela-latin-america-left-wing/.

45 Simon Romero, "An Exploding Pension Crisis Feeds Brazil's Political Turmoil," *New York Times*, October 20, 2015, https://www.nytimes.com/2015/10/21/world /americas/brazil-pension-crisis-mounts-as-more-retire-earlier-then-pass -benefits-on.html.

46 Sarah Toy, "Brazil Risks New Zika Outbreak 3 Months After End of Health Emergency," *USA Today*, July 5, 2017, https://www.usatoday.com /story/news/2017/07/15/brazil-risk-zika-resurgence-says-human-rights -watch/480705001/.

47 "Petrobras Elected Leading Ethical Oil and Gas Company," *MercoPress*, February 8, 2009, http://en.mercopress.com/2009/02/08/petrobras-elected -leading-ethical-oil-and-gas-company.

48 J. William Carpenter, "The Top 5 Petrobras Shareholders," *Investopedia*, June 19, 2016, http://www.investopedia.com/articles/insights/061916/top-5-petrobras -shareholders-pbr.asp.

49 Carpenter, "Top 5 Petrobras Shareholders."

50 Simon Romero, "Dilma Rousseff Is Ousted as Brazil's President in Impeachment Vote," *New York Times*, August 31, 2016, https://www.nytimes .com/2016/09/01/world/americas/brazil-dilma-rousseff-impeached-removed -president.html.

51 Joe Leahy, "What Is the Petrobras Scandal That Is Engulfing Brazil?" *Financial Times*, March 31, 2016, https://www.ft.com/content/6e8b0e28-f728-11e5-803c -d27c7117d132.

52 Andrew Jacobs, "Brazil Impeachment Debate Hinges on a Thorny Legal Question," *New York Times*, April 19, 2016, https://www.nytimes.com /2016/04/20/world/americas/dilma-rousseff-impeachment-brazil.html.

53 Jacobs, "Brazil Impeachment."

54 Patrick Gillespie, "Brazil Hit by More Punches Amid Historic Recession," *CNN*, October 4, 2016, http://money.cnn.com/2016/10/04/news/economy/brazil -economy-jobs-crisis/index.html.

55 Duncan Wood, "The Most Important 2018 Election for America May Be Mexico's," *National Interest*, http://nationalinterest.org/print/feature/the-most -important-2018-election-america-may-be-mexicos-24013?page=show.

56 Eduardo Salcedo-Albarán and Luis Jorge Garay-Salamanca, "Networks of Evil," *City Journal*, Spring 2016, https://www.city-journal.org/html/networks-of -evil-14333.html.

57 "El Chapo Speaks: A Secret Visit with the Most Wanted Man in the World," *Rolling Stone*, January 9, 2016, https://www.rollingstone.com/culture/features /el-chapo-speaks-20160109.

58 "El Chapo Speaks."

59 "El Chapo Speaks."

60 Jeremy McDermott, "How Organized Crime & Corruption Intersect in LatAm," *Insight Crime*, December 4, 2014, http://www.insightcrime.org/news -analysis/organized-crime-corruption-meet-latin-america.

61 Kyra Gurney, "Corrupt Mexico Police Concentrated in 10 States," *Insight Crime*, November 27, 2014, http://www.insightcrime.org/news-briefs/corrupt-mexico -police-concentrated-in-ten-states.

62 Gurney, "Mexico Police."

63 Carrie Kahn, "43 Missing Students, 1 Missing Mayor: Of Crime and Collusion in Mexico," *NPR*, October 10, 2014, http://www.npr.org/sections/parallels /2014/10/10/355140186/43-missing-students-1-missing-mayor-of-crime-and -collusion-in-mexico.

64 "Cartels, Corruption, and the Case of 43 Missing Mexican Students," *CBS News*, October 7, 2014, http://www.cbsnews.com/news/cartels-corruption-and-the -case-of-43-missing-mexican-students/.

65 "Missing Mexico Students: Case Unresolved Two Years On," *Al Jazeera News*, September 26, 2016, http://www.aljazeera.com/news/2016/09/160926160722158 .html.

66 Kahn, "43 Missing Students, 1 Missing Mayor."

67 S. Ramirez, "Former Mayor of Iguala and His Wife Arrested in Mexico City," *Justice in Mexico*, November 8, 2014, https://justiceinmexico.org/former-mayor -of-iguala-and-his-wife-arrested-in-mexico-city/.

68 Ed Vulliamy, "One Year Ago, 43 Mexican Students Were Killed: Still, There Are No Answers for Their Families," *Guardian*, September 19, 2015, https://www .theguardian.com/world/2015/sep/20/mexico-43-killed-students-.

69 "Missing Mexico Students."

70 "Missing Mexico Students."

71 Nina Lakhani, "'Journalists Are Being Slaughtered': Mexico's Problem with Press Freedom," *Guardian*, August 4, 2015, https://www.theguardian.com /world/2015/aug/04/journalists-mexico-press-freedom-photographer-ruben -espinosa-murder.

72 "Disastrous Toll—21 Latin American Journalists Killed in the Past Six Months," *Reporters Without Borders*, July 5, 2016, https://rsf.org/en/news/disastrous-toll -21-latin-american-journalists-killed-past-six-months.

73 Darwall, "Europe's Energy Crack-Up."

CHAPTER EIGHT: A GLOBAL ENERGY WAR?

1 Fensom, "America Is Smashing Russia and OPEC's Grip."

2 "U.S. to Undermine Russia's Gas Monopoly in Europe," *NASDAQ*, April 25, 2016, http://www.nasdaq.com/article/us-to-undermine-russias-gas-monopoly -in-europe-cm610811.

3 James Sherr, "How Russia's Relationship with Europe Has Evolved," *BBC News*, January 5, 2016, http://www.bbc.com/news/world-europe-35154633.

4 "Energy Production and Imports," *Eurostat*, June 2017, http://ec.europa.eu /eurostat/statistics-explained/index.php/Energy_production_and_imports.

5 "Nord Stream 2," *Gazprom*, http://www.gazprom.com/about/production /projects/pipelines/built/nord-stream2/.

6 "Gazprom CEO Sees Russian Dominance of European Gas Market," *RT*, April 25, 2017, https://www.rt.com/business/386081-russia-gazprom-miller-europe/.

7 Anca Gurzu, "Nord Stream 2 Fight Set to Heat Up as Countries Show Their Cards," *Politico*, September 4, 2017, https://www.politico.eu/article/nord -stream-2-fight-set-to-heat-up-as-countries-show-their-cards/.

8 Jeff Mason, "Trump Lashes Germany over Gas Pipeline Deal, Calls It Russia's 'Captive,'" Reuters, July 11, 2018, https://www.reuters.com/article/us-nato -summit-pipeline/trump-lashes-germany-over-gas-pipeline-deal-calls-it -russias-captive-idUSKBN1K10VI.

9 Robbie Gramer, "Is Europe Caving to Russia on Pipeline Politics?" *Foreign Policy*, February 8, 2017, http://foreignpolicy.com/2017/02/08/is-europe-caving -to-russia-on-pipeline-politics-european-union-nord-stream-two-gas-oil -energy-germany-baltic-poland/.

10 Kenneth Rapoza, "Russia's Baltic Sea Pipeline Scares the Life Out of Ukraine," *Forbes*, February 9, 2017, https://www.forbes.com/sites/kenrapoza/2017/02/09 /russias-baltic-sea-pipeline-scares-the-life-out-of-ukraine/.

11 James Marson, "Putin Exploits Europe's Divisions in Bid to Dominate Gas Supply," *Wall Street Journal*, March 30, 2017, https://www.wsj.com/articles /putin-exploits-europes-divisions-in-bid-to-dominate-gas-supply-1490866203.

12 Emre Peker, "EU Says It Can't Block Russia-Backed Nord Stream 2 Pipeline," *Wall Street Journal*, March 30, 2017, https://www.wsj.com/articles/eu-says-it -cant-block-russia-backed-nord-stream-2-pipeline-1490906474.

13 Rapoza, "Russia's Baltic Sea Pipeline."

14 Marson, "Putin Exploits Europe's Divisions."

15 Marson, "Putin Exploits Europe's Divisions."

16 "Germany's Russian Gas Pipeline Smells Funny to America," *The Economist*, June 22, 2017, https://www.economist.com/news/europe/21723822-angela -merkel-says-nord-stream-2-no-ones-business-germanys-germanys-russian -gas-pipeline/.

17 Tom DiChristopher, "Russian Energy Sanctions Bill Puts Another Crack in Strained US-Europe Relations," *CNBC*, July 26, 2017, https://www.cnbc.com /2017/07/26/russian-energy-sanctions-us-europe.html.

18 Steven Erlanger and Neil MacFarquhar, "E.U. Is Uneasy, and Divided, About U.S. Sanctions on Russia," *New York Times*, July 25, 2017, https://www.nytimes .com/2017/07/25/world/europe/eu-uneasy-about-impact-of-new-us-sanctions -on-russia.html.

19 Alissa de Carbonnel and Oleg Vukmanovic, "EU Gets Wake-Up Call as Gazprom Eyes Rival TAP Pipeline," *Reuters*, February 14, 2017, http://www .reuters.com/article/us-gazprom-eu-tap-idUSKBN15T1LC.

20 De Carbonnel and Vukmanovic, "EU Gets Wake-Up Call."

21 Holly Ellyatt, "How—and Why—Saudi Arabia and Russia Are Bonding Over Oil," *CNBC*, October 3, 2017, https://www.cnbc.com/2017/10/03/the-new-opec -bromance-how-saudi-arabia-and-russia-are-bonding-over-oil.html.

22 Liam Denning, "Russia and Saudi Arabia Keep Talking, but Who's Listening?" *Bloomberg*, September 5, 2017, https://www.bloomberg.com/news /articles/2017-09-05/saudi-arabia-russia-and-oil-talking-s-not-working.

23 "Saudi Arabia Ready to Extend Oil Output Cut Deal," *Reuters*, October 28, 2017, https://www.reuters.com/article/us-saudi-oil/saudi-arabia-ready-to-extend-oil -output-cut-deal-crown-prince-idUSKBN1CX0FD.

24 Zainab Calcuttawala, "How Russia Is Using Oil Deals to Secure Its Influence in the Middle East," *Oilprice*, February 26, 2017, http://oilprice.com/Energy /Energy-General/How-Russia-Is-Using-Oil-Deals-To-Secure-Its-Influence-In -The-Middle-East.html.

25 Elena Mazneva, Stephen Bierman, and Javier Blas, "China Deepens Oil Ties with Russia in $9 Billion Rosneft Deal," *Bloomberg*, September 8, 2017, https:// www.bloomberg.com/news/articles/2017-09-08/china-s-cefc-buys-stake-in -rosneft-from-glencore-and-qatar.

26 "Russia and China Quietly Build Business Bonds," *Financial Times*, https:// www.ft.com/content/38f0ce22-9dd7-11e7-8cd4-932067fbf946.

27 Mazneva, Bierman, and Blas, "China Deepens Oil Ties with Russia."

28 "Exclusive: Russia's Rosneft Aims for Big Boost in Oil Exports to China," *Reuters*, October 6, 2017, https://www.reuters.com/article/us-russia-china-oil -exclusive/exclusive-russias-rosneft-aims-for-big-boost-in-oil-exports-to -china-sources-idUSKBN1CB1KE.

29 Chen Aizhu and Olga Yagova, "Russia Set to Pipe More Oil to China, Stepping Up Race with Saudis," *Reuters*, September 21, 2017, https://www.reuters.com /article/us-china-russia-oil/russia-set-to-pipe-more-oil-to-china-stepping-up -race-with-saudis-idUSKCN1BW1M3.

30 Ed Morse, "Welcome to the New Oil Order," *Financial Times*, January 28, 2016, https://www.ft.com/content/63790fdc-c5ad-11e5-b3b1-7b2481276e45.

31 Naureen S Malik, "U.S. Becomes a Net Gas Exporter for the First Time in 60 Years," *Bloomberg*, January 10, 2018, https://www.bloomberg.com/news/articles/2018-01-10/u-s-became-a-net-gas-exporter-for-the-first-time-in-60-years.

32 Gregory Brew, "Analysis: Why Saudi Arabia Should Fear U.S. Oil Dominance," *USA Today*, November 18, 2016, https://www.usatoday.com/story/money/energy/2017/11/18/analysis-why-saudi-arabia-should-fear-u-s-oil-dominance/868990001/.

33 Fensom, "America Is Smashing Russia and OPEC's Grip."

34 Fensom, "America Is Smashing Russia and OPEC's Grip."

35 "Frequently Asked Questions About LNG," *California Energy Commission*, http://www.energy.ca.gov/lng/faq.html.

36 Srinivas Mazumdaru, "Western Sanctions and Languid Russian Economy," *DW*, February 5, 2017, http://www.dw.com/en/western-sanctions-and-languid-russian-economy/a-38668372.

37 Kenneth Rapoza, "Putin Admits Sanctions Sapping Russia," *Forbes*, October 21, 2016, https://www.forbes.com/sites/kenrapoza/2016/10/21/putin-admits-sanctions-sapping-russia/print/.

38 "The Hidden Consequences of the Oil Crash," *Politico*, January 21, 2016, https://www.politico.com/magazine/story/2016/01/oil-crash-hidden-consequences-213550.

39 "Hidden Consequences."

40 Elena Mazneva and Anna Shiryaevskaya, "Putin's Russia Seen Dominating European Gas for Two Decades," *Bloomberg*, March 1, 2017, https://www.bloomberg.com/news/articles/2017-03-01/putin-s-russia-seen-dominating-european-energy-for-two-decades.

CHAPTER NINE: RELIGION AND AMERICAN LEADERSHIP

1 John Adams, "Message from John Adams to the Officers of the First Brigade of the Third Division of the Militia of Massacusetts," October 11, 1798, http://www.beliefnet.com/resourcelib/docs/115/Message_from_John_Adams_to_the_Officers_of_the_First_Brigade_1.html.

2 Kelsey Dallas, "Russia Is 'Much More Religious' Than It Was 25 Years Ago: So Why Is Religious Freedom Under Attack?," *Deseret News*, May 11, 2017, https://www.deseretnews.com/article/865679764/Why-religious-tensions-are-rising-in-Russia.html.

3 Dallas, "Russia Is 'Much More Religious.'"

4 Nicolai N. Petro, "Russia's Moral Framework and Why It Matters," *National Interest*, September 24, 2015, http://nationalinterest.org/feature/russia's-moral-framework-why-it-matters-13923.

5 Petro, "Russia's Moral Framework."

6 Petro, "Russia's Moral Framework."

7 "Pope 'Loves China,' Vatican Official Says on Trip to China," *Reuters*, August 3, 2017, https://www.reuters.com/article/us-china-vatican-pope-loves-china-vatican-official-says-on-trip-to-china-idUSKBN1AK06K.

8 Alan Dowd, "Far from Civilized: Religious Liberty in China," *Providence*,

August 3, 2017, https://providencemag.com/2017/08/far-civilized-religious
-liberty-china/.

9 William McKenzie, "China's Latest Crackdown Target: Religion," *CNN*, June 2, 2014, http://religion.blogs.cnn.com/2014/06/02/.

10 Ian Johnson, "Focusing on Religious Oppression in China Misses the Big Picture," *CNN*, February 28, 2017, http://www.cnn.com/2017/02/28/opinions /china-religion-johnson/index.html.

11 Dowd, "Far from Civilized."

12 Alan Dowd, "Far from Civilized: Religious Liberty in China," *Providence*, August 3, 2017, https://providencemag.com/2017/08/far-civilized-religious -liberty-china/.

13 Tom Strode, "Religious Liberty in China 'Rapidly Deteriorating,'" *Baptist Press*, March 15, 2017, http://www.bpnews.net/48505/religious-liberty-in-china -rapidly-deteriorating.

14 Dowd, "Far from Civilized."

15 "Cracks in the Atheist Edifice," *The Economist*, November 1, 2014, https://www .economist.com/news/briefing/21629218-rapid-spread-christianity-forcing -official-rethink-religion-cracks.

16 Johnson, "Focusing on Religious Oppression in China."

17 Peter Feaver and Will Inboden, "We Are Witnessing the Elimination of Christian Communities in Iraq and Syria," *Foreign Policy*, September 6, 2017, http://foreignpolicy.com/2017/09/06/we-are-witnessing-the-elimination-of -christian-communities-in-iraq-and-syria/.

18 William McGurn, "Merry Christmas, Iraq," *Wall Street Journal*, December 18, 2017, https://www.wsj.com/articles/merry-christmas-iraq-1513642589.

19 John Kerry, "Remarks on Daesh and Genocide," March 17, 2016, https://2009-2017.state.gov/secretary/remarks/2016/03/254782.htm.

20 Sarah Pulliam Bailey, "Christianity Faces Sharp Decline as Americans Are Becoming Even Less Affiliated with Religion," *Washington Post*, May 12, 2015, https://www.washingtonpost.com/news/acts-of-faith/wp/2015/05/12/christianity -faces-sharp-decline-as-americans-are-becoming-even-less-affiliated-with -religion/.

21 "America's Changing Religious Landscape," *Pew Research Center*, May 12, 2015, http://www.pewforum.org/2015/05/12/americas-changing-religious-landscape/.

22 Bailey, "Christianity Faces Sharp Decline."

23 Bailey, "Christianity Faces Sharp Decline."

24 "America's Changing Religious Landscape."

25 Mary Wisniewski, "Americans Becoming Less Religious, Especially Young Adults: Poll," *Reuters*, November 3, 2015, http://www.reuters.com/article/us-usa -religion-idUSKCN0SS0AM20151103.

26 David Brooks, "The Next Culture War," *New York Times*, June 30, 2015, http:// www.nytimes.com/2015/06/30/opinion/david-brooks-the-next-culture-war.html.

27 Mercedes Shlapp, "That's Me in the Corner," *U.S. News*, April 18, 2014, http:// www.usnews.com/opinion/mercedes-schlapp/2014/04/18/the-decline-of -religion-will-hurt-america-in-the-long-run.

28 "Public Sees Religion's Influence Waning," *Pew Research Center*, September 22, 2014, http://www.pewforum.org/2014/09/22/public-sees-religions-influence -waning-2/.

29 Michael Lipka, "Is Religion's Declining Influence Good or Bad? Those Without Religious Affiliation Are Divided," *Pew Research Center*, September 23, 2014, http://www.pewresearch.org/fact-tank/2014/09/23/is-religions-declining -influence-good-or-bad-those-without-religious-affiliation-are-divided/.

30 Frank Newport, "Most Americans Say Religion Is Losing Influence in U.S.," *Gallup.com*, May 29, 2013, http://www.gallup.com/poll/162803/americans-say -religion-losing-influence.aspx; Shlapp, "That's Me in the Corner."

31 "Moral Issues," *Gallup.com*, May 4–8, 2016, http://www.gallup.com/poll/1681 /moral-issues.aspx.

32 George Washington, "Farewell Address—Transcription," *The Papers of George Washington*, http://gwpapers.virginia.edu/documents_gw/farewell/transcript .html.

33 Adams, "Message from John Adams."

34 Nicholas Bakalar, "U.S. Fertility Rate Reaches a Record Low," *New York Times*, July 3, 2017, https://www.nytimes.com/2017/07/03/health/united-states-fertility -rate.html.

35 Patrick J. Buchanan, "The West Dies with Its Gods," American Conservative, http://www.theamericanconservative.com/buchanan/the-west-dies-with-its -gods/.

36 Matthew Continetti, "The Theological Politics of Irving Kristol," *National Affairs*, Summer 2014, http://www.nationalaffairs.com/publications/detail/the -theological-politics-of-irving-kristol.

CHAPTER TEN: ASSERTIVE DEMOCRATIC IDEALISM

1 Daniel W. Drezner, "America the Unexceptional," *Washington Post*, February 1, 2017, https://www.washingtonpost.com/posteverything/wp/2017/02/01/america -the-unexceptional/.

2 Erica R. Hendry, "Read Trump's Full Speech Outlining His National Security Strategy," PBS, December 18, 2017, https://www.pbs.org/newshour/politics/read -trumps-full-speech-outlining-his-national-security-strategy.

3 Zbigniew Brzezinski and Paul Wasserman, "Why the World Needs a Trump Doctrine," *New York Times*, February 20, 2017, https://www.nytimes .com/2017/02/20/opinion/why-the-world-needs-a-trump-doctrine.html.

4 Susan E. Rice, "When America No Longer Is a Global Force for Good," *New York Times*, December 20, 2017, https://www.nytimes.com/2017/12/20/opinion /susan-rice-america-global-strategy.html.

5 Hendry, "Read Trump's Full Speech Outlining His National Security Strategy."

6 Judy Shelton, "A New Trumpet for Democracy," *Wall Street Journal*, December 20, 2017, https://www.wsj.com/articles/a-new-trumpet-for-democracy -1513812104.

7 Gordon Chang, "Trump's National Security Strategy: Global Force for Principled Realism," *The Hill*, December 27, 2017, http://thehill.com/opinion /national-security/366499-trumps-national-security-strategy-global-force-for -principled.

8 Hendry, "Read Trump's Full Speech Outlining His National Security Strategy."

9 Chang, "Trump's National Security Strategy."

10 Chang, "Trump's National Security Strategy."

11 David P. Goldman, "Trump Offers a Daring Program to Restore US Dominance," *Asia Times*, December 18, 2017, http://www.atimes.com/article /trump-offers-daring-program-restore-us-dominance/.

12 Goldman, "Trump Offers a Daring Program."

13 "Israel Is Not the Cause of Middle East's Problems, US Security Strategy Says," *Times of Israel*, December 18, 2017, https://www.timesofisrael.com/israel-not-at -heart-of-middle-east-turmoil-new-us-security-strategy-says/.

14 Tyler O'Neil, "Former Obama Official Calls Obama Un-American on Iran Protests," *PJ Media*, January 3, 2018, https://pjmedia.com/trending/leon-panetta -obama-should-have-helped-2009-iran-protesters-thats-what-the-u-s-is-all -about/.

15 Donald J. Trump, *Twitter*, January 2, 2018, https://twitter.com/realdonaldtrump /status/948164289591902208.

16 "Remarks by President Trump on the Administration's National Security Strategy," *White House*, December 18, 2017, https://www.whitehouse.gov /briefings-statements/remarks-president-trump-administrations-national -security-strategy/.

INDEX